On Being Catholic

Thomas Howard

On Being Catholic

IGNATIUS PRESS   SAN FRANCISCO

Cover art: *Christ Giving Communion to the Apostles*
(*The Institution of the Eucharist*), detail
Fra Angelico
From the Museo San Marco, Florence
Scala/Art Resource, N.Y.

Cover design by Roxanne Mei Lum

ISBN 978-0-89870-608-6
Library of Congress catalogue card number 96–75716
Printed in the United States of America ∞

To my daughter, Gallaudet,
and my son, Charles,
who, with my wife, Lovelace,
are my chief joys

Contents

Foreword

In these times of crisis and discussions on religion and liturgy, often limited to secondary aspects, this book, written with the realistic intelligence of living faith by a Catholic convert, is a refreshing and renewing document. It is a beautiful book, a book of great relevance and of lasting value; it is life and contemplation put into words, based on the truth of God's gracious gift to us in his Church.

It recalls to us the very essence of the grace of *being Catholic*, as the author summarizes: "To be Catholic . . . is to live one's whole life 'in' the gospel", "to rest one's case in the pierced hands of Jesus Christ the Savior"; "to think of oneself as having been adopted into 'the whole family in heaven and earth' as St. Paul teaches", "to be profoundly conscious of one's place in an immensely ancient tradition . . . that stretches back to the beginning". It is to have been set free by Christ for "the Dance" called Charity—with its healing rules of renunciation, self-mastery, and virtue, and its fruits of freedom and joy, glimpsed in the Beatitudes. "The image of Christ. That is a very taxing assignment", our configuration to Christ. "To be Catholic is to confront all of this in the presence of the Crucifix."

The author first of all recalls the invisible depths of the divine mysteries present in the Holy Liturgy, above all in the Lord's unique and everlasting Sacrifice, which unites heaven and earth in the Assembly of the Eucharist, Center of the life of the Church and of each of the faithful. To be Catholic is to live from this infinite love of the Lord Jesus Christ, inviting us to eat his Flesh and drink his Blood, and so to enter into a growing partaking of his divine life in the communion of the Most Holy Trinity, to live in this love and peace throughout all our daily life, "to the glory of God and the salvation of the world" (Liturgy of the Eucharist).

The reading of this precious little book, so truly Catholic, makes one rejoice greatly; one's spirit is enlightened, and one's heart is opened up in contemplating the everlasting presence to us of the overwhelming love of Jesus Christ, of the Blessed Trinity, which is the Truth and Life of the Catholic Church, and of *being Catholic*.

✠ Christoph Schönborn
Archbishop of Vienna, Austria

I

The Glad Tidings

To speak of the Roman Catholic Church as glad tidings is to rouse scandal and incredulity in some quarters.

For example, some who were born into this Church will urge that their whole experience led them to conceive of the Church as of a tyrant. Whether it was a matter of having rote replies to the Baltimore Catechism drummed into their aching ten-year-old heads, or of their little knuckles being cracked with a ruler wielded by a fierce nun, or of guilt and confusion being compounded upon them in dire homilies Sunday after Sunday—one way or another, they will tell us, this Church can by no stretch of fancy be thought of in connection with any very encouraging tidings. Darkness and cringing bondage would seem to them to strike the note more exactly.

Others, especially zealous non-Catholic Christian believers who have watched this Church from the outside for a lifetime, will volunteer that, far from glad tidings, what Roman Catholicism purveys by way of gospel is a travesty. Instead of the invitation to come and be set free from your bondage and sin, they will tell us, Catholicism tangles one ever more deeply in guilt and uncertainty. Instead of the bright assurance that attends the conviction that one has at last been "saved", we find Catholics toiling along wondering if heaven is too much to hope for. Instead of "let us therefore come boldly to the throne of grace", which we hear from St. Paul, we find peasants and Montagnards and crones in babushkas lighting candles and offering prayers at squalid shrines and grottoes in a forlorn attempt to find some modest toehold on the fringes of the Divine Mercy.

And yet others will point to history and ask what sort of gladness may be said to attach to crusades, inquisitions, revoked edicts, Borgia popes, and crafty diplomacy.

And besides all this, it is sometimes remarked, look how the simple message that brought joy to shepherds, to the poor, to the jailer in Philippi, and to the Ethiopian in his chariot, of "Fear not!" and "Believe!"—look how this has been choked with penances and confessions and obligations and anathemas and Purgatory. Where are these glad tidings?

Where indeed?

The effort to mount a rejoinder to such observations must allow for the earnestness of the observers. No one has cobbled up such remarks about the Catholic Church out of thin air. Something lies at the root of all these strictures. The Church's interlocutors can point to many things that have aroused their confusion and even their wrath. Protestant witnesses, for example, have in times past cried out in agony from Catholic bonfires; and concordats have been signed between the Vatican and various states depriving powerless multitudes of their freedom to worship as non-Catholics; and too many of the Catholic faithful themselves have, no doubt, gone to Christian graves never having quite grasped the "glad" aspect of the tidings.

It is with these anomalies in mind that I attempt the apologia that occupies the following pages. I myself am a late comer to the ancient Roman Catholic Church. My Christian nurture occurred in a wing of Christendom that stands at a polar remove from Rome; but it is to that Protestant Fundamentalism, ironically, that I owe my having at last found my way into the Church, for it was the Fundamentalists, most notably the figures of my father and mother, who taught me the apostolic faith. They taught me that there is nothing—nothing at all—that may be compared to the excellency of the knowledge of Christ Jesus the Lord. They instilled in me the immense gravity of the matter, that to obey and serve God must swallow up all other contenders for one's attention. And they taught me, I think, that the peace and order that follow upon such obedience and service, both in one's inner man and in one's household, are a treasure to be desired and sought most sedulously. Everything else is ultimately illusionary, fugitive, and perfidious.

It was from such a beginning that I set out on the itinerary that brought me eventually to the Catholic Church. I have told that particular tale elsewhere,[1] and it is not my task to repeat it here. I would like, if I can, to put forward the senses in which it may be said of the Roman Catholic Church that, despite the most baleful charges that can be brought against her, nevertheless, to hear what she teaches is to have heard glad tidings, and to have entered truly into her life is to have found the tidings to be true. It is to have come to that fullness of the faith toward which all other renderings of the Christian gospel tend.

To assert that the Catholic Church constitutes that fullness toward which all other forms of Christian profession tend is to send us back to the question of whether man is, in his essence, religious, and if so, in what does his "religiosity"

---

[1] *Evangelical Is Not Enough* (San Francisco: Ignatius Press, 1988); *Lead, Kindly Light* (Steubenville, Ohio: Franciscan University Press, 1994).

consist? The assertion here is that it is only in the Roman Catholic Church that mankind may discover *all* that is implied in his native religiosity.

Is Man Religious?

Is man religious? The testimony of anthropology, archaeology, history, mythology, and art would seem to oblige us all to answer Yes to such a question. Temples, altars, statues, tombs, frescoes, scrolls, mosaics, murals, barrows, ziggurats, minarets, inscriptions, dances, amulets, sacrifices, mumbo-jumbo: it would be a highly idiosyncratic view of man that reached any conclusion here other than that we are deeply religious creatures, quintessentially and incorrigibly so.

But do we not see the emergence in our own time of postreligious man, or a-religious man? Man-come-of-age was thought to be a useful category in the years following World War II, when the works of Dietrich Bonhoeffer were disseminated widely among theological colleges in Europe, England, and North America. The notion here was that it is all very well for man to be erecting great temples in honor of Athena, or invoking Baal with slaughtered bullocks, or kneeling, all gloved and brushed, for Matins in British India: but this all arises in the childhood of the race. To accept the yoke of our adulthood as *homo sapiens* is to come to terms with the bleak awareness that the only "gods" there are, are those of our own making. To be free is to take responsibility for one's own existence and destiny. Human dignity derives from our having come to grips with our solitude. There is no one there speaking to the sibyl. There is no one there receiving all the supplications and invocations. There are no divine nostrils being regaled with the smoke of the incense and the burned fat. All of your *Te Deum*s and *Exaudi*s evaporate into the ether.

Timorous and unwilling souls recoil from the bleak tidings. But we men-come-of-age, we citizens of the Secular City, greet the news as the very herald of our enfranchisement. Today, for the first time, we stand tall. Now we take up our true task, as postreligious Man.

There is a massive sense in which the priests themselves must admit that such indeed would at least appear to be the case. The temples are emptying. Only a few heads, white and bowed, dot the nave. And outside bustles Contemporaneity, with its exhilarating agenda.

In other periods of history your skeptics and atheists were your odd men out. Zeno, Lucretius, Voltaire, Huxley, Russell: they stood out. But one has only to visit any faculty club, coffee shop, or quad in any university in the West or take soundings among the vastly urbane singles and couples hurrying out of Paris, London, Rome, or New York for the weekend, or to thread one's way through the crowds in any high-school corridor to find oneself asking whether it might not after all be the case that you *can* have a species of human being that is not religious.

So far has the religious question ("Who art Thou?") receded from contemporary consciousness that the term postatheist might be brought into play. The question of whether there is a god is not a question for this generation. People aren't atheists: they don't admit, or even so much as dream, that there ever was a category God. No shouting match at Marble Arch will be stirred up over the matter from this generation. It cannot even be said that they are bored by the religious question. There is no such question.

This would seem to be the case in our own epoch. To be sure, millions of people still troop off to churches. And they are not drawn solely from the ranks of the valetudinarians. There is a whole breed of householders who, upon finding themselves raising children, have reanimated the religious question for themselves. There has got to be some center of gravity for human existence, they tell themselves. The din scattered abroad by the culture of rock music can't possibly be a trustworthy guide toward authenticity. Perhaps the Church might help.

But this mass of people lives its life where such masses have always lived their lives: outside the pale of influence and power. It took only a few *philosophes* in France to create an entire culture of unbelief. It took only a few thousand Bolsheviks to replace tsarist Russia with atheist Russia. Thus it is in our own epoch. No one knows which are the chickens and which are the eggs: but affluence, drugs, rock music, feminism, "humanism", deconstruction, the media, and various sexual lobbies, along with the phenomenon known as "multiculturalism", have a generally antireligious power in modern culture that the great ballast of "the people" lack. In this connection, by way of an example of a tiny minority obliging a whole culture to conform to an ideology, one need only consult the grammatical rigors that have been clamped on our own culture by a small cadre of people: all broadcasters, ministers, academics, and public speakers have to pick their way gingerly along among the traps of *he* and *she* and *persons*, and so forth, at peril of awful litigation.

It might, then, be said of contemporary Western culture that it has been made postreligious, and even postatheist. All the signs would seem to suggest such a state of affairs. Perhaps mankind itself is on the point of emerging, once for all, from its religious phase.

But then doubt is cast on the matter straightaway when we recall that we are speaking here of only a very small scrap of time—shall we say twenty years, from 1975 until the present? Who knows? Certainly the roots of unreligion can be traced back through mid-twentieth-century French existentialism, nineteenth-century scientism and German romanticism, eighteenth-century rationalism, seventeenth-century inductionism, and so on. The more you ferret, the farther back the quarry recedes. (I had a Jesuit polymath for a professor once who demonstrated fairly convincingly that he had located a crux in the figure of Petrus Ramus in the sixteenth century.)

But unreligion, if we may bring such a term into play, was very far from corralling the whole of humanity in any of those eras. Your ordinary citizen got on with his life, if not exactly pursuing sanctity with any great zeal, nevertheless vaguely assuming that God was in his heaven. Unbelief was the province of academia.

Now things look different. Has man himself undergone a massive overhaul at the hands of modernity, and may we now look for the final atrophy of religion?

Not altogether so. *Pieta*s will not go away so easily. If you destroy our temple, we mortals seem to say, we will make for the woods. If you chase us from the woods and hound us into prison, we will cry out *"Domine!"* from our chains. On the gibbet we will sing out *"Kyrie!"*, even as you fix the great knot. And when you have eliminated all of us, so that no crone may be found left in any Sicilian or Balkan or Irish village, munching toothless gums and mumbling over her beads, and no psalms ring out from any convent, then . . .

Then some savage will creep out with punk and flint and kindle sacred fire somewhere. Or some woman will lift up a prayer as she keeps vigil at the fevered cot of her infant. Or some physicist at his chalkboard will stand back, eyes starting out at the symmetry he has stumbled upon, mop his brow, and whisper "*O altitudo!*" And finally, with a great roar, all the dragons and great deeps that you have lulled with your drowsy mantras appealing to Secular Man will leap and boil upon you in a titanic religious apocalypse.

Overblown rhetoric? Yes. But if we reached for the flattest possible prose, we would have to find a way to speak of the might, the ubiquity, and the depth of the religious impulse in us mortals. A scant and hasty few, especially theologians, may chase fatuity to the point where they announce briskly to us all, "Man has come of age! God is dead!" But the brave parade organized to celebrate the news trails off into the side streets presently. The very youth so ardently recruited by the no-god theologians are found buying amulets to hang around their necks and invoking the spirits of owls and polar bears. When Marxism finally keels over like a palsied brontosaurus, the celebration of the Divine Liturgy in the Cathedral of the Assumption in Moscow finds itself suddenly packed with the wards of the state who have been drilled for seventy years in the credo of unreligion. And, almost more piquant if possible, we find, now and again, but often enough to make an inquirer wonder, refugees from success itself—the men and women whose world has been the board room, the yacht, the Lear jet, and the chambers of academe, government, industry, and communication—decamping to ashrams and desert monasteries and therapists in the effort to simmer down, slough off illusion, and get in touch.

With what? Oneself? Many go to the desert or to the therapist with just such a quarry in mind. But "myself" turns out either to be eluding me, like the egg in *Alice in Wonder-*

land, or to be a less satisfactory prize than I had supposed, our own epoch having drilled into me the notion that the question "Who am I?" is the Golden Key.

Not so, says history. Not so, say the sages. Not so, say all the myths. And above all, not so, says religion. The quest for yourself leads to solitude. It is a vortex from which escape is almost impossible. On and on you will go, from therapist to medicine man, rifling into your viscera, swallowing the pills, identifying the syndromes and neuroses, discovering how you have been victimized and abused, and embarking on ever fresh techniques. But, like Palomides chasing his chimaera, never apprehending your quarry.

Alas! you mortal soul, the voice of the bard cries out to us. It is not yourself but rather the Apples of the Hesperides that you seek. It is Arcadia, say the poets. It is the Garden of Adonis. It is the Well at the World's End. It is the Grail.

No, no, whisper the therapists: those are illusions, wrought from the fever of your own estrangement from yourself.

Wrong, say the bards and the prophets, the sages and seers: you lost yourself because you had, long before, lost the god.

Who is he?

The answer, from far beyond the myths and oracles and pantheons, comes to us from the burning bush: I AM THAT I AM.

The ineffable Name, so holy as to place in great peril the man who even presumes to pronounce it. It is the name of the One above the many. Baal, Ashtaroth, Phtha, Ahura-Mazda, Zeus Pater: these must flee from his presence. It is I whom you seek, he says to all the priestesses and sibyls at their braziers. It is I whom you seek, he says to the savage with his punk and flint, to the woman with her child and the physicist at his chalkboard. I am the One who made you, who has redeemed you, and who seeks you like a shepherd among the crags looking for a lost sheep.

Jews and Christians agree that the One speaking to Moses from the bush is indeed the One. Oh, to be sure, there are other powers in the universe: but they are either obedient to him, like the seraphim and dominations, or they are in rebellion, like the devils. (Was Satan himself behind the cults of Baal and Moloch? Some of the Fathers of the Christian Church suspected as much. No one can say.)

And Christianity goes on to say that this One came among us at the Incarnation. In his *Introduction to Christianity*, Cardinal Ratzinger puts the matter this way:

> The notion that God names himself, that it becomes possible to call on him by name, moves, together with "I am", into the center of [St. John's] testimony. In John, Christ is compared with Moses in this respect too; John depicts him as him in whom the story of the burning bush first attains its true meaning. All Chapter 17—the so-called "high priest's prayer", perhaps the heart of the whole gospel—centres round the idea of "Jesus as the revealer of the name of God" and thus assumes the position of New Testament counterpart to the story of the burning bush. . . . Christ himself, so to speak, appears as the burning bush from which the name of God issues to mankind. But since in the view of the fourth gospel Jesus unites in himself, applies to himself, the "I am" of Exodus 3 and Isaiah 43, it becomes clear at the same time that *he himself* is the name, that is, the "invocability" of God. The idea of the name here enters a decisive new phase. The name is no longer merely a word but a person: Jesus himself.[1]

All Christians agree on this. Jesus Christ is Immanuel: God with us. We find this affirmed by all Christian bodies.

In some of these bodies all the usual paraphernalia of "re-

[1] Joseph Cardinal Ratzinger, *Introduction to Christianity* (San Francisco: Ignatius Press, 1990), 90–91.

ligion" has been jettisoned in the effort to distinguish Christianity from heathendom. Smoke, bells, muttering, bowing, holy objects, ceremonial: the house has been fumigated and we have, no longer the temple or the shrine, but the building understood as the structure where the faithful convene, not for mumbo-jumbo, but for the Word. Ceremonial belongs to the *antiquum documentum*, the "old" Covenant with Israel, where the One himself had dictated the elaborate furnishings of his sanctuary and had actually taken up his place mysteriously between the golden cherubim on the Ark. But when he became incarnate and lived and died among us and rose from the dead, why, then he put all the furniture of "religion" away. He does not dwell in temples made with hands; and there is no longer any need for altars. In His own self he has both fulfilled and put away all of that. Now, "we see Jesus" and have no need for anything supplementary.

Vast sectors of the Christian faith organize themselves along such lines. While there was a thin thread of tradition of this sort all through Christian history from the beginning, this outlook mushroomed into prominence five hundred years ago, at the beginning of the modern epoch, with the Protestant Reformation.

In its early stages, and to this day in many groups, the faith was articulate and robust. The Bible (*sola Scriptura*, said Luther) constitutes the center of gravity here, although in a deeper sense, of course, Christ himself is the center. The stress in Reformed Protestantism, and in its stepdaughter Evangelicalism (and, a fortiori, in Fundamentalism), is on the individual Christian's conscious, intelligent, and volitional response in faith to the gospel of Jesus Christ, that is, to the summons put by St. Paul to the jailer in Philippi, "Believe on the Lord Jesus Christ and thou shalt be saved." Christians of all descriptions have been made familiar with this rendition of the faith in the preaching of Billy Graham. Salvation is overwhelmingly a personal matter, having its inception in an explicit transaction and flowering in the individual who, with his inner man suffused by Scripture, associates himself with that great, loose, invisible global skein of other believers that Protestants call the Church.

In Protestant churches we find the worship exercises proceeding from this bibliocentric faith. The reading of Scripture, the singing of hymns, and the preaching of Scripture constitute the characteristic activities. The very architecture indicates the vision: row upon row of the people, ranged below a great lectern, seated most of the time, *listening.* Immense quantities of data—biblical, theological, and spiritual—form the staple, and all of it urged upon the faithful in an earnestly hortatory fashion. The whole point is that Scripture be taught and that the Word thus spoken be vouchsafed to each hearer and, in turn, translated into Christian fidelity and piety in those hearers' beings.

What may look to Catholic or Orthodox Christians like a spareness even to the point of gauntness in Protestant worship is the very thing sedulously sought by Protestants for their public worship, for two reasons, really: first, they would urge that Christian faith is a wholly interior matter, and in Jesus Christ we have both the fulfilling and the putting away of all ritual and ceremony; and, second, Christian worship ought to be starkly distinguished from the steamy jungle of ceremonies we find in pagan worship.

In behalf of the Reformers, it should be pointed out that their sweeping away of the external paraphernalia of piety and their insistence that the holiness sought by Catholics through Masses and medals and pilgrimages and candles is to flower in the inner man alone and is therefore to be sought strictly by faith, that is, by interior exercises—their stress on this did, in fact, foster a vastly impressive rectitude, industry, and purity among their people (my own father is the icon of this for me) that not infrequently stood dramatically over against what looked to them like the laxity, not to say squalor, that seemed to obtain in Roman Catholic circles. It should also be pointed out that the Reformers were far from being the only protesters: St. Thomas More, Erasmus, and, long before them, Chaucer and the author of the enormous poem *Piers Plowman* railed savagely over Roman impurities. Ignatius Loyola was horrified at the dionysian romp he found in Rome.

It was the effort at a clean sweep in this connection that produced the nonceremonial character of Protestant public worship.

What does Rome say in the face of all of this? It is hard to argue against simplicity and purity.

Two matters might be put forward in Rome's rejoinder here. The first is that Catholic ceremony, ritual, sacraments, and sacramentals, rightly understood, not only do not do violence to the faith opened up to us all in the gospel: all of this (again, rightly understood) is the very flowering of the faith. This point, in one sense, forms the rest of the content of this book so is not elaborated here.

Secondly, we mortals, *homo religiosus* that we are, *will* sooner or later give visible shape to what is in our hearts. Another way of putting this would be to point out the obvious, namely, that we are ceremonial creatures. What we find in the ceremonies of Roman Catholicism is nothing more than what we find ebulliently at work among us all, all the time.

Let us reach outside of religion for an example. Our awareness that something has happened with the birth of a child that reaches far beyond what mere obstetrics and gynecology offer takes external and ceremonial and even concrete shape: we have, on the one hand, cigars and popping corks and gifts, probably running to pink (a girl) or blue (a boy). On the other, a year later, when our memory (a wholly interior quality, it must be kept in mind here) recognizes the anniversary of the event, we give visible, external, even concrete shape to the matter with (1) cake, (2) candles, and (3) gifts again.

Somehow the interior and unseen (our consciousness of significance for a start, and then our memory) will "out", so to speak. It cries out for a form and a presence in the world of ceremony.

Or put it the other way round: we humans, as opposed to the dogs and the crows, *will* mark our awareness of significance in a visible, external, and concrete way. And, more than this, our marking of significance seems to take on a formal—even a ritual and ceremonial—shape. That is, rather than simply leaving things with spontaneous exclamations of joy and congratulation, we all reach for the ritual (that is, precast text) of "Happy Birthday to You!" Somehow, oddly, this hackneyed and not especially impressive ditty, precisely because it is traditional, takes up our interior responses to the event, gives them an external shape, and thereby satisfies something in us that springs from the deepest mysteries of our humanness.

"Our humanness." The dogs don't organize their responses in this manner. No one has ever seen a terrier scampering along with a bone done up with a pink bow to bring to the neighboring shi-tzu on the birth of her litter. The dogs don't even bark in this connection: certainly there is no synchronized barking, as in our own "Happy Birthday!"

It is we who do this, and we suspect that the oddity belongs to our humanity itself. We are ritual creatures. We are ceremonial creatures. We give concrete shape to that which wells up in our innermost being.

Otherwise how shall we give an accounting of all the elaboration with which we deck the joining together of a young man and woman in marriage—an event, surely, that exists solely in their interior feelings about each other and that takes physical shape in a form to be closely veiled from any public participation? And what shall we say of the obsequies with which all civilizations have decked death—again, surely an individual matter, to be taken care of as quickly as possible by getting the man or his ashes into the ground? But no, we insist: the matter won't rest there. We must *do* something formal, something traditional. We will submit ourselves to the rites and ceremonies (slow processions and lowered voices) that our culture offers to us. The last thing we want is spontaneity. That will do for the outbursts of emotion that rush upon us as we see each other for the first time after the death in question. But then the tumult must be quieted. And the best (the only?) way to do this is to permit ourselves to be taken up by the formal ceremony. Paradoxically, it is this rigid structure, and not our heaving sobs, that summons us most accurately to our own noblest being.

The dogs don't do this. We do.

This is a point on which the Protestants will agree with the Catholics.

There is nothing more than this at work in Catholic worship. What you see in the Mass is nothing but what we have agreed upon. It is the visible, external, concrete shape we Christian believers give to matters that reach to the very center of things and that cry out to be given such a shape.

But surely *words* are the form to be brought into play here, our Protestant inquirers might urge. It is interior faith that grasps the great panoply unfurled for us in the Gospel—of God's majesty and holiness, of man's sin, and of that Love which came down from heaven. And faith is most appropriately expressed in words.

Yes. In fact words keep us all close to the center of the mysteries, for it was a word—*the* Word—that spoke to us mortals in the gospel. So indeed, words are of the essence.

And how did that Word speak? *Et verbum caro factum est.* And the Word was made flesh. God, who at sundry times and in divers manners spoke to us in times past by the prophets hath in these last days spoken to us in his Son. And this Son not only spoke the words of God: he *was* (is) that Word. The Word becomes incarnate. Words tend toward concretion. Audible articulation and syntax do not exhaust the matter.

Hmm. The Catholic Church would believe that we need only consult our own humanity to discover this principle at work. We, for example, do not leave matters with a mere "How do you do": we grasp each other's hands. We will not leave things at "Good-bye": we bring our hands into play with a form (physical gesture) and wave. We cannot leave things with a mere "I love you": we embrace and kiss. We do not settle for the mere sound of our "No"· we shake our head.

And not only this. We very quickly come to admit that this oddity, of words finding embodiment in gesture and concrete form, is not simply convenient: it is inevitable. It belongs to our humanity, which is nothing if not physical. We are not ghosts. We are not pure intellects, like the angels. The very distinctiveness, and glory, of our humanness is bound up with the fact that we are physical.

The gnostics and Manichaeans deplore this. They want us to be disembodied. Flesh belongs to the lowest echelons of the universe, they tell us, and even to evil. We humans, trapped sadly in these bodies, strive to surmount the trammels of flesh and to escape into the ether.

No, say the Catholics. And no, say the Protestants. To decry our flesh is to set oneself over against the creation, which is to set oneself over against the Creator. We not only do not grudge our flesh: we extol it as the particular badge of our identity as Man, who is the crown of creation. This "incarnacy"—of intelligent spirit appearing under the modality of flesh—is said to exhibit the "image of God", as this is not said even of the seraphim themselves, glorious as they are.

Word becomes flesh. The word of God, spoken into the abyss, took on solidity in the stars and worlds. Even light, thin as it seems, is not an abstraction or a mere idea evoked by the words of God. It is physical, although whether it is to be spoken of as waves or particles seems to be a matter the physicists find difficult to make clear to us laymen. And the prize "product", if we may so speak, of the creating Word of God steps forward as Man and Woman. God's words do not merely reverberate through the vaults of the universe, although they certainly do that: they lodge themselves in orbs and granite and water and cheetahs, and in Man. It is of the nature of words to do this.

In the concreteness of the Mass, we see this truth at work. We may see it in the color of the priest's chasuble: red for martyrs, green for "ordinary time", and so forth. We may see it in the postures of the congregation: they kneel briefly as they enter, thus articulating the truth that we mortals ought indeed to humble ourselves in the presence of the *Mysterium Tremendum*. Every object and action points to that which is true. To be sure, words also point to that which is true; and certainly words constitute the articulating par excellence of that which is true. Pantomime won't quite suffice, rich as pantomime is. On this point again, the Catholics and the Protestants stoutly agree. There is no substitute for the verbal in all of its particularity.

But in the Roman Mass we find a shape, a texture, given to the corporate worship of Christian believers that issues directly from the mystery of the incarnate Word and bespeaks that mystery in every word, gesture, and object. The model here is not the classroom, or the lecture, or the town meeting, with a man presiding from a desk at the front and an audience ranged before him in rows. What we find, rather, is an *enactment*.

At this point the whole mystery opens up before us. For one thing, we must pause over this word "mystery". It is a word not commonly brought into play when we speak of the weekly public gatherings of the Christian faithful among the heirs of strictly Reformed teaching, at least among those who look to Geneva, Zurich, Amsterdam, and Edinburgh for their roots. In the German Reformation, of course, Luther did preserve a shape for worship recognizably analogous to the Mass. But most Protestants would find it odd to hear someone referring to their Sunday morning activity as "the holy mysteries".

The term is apt when speaking of Catholic and Orthodox worship, since these ancient and apostolic churches understand that the liturgy is an enactment. It is worth noting that Catholics and Orthodox do not speak of "a beautiful worship experience". This is significant. They understand themselves to be gathering to *do* something, not primarily to experience something; they are a congregation, not an audience. The ancient Church teaches that in the act of worship we enter into the mystery of Christ's own self-offering at the Cross, which he opened up to his disciples at the Last Supper, and which he inaugurated as the pattern for the Church's worship for as long as history lasts.

On this point great confusion has prevailed for the five hundred years since the Reformation. The general notion outside the Catholic Church (and, alas, among millions of the faithful themselves, it seems) is that in the Mass Jesus Christ is sacrificed again and again.

No, says the Church. Here is how the *Catechism of the Catholic Church* speaks of the matter:

> God's saving plan was accomplished "once for all" by the redemptive death of his Son Jesus Christ (571). . . . This sacrifice of Christ is unique; it completes and surpasses all other sacrifices (614). . . . When the Church celebrates the Eucharist, she commemorates Christ's Passover, and it is made present: the sacrifice Christ offered once for all on the cross remains ever present (1364). . . . In the sacrifice of the Mass they make present again and apply, until the coming of the Lord, the unique sacrifice of the New Testament, that namely of Christ offering himself once for all a spotless victim to the Father (1566).

It is crucial to recall that the word the Lord used at the Last Supper when he said, "Do this for a remembrance of me", is the word *anamnesis*, which signifies, not a mere remembering of a past event, as we remember the signing of the Declaration of Independence on July 4, but rather a remembering *that is a making present*. This crux lies at the root of the Protestant confusion over the Mass as "making present" (not repeating) the unique sacrifice of Calvary.

This is a point of such weight that we may be excused here for quoting at some length the explanation given for the matter by F. X. Durrwell:

> That death which St. Paul speaks of and Christ speaks of, is Christ's death, the one and only death, *sub Pontio Pilato*. The Mass is Christ present in his one and only redeeming act, the sacrifice of Calvary becoming a reality of our lives too.
>
> "How can it be a sacrifice?" ask Protestants. There is only one sacrifice of Christ: "By his own blood he entered once

into the holies, obtaining eternal redemption" (Heb 9:12). "By one oblation he hath perfected forever them that he hath sanctified" (Heb 10:14). There is one of the key ideas of the epistle to the Hebrews: the sacrifices of the Old Testament had constantly to be renewed because they were always ineffective, incapable of "sanctifying" man, of immolating him to himself and bringing him into the life-giving holiness of God. Christ, on the other hand, has offered a single sacrifice, perfect and sufficient, the sacrifice of the end of time, which fulfills and crowns all mankind's longing for salvation and sacrificial actions. By his death, Christ entered once for all into the sanctuary of divine life, and takes with him all his followers.

The Protestants are therefore quite right in their dogged affirmation of the absolute uniqueness of Christ's sacrifice. There is but that one, which took place once and for all, never repeated, never repeatable. Yet the Church believes that the Mass is a sacrifice. She believes it because of Scripture, and because of her own uninterrupted and most ancient tradition, through which the Holy Ghost speaks. . . . She is faced with two apparently contradictory truths: the fact that Calvary is unique, and the fact that the Eucharist is a sacrifice. . . .

Of these two truths, the prime and essential one is the uniqueness of Christ's sacrifice; the Church must hold this in all strictness. The Mass cannot be another sacrifice, a reproduction or repetition, a second, third or hundredth sacrifice following the one offered under Pontius Pilate. If it is a sacrifice, it must be that one and only one, made two thousand years ago, never repeated, never repeatable, but mysteriously brought into our lifetime.[2]

All of this is present in the Mass. Hence, Catholics do not see their coming together for worship as a "meeting", with

[2] F. X. Durrwell, *In the Redeeming Christ* (New York: Sheed and Ward, 1963), 55, 56.

the principal feature being the sermon. Rather, they believe they have come, in a mystery, to the frontier that lies between the seen and the unseen, or between heaven and earth—as we all do when we pray, for example. No Christian will balk at the notion that he is, at one and the same time, kneeling beside his bed *and also* standing before the Throne of Grace. Faith is full of paradoxes like this, which appear to outsiders to be contradictions and hence nonsense but to believers to be mysteries.

But we were speaking of the obvious differences between Protestant worship services and the Mass, the most immediately obvious one, to a casual glance, being the difference between a meeting, on the one hand, organized around the idea of people listening to a lecture and, on the other, an enactment. And enactment, of course, takes ritual and ceremonial form—a principle we see when we mortals come up to the great moments of human existence, namely, birth, marriage, and death, and attempt to "enter into" the mysteries at stake in these events. We do not settle for speaking to each other about these things. In some profound sense that belongs to our humanity itself, we know that we must "enter into" the significance of the events, and this entering into, inevitably, takes ritual and ceremonial form.

There may be some unhappy sect somewhere that sticks rigorously to the exclusively verbal and propositional, but such a state of affairs is almost unimaginable to the rest of us. Protestants and Catholics alike energetically play out the ritual and ceremonial ordering of things.

Protestants? Yes. It is worth noting that, despite their laudable stress on *word*, nevertheless Protestants cannot live without ceremony. The irony here, of course, is that there is very little comfort given in this connection from their theology and preaching. To hear some teaching, one might indeed conclude that "the Word" alone is sufficient to our humanity and that therefore Christian worship must restrict itself to the reading, singing, and preaching of this Word.

But then, of course, their ministers show up in academic regalia in the pulpit. Pure ceremony. Velvet strips, billowing sleeves, and brilliant color: nonverbal ways of saying, "I have a Ph.D.", or at least, "I am an educated man, and it is appropriate for us all to be reminded of this as I stand before you teaching." Or again, even among the groups that wish to pursue the greatest possible simplicity, namely, the Quakers, the Brethren, and the various Anabaptist denominations, a palpable sense of ceremony presides over the coming together of the people. Things get quiet, for one thing: a nonverbal manner of saying, "Stillness is of the essence as we mortals present ourselves before the Most High." And a strict order is observed: even in the assemblies that allow for anyone "moved by the Spirit" to rise and offer what is on his heart, the gathered believers would be greatly put off their stride if someone rose and suggested ring-around-the-rosy, or a clambake. Not here. Those wholly praiseworthy activities do not come under the strict rubric that dictates what we may and may not do here. Indeed, even in the groups that extol spontaneity as the very cockade of worship and propose that the clapping of hands, the calling out of *ad hoc* exclamations of joy, and even jigging are all acceptable—even these groups would draw the line at someone's proposing gymnastics or cigars. Not according to the ceremonial.

Certainly in the sectors of Christendom that teach the overriding primacy of word over all else, even in such circles, there comes an unabashed acknowledgment of the ceremonial principle on special occasions. Some Protestant churches have moved the once-central pulpit to one side, thus exposing the Communion Table and thus invoking the ceremonial rather than the strictly verbalist principle. Others have restored candles. Crosses (rarely crucifixes) now appear in many Protestant church buildings. And at Christmas and Easter, holly and lilies overleap the verbalist rubric in a most embarrassing fashion. Good Friday itself has, timidly, edged its way back into some non-Catholic purlieus, with things going so far as to exhibit the cross draped in a black scarf (this outside the evangelical Baptist church near my home).

We mortals are ceremonial creatures, and the most sparse sect cannot go forward on terms other than these. The classroom will not do. Indeed, we cannot so much as open our mouths in a psalm or song without giving the entire game away: tune and melody and rhyme lie wholly outside the circumference of the strictly verbal (even though rhyme, of course, is a property attaching to the *sound* of those words). Song takes the verbal up into the region of ceremony and lends to words the wings they cry out for.

In one sense, nothing more than this need be put forward as the rationale for the ceremonial aspects of the Roman Mass. In it we see what belongs to our very humanity taken up into the service of Christian worship, which, along with birth, marriage, and death, reaches to the profoundest depths of that humanity.

This, then, brings us to the threshold of a further consideration. The Roman Mass is not simply "a" ceremonial ordering of Christian worship, as though additions had been affixed to the matter by various "coordinators of worship" over the years. Nor has the topic the smallest connection with taste: it will not quite yield to the remark, "Oh well, some people like elaborate worship ceremonies, and some of us like simplicity." That is irrelevant. There is nothing, actually, simpler than the Mass, since everything is explicit. No nuances or subtleties veil things. All is stark and apparent. But this brings us up to the next threshold.

3

The Unity of the Church

What about the question of varieties of worship? Could it not be urged that the multiplicity of styles to be found across the Christian spectrum is itself the very sign of vigor? Surely this riotous fructifying of fashions in public worship suggests something deeply significant about the gospel, namely, that it is a seed of such glorious vitality that, when it is planted anywhere among us mortals, it will sprout, burgeon, and bear good fruit? And more: in the colorful heaps displayed in this harvest we find the rich and particular genius of each tribe and people, redeemed, purified, raised, and touched with eternity itself. What you find in Spain and Latin America differs greatly from what you find in the Netherlands or Norway. Sicilians do not order their worship as do the Watutsi; nor does Irish Catholicism yield just the look given things by the Filipinos.

What can one do but assent to all of this, and even applaud it. Who will carp? Who will be so parsimonious as to begrudge the human race such a splendid panoply? By all means let Philadelphia Quakers guard the stillness and austerity of their venerable meeting houses. Let the rococo flower among the Bavarians and Austrians. Who will deny to the Pentecostalists their ebullience, and to the Presbyterians the rectitude and sobriety coming to them from Scotland, and to the Russians their gold and incense? Come.

Yes. One is inclined to echo Gerard Manley Hopkins here: ". . . all trades, their gear and tackle and trim./All things counter, original, spare, strange;/ . . . He fathers-forth whose beauty is past change:/Praise him."

In gazing on this variety exhibited in the forms of Christian worship we find ourselves drawn past the question of mere taste to matters of thicker substance. The faithful from every one of the sectors that together constitute the variety presenting itself to us would wish us to understand that the "shape" of their worship is very far from having been arrived at simply in answer to questions of taste. To be sure, the Quakers no doubt do, in fact, "like" the shape their worship has taken on, as do the Bavarians, the Scots, and the African American Baptists. But they would all justly demur if an observer chalked up what he saw among them as mere taste. Not altogether, they would all wish to impress upon him: what you observe among us is the purest and fullest rendering that can be given to the Christian gospel in all its richness.

That is, the Calvinists do not run to long sermons simply because Swiss, Dutch, and Scottish tastes run along such lines: you have opened up an immense theological matter when you note this about their worship. The preaching of the Word: this is the central and characteristic activity of the Church, and it is under this mode that God is pleased to instruct and bless his people. Our worship evinces this towering consideration, in all the details of the shape we have given to our practice in this connection, they would tell us. Or again, the Pentecostalists among American black communities would urge upon us the crucial place that vital, felt, and spontaneous experience must hold in true Christian worship. The Spirit is free and sets us free, they would tell us: do not clamp us into the stocks and manacles of ritual. How shall we truly praise the Redeemer under those gaunt restraints? And yet again George Fox, father of the Quakers, would want his followers to maintain that stillness which must guard the soul's opening of itself to the Inner Light and that openness to the Spirit that alone authenticates the Christian soul's approach to God.

The "shape", then, that public Christian worship takes on exhibits two things: first, the particular genius of the group in question (whether this is ethnic, socioeconomic, or geographical) and, second, the substance of the faith as that group apprehends it.

How, then, can the Roman Catholic Church insist that the shape that Christian public worship must take, always and everywhere, is found in the Mass? Surely this is a highhanded attitude?

It would seem so, *if* worship were an abstraction afloat in the ether around us, so to speak, to be distilled by any of us and wrought into a shape that pleases us. On that accounting the great thing would be for us all to come at the matter perennially, tapping and tinkering, and ever and anon coming up with yet new shapes. Our tribal or cultural genius would be given wide scope, and our spirits would be perpetually regaled by novel and unpredicted challenges and thereby kept on their toes. A vastly appealing case can be (and is) made in behalf of this approach.

But worship is scarcely such an abstraction. It is far, far more than the expression of our spiritual aspirations or of the Godward proclivities of our spirits. To be sure, these aspirations and proclivities are caught up, channeled, and energized in our acts of worship: but these are not the primal matter of worship. These are only properties in us that answer to the primal matter that is God.

All religions testify to this. Hinduism does not leave it to the Hindu faithful to cobble up infinite varieties for Hindu worship: whether you are a Tamil from South India or a man from Assam, you must do so-and-so if you wish to present yourself to the gods in our temples. Islam does not leave it to the Sudanese or the Persians to consult their own inclinations and thus fashion their cult of Allah. The Jews would also testify to this.

It would seem, then, that there is a source other than ourselves from which proceed the form and content of worship. The question for the believer from any religion is not, first of all, "How do I feel about this?" but, rather, "What am I to do when I come to the Holy of Holies?"

That is the question that reaches deeper than my ethnic or cultural or historical identity. I may be a young, well-off American of Swedish ancestry living in the suburban colossus around Chicago, and it may greatly appeal to me to drive my family to an immense "seeker-friendly" emporium as my weekly religious exercise. There is much to be said for it. But does it address the question that comes to me from the immensities of the creation, the fall, and redemption, namely, what am I to do when I come to the Holy of Holies? How am I to dispose myself here, mortal that I am?

Or again, I am bubbling with joy over my status as one of the saved, and it comes naturally to my sort of people to shake out our joy by dancing, waving our arms, and calling out with bursts of adoration to the holy Name of Jesus. There is a very great deal to be said for this. Let it attend our worship, by all means. Let it find its expression in the midst of the assembly of the faithful. But does it exhaust the whole matter that looms upon us when we mortals come to the Upper Room, Golgotha, the Tomb, and the Sapphire

Throne? Is the whole of our action here ordered to the whole of the mystery?

And yet once again: there is much to be said for spareness and stillness as the particular note of public worship. But we must ask: Does the aggregate of meditations and aspirations rising to heaven from the hearts of the gathered faithful compass the matter? Are our bodies drawn into the mystery so that by standing, sitting, kneeling, and bowing, we address that which we know in our hearts to be fitting for us mortals in these precincts?

To speak of physical postures is to open a question that touches closely upon this matter of public Christian worship. It might be put this way: Since God seeks those who will worship him in spirit and truth (rather than upon this mountain or that), is there any requirement at all for public worship other than that the faithful raise their hearts to the Most High? Surely such raising, which must be the final test of whether worship is occurring at all, can be achieved sitting, standing, kneeling, or, in the case of the infirm, supine, not to mention by the hiker in the mountains as he strides along with the song of the winter wren in his ears, offering his acts of praise to heaven.

Yes. The locale of true worship is the heart of man, and worship can ascend from the foxhole, the anvil, or St. Lawrence's very griddle, if it comes to that.

But we are speaking of the public ordering of the worship of the Christian faithful, day by day, week by week, century after century, for all tribes and cultures, in a shape such that all that ought to present itself to them is presented, so that they will be drawn, body, soul, and spirit, into the totality of the mystery that worship approaches.

If these considerations are taken seriously, we begin to see that much more is at stake than tends to be available to mere taste or inclination—even if that taste and inclination arise most poignantly from a given people. "We like to sing these songs" may be volunteered in this connection; and "We like our ministers to be affable, and even colloquial", or "The whole point for us is the preaching of the Word", or "Spontaneity is the crucial thing for us."

All of that, to be sure. But it is to be remembered by us all that the discussion of these nettlesome topics has not been left to the perennial open forum, with delegations from all concerned groups striving to lodge their special priorities in the agenda.

Christian worship did not simply proliferate randomly. There was a shape given to it in the beginning. Actually, it *took* this shape: it is not as though the apostolic community cast about for ingredients that might be appealing to local Jewish converts, or to Greeks, or to Scythians, Romans, Egyptians, or Parthians, least of all to that ubiquitous figure, "contemporary man". No market research was brought into play. No caucuses—of youth, or of senior citizens, or of the affluent or the indigent, or of women, or men, or of anyone else—were heard from. No theologians or reformers or charismatic leaders or prophets dictated the shape of things.

The particular act that was understood by the apostolic and patristic Church to constitute worship for the new cult (soon enough labeled "Christian" at Antioch) had been received from the hands of Jesus Christ himself. And it was a particular act. What he had done on the night before his betrayal in the Upper Room was received by the apostles as his ordering of the act of Christian worship. He took, blessed, broke, and gave bread to them, and he blessed the cup of wine; and by his word he inaugurated this strange quasi meal as the act that would "make present" (his word—*anamnesis*) for them, until history ended, the entire mystery of his redeeming self-oblation to the Father, that is to say, the entirety of revelation. The whole of the Law and the Prophets and of the history of Israel, and of his own coming into the world, passing through it (it is *pasch*—passing), and returning to the Father is opened up in this rite. It can never be exhausted or wholly comprehended. It will never run dry, for as long as Christian people gather for worship.

The Roman Catholic Church (and, it may be remembered here, the Orthodox) offers no other apologia for the shape of her regular public act of worship. She has no warrant—no warrant at all, she would stress—to alter things in the interest of some doctrinal point (the Inner Light, or the importance of the Bible, or spontaneity), and least of all of some lesser notion, such as "We *like* informality", or "Our tradition is four hundred years old and comes to us from the Old Country."

It is often put forward in this connection that Catholic worship cannot possibly be of one piece with the spare and humble simplicity that obtained in the Upper Room, and among the apostles, the believing women, and the others who gathered after the Ascension. Look at the sumptuousness and complexity of the Mass. My word—brocaded vestments and bowing and mumbling and bric-a-brac: How can Rome possibly maintain that *that* is to be understood as "primitive"?

Many Christian denominations make the claim that theirs is nothing more than New Testament worship. "We just go back to the Book of Acts for our pattern", it is said.

The difficulty here is that the Book of Acts scarcely hints at what the believers actually did when they gathered. We all know Acts 2:42: "And they continued steadfastly in the apostles' doctrine and fellowship, and in breaking of bread, and in prayers." Certainly this touches on the content of their gatherings.

But what did they actually do in these gatherings? We find presently, in the writings that we have from the Church, written, often, by men who had themselves known and been taught by Peter and John and Paul, that indeed the "bishop" expounded the Scripture to the gathered faithful in a homily that followed certain readings from Scripture. The sermon, in all Christian churches, can trace its taproot straight back to this custom.

And what shape did "fellowship" take? Newly composed hymnody? Testimonials? Sharing? Extempore prayers? All of these items form staple ingredients in many of the groups that seek to remain close to the simplicity glimpsed in the Book of Acts. But of course Acts does not spell out any of this. We Christians, late in time, have to guess here. No one can claim that such activities have undoubted biblical pedigree.

But "the breaking of bread". Here we are on firmer ground. We do, in fact, know something more about this aspect of the apostolic Church's worship. The Book of Acts, of course, tells us nothing about the actual pattern. Did they use little squares of leavened bread? Little thimble-cups with a drop of grape juice in each? Did they look on the matter as strictly a memorial of the Lord's death? We can say nothing to the purpose here as long as we rummage only in the pages of Acts or of the "pastoral epistles". If we wish to stick close to what the believers did in this connection, we must consult the writings of Ignatius, Justin, Irenaeus, and other early writings. These texts are not Scripture, to be sure: but they are first- and second-century reports, and they are "Church", so to speak. If we wish to dismiss these reports with, "Oh, the Church very early strayed from 'the simplicity that is in Christ'", then we are left to our fancies, that is, to how we, fifteen hundred or two thousand years after the fact, are pleased to imagine things. (How it is that such late notions are to be taken with a confidence we deny to Clement and Ignatius and Justin is a question to set the most fervent sectarian to wondering.)

And in these reports from that very early Church, we find "the shape of the liturgy", to borrow the phrase from the Anglican scholar Dom Gregory Dix. Greetings, readings from Scripture, homily, and prayers formed the first part of the Christians' gathering (the so-called *synaxis*, which means gathering); then any visitors and inquirers, and even not-yet-baptized believers, were sent out, and the believers embarked upon the *anaphora* (the offering). In the very earliest records we have of what was said by the "president" (the bishop or, later, one of his presbyters), we find the Mass; or, if we wish to put the matter less controversially, we may say that we find the phraseology and the sequence that may still be heard in the Mass.

None of this is controversial matter, actually. Anyone can read and find all of this for himself. Scholars from all sectors of Christendom agree that, yes, certainly this is how things were as the Church moved out from the morning of Pentecost into the long haul of history. The record is there. We have only one precedent, if we wish to tailor our public worship according to the early pattern.

We are free to jettison this pattern and to design a wholly alternative scheme for Christian gathering. This is what has been done in many of the Protestant churches. They themselves would say stoutly that a clean sweep was necessary, given the havoc in the late mediaeval Church, and that all apostolic, patristic, and historic precedent must be overridden in the interest of locating the preaching of the Word as the *pièce de résistance* of worship. Yes, it is a novel pattern, they will tell us: but it was necessary at the time to make this purge, and now, five hundred years later, we see no reason to reconsider the matter.

In one sense all discussion halts at this point, since it is impossible to find a common footing upon which to proceed. Non-Catholic Christians do not wish to be obliged to test things with these "apostolic" and "patristic" and "catholic" touchstones that govern the teaching and practice of the Catholic Church. *Sola Scriptura*, they urge. The great difficulty here for Catholics is that Scripture itself is silent on this *sola* point, for a start, and, further, no one had heard of this stricture until a millennium and a half had gone by after Pentecost. St. Paul called the Church "the pillar and ground of the truth" (1 Tim 3:15). How can this be set on one side, Catholics might ask. What Church is that? Well, the only one there is, St. Paul might reply.

But this last is a remark almost incomprehensible to non-Catholics in these late years of history. The only Church there is? Fie! Here, let us fetch the directory of churches: let's see, starting with A . . .

We all know the list of denominations. And no one, of course, can dismiss in a cavalier way the agonies, sunderings, debates, and even wars from which that very long list of "churches" derives. Alas. All of us read the Lord's "high-priestly" prayer recorded in John 17 and wonder wistfully how his petition for unity might be recovered in our own epoch. Some Christians, of course, will venture that we do, as it happens, already enjoy that oneness for which Jesus Christ prayed: all true believers in Jesus, scattered as they are, constitute the "invisible church", which is united by that common belief in a profound fashion that no ecumenical synods can ever hope to achieve. Hence, unity is not something for which we need pray. We have it, not visibly or organizationally, to be sure, but nonetheless truly. Jesus Christ's true followers know each other and, when the test comes, will stand forth in a solid phalanx that no foe foresees. Meanwhile, the variety in Christendom is healthy. Let a hundred flowers bloom, they might say, giving Chairman Mao's words a meaning he cannot have imagined.

This is an appealing picture. It has the cachet about it of diversity, which in turn suggests good health.

The difficulty here is that, whatever accolades we may wish to accord to such a picture, it is not, in any sense ever imagined by our forefathers in the faith, most notably the apostles and the believers who gathered about them in the early decades after Pentecost—it is not "the Church". It may be a praiseworthy and admirable aggregate of assemblies or of task forces or even denominations: but it is not "the Church", again as that term was understood by our forerunners. This brave array of ecclesial groupings may exhibit zeal and fidelity, energy and resourcefulness, and even enormous success in preaching the gospel and winning converts to Christian belief. Nevertheless, it is not the Church. Or at least, to spare ourselves shouts of dismay and ire, it is not the thing called "the Church" by the men to whom we all owe this ancient faith.

For them, "church" did not refer to a scattered aggregate of individuals, each of whom had professed faith in Jesus. There certainly was such an aggregate, if one wanted to count believing noses, so to speak, in Smyrna and Philadelphia and Sardis and Ephesus. But "church" was a word that referred to an entity—a mystery, really—with a specific content and with an embodied visibility. It was, on one level, the Body of Christ, or the New Israel of God, or the Bride of Christ. All these terms pointed to the mystery, hidden in God from former ages and now disclosed, of a new people, "born again" by the Spirit of God, citizens of the Kingdom of Heaven even while still here in history. But on the level of the (literally) mundane, this mystery could be seen in Smyrna or Sardis. Where? How?

One found "it", not by canvassing the shops for believing shopkeepers and their families or hunting through the legions for believing soldiers or inquiring at the academy for believing pedagogues and then tallying the list. This technique would, of course, have yielded a noble list and, to that extent, what might be called, loosely, a directory to an "invisible" church.

But the believers themselves would not have wanted you to identify your list with the Church. You can find "her", they would have told you, by finding our bishop and by observing us at our worship, that is, at the liturgy. There we may be found gathered around our bishop, obedient to him, recognizing him as bearing apostolic authority, and, in some sense, embodying in his person the unity that we—believers usually scattered out across the city but now, precisely, gathered—constitute. We are all one in the Lord, they would tell us, not merely in the abstract sense of agreeing with each other that we share a common faith, but rather insofar as we attest to that unity by our unity with the bishop. For us here in Smyrna, it is Polycarp, the disciple of John.

Yes. Very good, we might begin. Now could you show us to the other denominations here in Smyrna?

Blank. Silence. Presently, out of politeness, one of them asks us what it was, again, that we had requested.

The other churches.

But this is the Church. We are the Church. This is the Church in Smyrna.

And we would find, if we pursued things far enough, that various companies had from time to time hived off but that there was a distinction, clear enough for Christians and pagans alike to grasp, between the believers here in Smyrna under Polycarp and those in Antioch under Ignatius and those in Jerusalem under their bishop—between these, on the one hand, who are known as "the Church"—and the others who had sundered themselves from that unity in the interest of following someone who had come along with a fascinating variation on the gospel of Jesus and who had busily collected about himself his own cadre. They were called heretics in those brisk days.

That sounds harsh to us, two thousand years later. We believe in being good neighbors, religiously as well as on the street where we live. Christendom has diversified itself, we admit, and, since we are all undoubtedly united by a common faith in Christ Jesus, we will, despite superficial (or profound) differences, agree to live in amiable proximity to each other, hoping for the day when a way will be found for us to enter once again into that unity that was so visible in the early centuries of the Church.

This attitude is far more to be extolled than warfare, to which Christian believers have resorted from time to time over the unhappy history of the Church. We might say that hatred, strife, and war are the ditch on the one side of the road: but this, of course, sets up a picture that makes us all want to know what the ditch on the other side might turn out to be.

Certainly that ditch must in some sense imply the opposite of the zeal that takes up arms against fellow Christians. We should all have an amiable attitude toward our fellow believers.

But is there such a thing as a culpable amiability? Is there such a thing as a blameworthy ignoring of distinctions?

No one has the luxury of taking up a highhanded attitude here. Everyone is under the most somber obligation to look to his own knitting, so to speak. The Mennonites do not break bread with the Lutherans, nor the Cumberland Presbyterians with the Campbellites, nor the Moravians with the Countess of Huntingdon's Connection. What is wrong? Who is guilty? Who will insist that *he* has it right? On the other hand, we are no longer marching out against each other with swords and staves.

But alas. There is a sense in which everyone does, in fact, insist that he has it right, although *politesse* ordinarily inhibits us from trumpeting it too loudly at each other. But, in the bosom of our own assembly, there presides the rock-solid conviction that indeed, indeed, we *do* have it right. Let the others come as supplicants to us. We will gladly receive you, if you repent, mend your ways, acknowledge your errors, and submit to our teaching and discipline.

No one actually talks this way. Scarcely anyone spells things out quite so starkly even in his own heart. Nevertheless, we would all probably have to admit to some such posture, if we were ruthlessly candid with ourselves.

The Roman Catholic Church seems to hold herself aloof from all such questions. It often looks as though she waits, serene and patient, for the vendors in the stalls and kiosks of the fair to pull themselves together, close up shop, and come to her door. Then she will, with lavish condescension, open her arms to receive these supplicants.

Such a picture puts us all off. Nevertheless, it is a picture many suppose to be a true one. Certainly it is not a picture likely to move many to join the petitioners at Rome's doors.

How are we to speak of the matter, so perilous and delicate, so laced with passion, in any helpful way?

There is one sense in which nothing new can be said. Undergirding the sturdy convictions, partisanship, and even jingoism that many bring to this matter of what the Church is, there lie, as we all know, not only half a millennium of bale and woe, but also whole theological systems that were not erected in a day and that will not be dismantled in a day, or in a century.

For Catholics, of course, it seems difficult to think about the matter at all without laying their own souls open to superior, and even inquisitorial, attitudes. After all, we say, we are the Church founded by Jesus Christ himself. We don't know who these other church founders are; but we offer no apology for our own pedigree.

At this point we find ourselves facing the question of attitude, for which we are responsible and for which we will be judged. How is one to be at one and the same time intransigent and meek? It comes to that, really. Intransigence, although it is not a sympathetic word, has eventually to be brought into play by anyone when it comes to matters of truth. But how is a good man to do so? Is it not better to be pliable and irenic?

Irenic, yes. Pliable, no—at least where truth is at stake. The martyrs, peaceable as most of them wished to be, finally found themselves at the point where they had to say, No: we cannot agree. We wish most fervently to live harmlessly and unobtrusively here in Rome and to be at peace with all men. But we cannot offer incense to Decius or Diocletian. Their warrant for this behavior was, of course, the Lord himself, who could not modify what he said in the interest of *bonhomie* all round in Jerusalem.

The belief of Catholics is that the Church issued from the wounded side of Christ at Calvary and that the coming of the Holy Ghost at Pentecost ratified and vivified this mystery, galvanizing the apostles and the others into a company that quickly took on a shape discernible by all and sundry, pagan or Christian.

It was a body under authority, for one thing, not a democracy. The apostles, having had authority bestowed on them by the Lord to teach and rule in the Church, were in charge. They taught doctrine, and they governed the assemblies that began to sprout, first in Jerusalem, then in all Judaea, then in Samaria, and finally unto the uttermost part of the earth. When the time came for a man to be raised up in a given locale to bear apostolic authority for his region, hands were laid on him. His was the office of "bishop" (*episkopos*).

The Catholic Church believes that this office of bishop was (and is) a particular one, derived solely from the original fountainhead of the apostles, and unavailable in any way other than the apostolic laying-on of hands. Most Christian churches recognize some such office, and most practice the laying-on of hands for various ministries. In the Catholic Church, the belief is that this "episcopal" lineage, originating from the Savior's own choosing and anointing of the Twelve, and passing thence, from that Twelve, on to the next generation, and the next, has continued unbroken until our own day and will continue uninterrupted until the Second Coming.

The history of the early Church makes clear that they all accepted this picture and that these bishops, all around the Mediterranean as the gospel advanced, recognized each other as sharing in the unique apostolic ministry. The Church was "one" under them, scattered as the churches were, inasmuch as teaching and discipline had to be agreed upon by these bishops in council. No one had to linger marooned in doubt as to which men were the true bishops and which were interlopers, mountebanks, and heretics. Confusions arose early enough: but when a teacher like Marcion or Apollinarius arose, or when someone started up his own "church" without this apostolic pedigree, the matter was settled sooner or later, so that what one found as the Church moved out into history was common knowledge as to who constituted the Church and who were schismatic.

Church history is not a smooth-surfaced road. Pebbles, rocks, potholes, cave-ins, and collapses of all sorts mar things. But the road is there, or so Catholics believe. Or, to put the matter in a different way: any one of us, Baptist, Catholic, Orthodox, or independent, will discover the same record if he will read about the early Church. Polycarp became bishop in Smyrna in the first century. Ignatius was bishop in Antioch. Clement was bishop in Rome. They and everyone else understood their office as having derived directly and organically from the apostles. So all of us discover an "episcopal" Church there. For good or ill, that is what took shape.

Some non-Catholic Christians urge that the whole Church went off the rails by about A.D. 95, and hence that "Church history" is really the record of an immense botch. These Christians would urge that the Church of Jesus Christ, made up as she is exclusively of true believers, pursued its humble and obscure way in little assemblies here and remote groupings there, quite apart from the brontosaurian imposter that, early on, took unto herself the name of The Catholic Church.

The difficulty of maintaining this view arises from the nature of the topic itself. The Christian believers who were under the authority of the apostles and then under the bishops appointed by them understood this episcopal entity to be the Church. All the writings we have from the first and second century attest to this. If we will read the letters, sermons, and tracts of Ignatius and Clement and Justin and Irenaeus, we will find a church that, if she is not *the* Church, is certainly the only one anyone had any knowledge of. If we wish to forego any connection with this lineage, then we find ourselves obliged either to link ourselves with the Montanists, the Marcionites, or the Nicolaitans or to postulate some fugitive network of assemblies of which there is no record. That is, we must identify either with heresy or with a lacuna in the record.

In this sense, Roman Catholics at times find themselves thought to be arrogant in their claim to such ancient lineage, whereas in their own imagination it is a matter for plain humility. We are merely the heirs to that noble lineage, they would say. No merit or glory attaches to us for what the apostles and Fathers did. We cannot "claim" them, if by that we mean that they are ours in some proprietary way. They are ours only in the sense that our great-grandparents are ours.

Catholics find themselves at a loss when a fellow Christian identifies himself as a follower of a man from the sixteenth or seventeenth century. No Catholic makes any such claim. There are in the Catholic Church, to be sure, Benedictines and Augustinians and Franciscans: but the names of the men in these titles simply specify the orders in the Church to which men and women identifying themselves thereby belong. These names do not refer to the kind of Christian our Benedictine or Franciscan is. For that, there is only one category: "catholic".

This word came into play within the first hundred years of the Church, precisely to point to the nature of the Church, namely, that she is the only "church" there is in the whole world and that she is discernibly and organically linked with the bishops who have been consecrated by the apostles. If I say that I am a Marcionite or an Arian or a Lutheran, to that extent I seem to distinguish myself, for whatever reasons, from the immense and plain category in which apostolic Christians see themselves.

To be Catholic, then, is, in a sense, to make a claim that can readily be interpreted as a barefaced attempt to "trump" all others in the discussion about what the Church is: "Well, I don't know about the rest of you; but I simply belong to the Church founded by Jesus Christ. I am in the Ark, so to speak, and the rest of you in your small craft may climb aboard whenever you are ready." It is an attitude of which Catholics are not altogether innocent; and it is certainly an attitude that understandably vexes non-Catholic Christians.

Two matters call for clarifying at this point. First, every non-Catholic group in Christendom sees itself as a simple, even obvious, return to "New Testament Christianity". Very few groups claim to offer something *new*. Insofar as they do, they find themselves regarded by the rest of Christendom as heretical or, at best, sectarian: Mormons and Jehovah's Witnesses would be the most well-known groups here. But Lutherans, Calvinists, Mennonites, Wesleyans, and all the other bodies to which a man's name is attached will tell us, "We didn't take up that name. We are simply New Testament Christians. Outsiders designated us with that name, and if it helps to identify the particular biblical emphasis that our group brought into the historical jumble, then we accept the name." In some cases, as with the Plymouth Brethren or the Christian Church, known respectively by outsiders as Darbyites and Campbellites, the believers themselves demur over any title, strongly emphasizing that what you see among them really is nothing at all but simple New Testament practice. And all Baptists hold that they have no special historic axe to grind: look into the New Testament, and you will find the Baptist Church, they tell us.

This brings us to the second matter, namely, the title "Roman" for the Catholic Church. Is not this the most unabashed admission of some late-arriving loyalty or identity, wholly unknown to the disciples, the first women, and the early converts?

What needs to be brought into play with respect to both of these matters—the claim of many non-Catholic groups to be simply the Church as the Bible anticipates her and the odd Roman identity that attaches to the Catholic Church—is the distinction between the effort, on the one hand, to hark back strictly to the text of the New Testament for a pattern thought to be visible there and, on the other, the view that sees the first decades in the apostolic Church, in all her rudimentary simplicity, as very much like an acorn from which an immense oak eventually rises (or, to reach for the Gospel image, a mustard seed).

That is, the thing (say Catholics) that was inaugurated, or planted, by Jesus Christ was a healthy organism, and like all healthy organisms she developed and grew. To find out what she looked like as she began to grow, we have to consult the record that follows immediately from the New Testament itself, namely, the writings of the men who had been disciples of the apostles and into whose charge the Church had been committed by the apostles. In the matter of the Christians' worship, for example, we have already noted that the Book of Acts and the pastoral epistles barely glimpse what actually occurred: similarly, a Catholic would remark, the whole matter of the government, or "polity", of the Church, barely glimpsed in the New Testament, emerges organically within a few decades as the "episcopal" church of Ignatius, Polycarp, and Clement, who, it is to be recalled always, were themselves taught by John and Peter and Paul. In their writings we will find, as we have already noted, both episcopal discipline and eucharistic worship. We will also find, fiercely insisted upon, the notion that the Church is one and that no one may start something afresh, any more than an Old Testament

Hebrew might start Israel afresh, even if Israel herself were
whoring away most brazenly.

Briefly, to be Catholic is to see the Church's early itinerary
as looking like this—or actually, we might say, to be any sort
of inquirer at all is to observe such an itinerary: the Church
formed herself, in response to apostolic preaching, in city after city around the Mediterranean as the decades passed, and
in each city that company of Christian believers, or church,
was visibly, organically, obediently in fellowship with, and
under, the bishop. Antioch, Smyrna, Alexandria, Carthage,
Lyons—in every place you could find the Christian Church,
and where you found the Church, you found the bishop.
(Actually, it was often expressed the other way around:
"Where the bishop is, there is the Church.") The people
who followed and formed themselves under Marcion, Mani,
or Montanus were not catholic Christians: the term "catholic" was the term that distinguished the Christians who saw
themselves as linked to Jesus Christ via the apostolic link he
had forged.

The bishops were in touch with each other and met in
council intermittently, as the apostles had done, to decide
matters of teaching. or discipline (we may all recall here the
first such council, under James in Jerusalem, where they de-
cided what to teach converts, Jewish and Gentile, about the
law). When the council met, and then spoke, the topic in
question was concluded, so to speak. Debate did not go on
and on and on.

At the same time, everyone took quite soberly the singular
words spoken by Jesus Christ to Simon Peter: "Thou art
Peter, and on this rock I will build my church", and "I will
give you the keys of the kingdom", and "Feed my sheep."
These texts have long since been raked raw in the attempt to
find a "non-Catholic" construction to put upon them: but it

must be acknowledged by all of us that the "Petrine" nature of the Church came into view early. The office of Peter was seen to be the pledge (or the "sacrament"), so to speak, of the Church's visible unity, here in this world, for as long as history lasts. Jesus Christ is, of course, the chief Cornerstone. Other foundation can no man lay than that which is laid in Christ Jesus: all Christians must acknowledge this. But the Roman Catholic Church believes that those peculiar charges given to Peter were what they seem to be. This has been her understanding from the beginning. Peter is, in some sense, that visible "sacrament" on earth, for as long as history goes on, of the unity that binds the Church together and to Jesus Christ her Head.

But this leaves the question of Rome still unanswered. Why Rome?

Peter went to Rome, as we know, and the Church has, from early on, understood his apostolic ministry to have constituted the first episcopal ministry there. There is no such claim made by anyone for St. Paul's preaching and teaching role at Rome.

This Petrine presence in Rome, coupled with the strange fact that, before long, the bishops around the Mediterranean found themselves looking to Rome as if it in some sense represented a "chief" see (bishop's seat), is what lies at the root of the Catholic Church's teaching on the papacy. This sketch of the matter is only that, a sketch, included here, not by way of convincing non-Catholic Christians in the matter, but rather simply to put forward enough bare data so that both Catholics and non-Catholics may at least agree on what exactly it is that Rome thinks about Peter, and hence why this church is called the Roman Catholic Church. It is not a church *other than* the church of Jerusalem and Antioch: it is *how that church grew.*

In this connection, it is not without significance that the phrase *Roma locuta est* (Rome has spoken) began very early to be heard, in matters involving the sort of question taken up by the bishops in their councils. The bishops in Rome— Linus, Anacletus, Clement, and so on—were believed to be the successors to Peter and, thereby, to have inherited the particular office that was his, to teach and rule in the Church. They sat in Peter's seat (see), in this view. In them the Church pointed to the unity that was more than a fantasy and that is dissipated, or violated, every time a man starts the church anew, as it were (again, the precedent of the undoubted unity of Israel, bad as she was, is always in view here). For the apostolic and patristic Church, there was no such thing as any "invisible church", except in the sense that God alone knows who is truly regenerate among catholic Christians in the only Church there is, namely, the visible one. Catholics have always accepted the melancholy fact that there are "unsaved" people in the Church. The Lord's frightening words about the angels burning the sheaves (Mt 13) are always there, judging Roman Catholic ecclesiology.

The notion of a loose network, or aggregate, of assemblies and task forces across the world linked solely by common affirmations about Jesus Christ would have been incomprehensible to them. There was no such thing as an independent Christian, much less an independent assembly of Christians. If you were the believers in Antioch, you were under Ignatius, visibly, organically, and obediently: or else you were schismatics or heretics.

That is ferocious language, not appealing to our ears now. But this sort of terminology seems to have supplied the vocabulary of the discourse, as the Church made her way out into the long haul of history.

It will have long since been clear that another supposition

is at work in all of the foregoing. You are speaking, it may be pointed out, as though the Church herself were some sort of source and authority for things. But we in our group hold fast to a principle that, if lost, casts all into confusion. It is the principle *sola Scriptura.* The Bible alone.

At this point stirrups are checked, lances leveled, banners hoisted, bugles blown. Charge!

It is not, of course, a question to be either trivialized or laid to rest with a colorful metaphor. It is a very high peak in the watershed between the Catholics and the Orthodox, on the one hand, and Protestantism, on the other. Blood as well as ink has flowed in this connection.

St. Augustine has condensed the matter as well as can be done in a very brief rendering. For him, Christians were to look to the Church for authority. Those who accepted "the authority of the Scriptures as preeminent" must, says Augustine, also recognize "that authority which from the time of the [earthly] presence of Christ, through the dispensation of the apostles and through a regular succession of bishops in their seats, has been preserved to our own day throughout the world". This authority, "inaugurated by miracles, nourished by hope, enlarged by charity, established by antiquity", was so powerful as even to validate the authority of the Bible. "For my part, I should not believe the gospel except as moved by the authority of the catholic Church." [1]

Augustine's words echo St. Paul's view of the Church as "the pillar and ground of the truth" (1 Tim 3:15).

Roman Catholic and Orthodox Christians are bemused by the oddity that *sola Scriptura* is itself a non-scriptural

[1] Quoted in Jaroslav Pelikan, *The Christian Tradition: A History of the Development of Doctrine*, vol. 1, *The Emergence of the Catholic Tradition (100–600)* (Chicago: University of Chicago Press, 1971), p. 303.

notion. It is not taught in the Bible. No one had heard of it in the early Church.

To be Catholic is to be conscious of the immense weight to be attached to the teaching office of the Church, known as the Magisterium. There has never been a wedge driven between the Bible and the Church's Magisterium. On the one hand, there was no Bible as we know it—certainly no New Testament—in those early years of the Church. The Gospels and letters were being written; but the believers were instructed by the apostles' teaching. St. Paul keeps adjuring them to hold fast to what they have heard from him and the other apostles. This state of affairs is understood by the Church to be the origin of the authority to teach found in the Church: it is apostolic, and was never abandoned or canceled.

On the other hand, there is the Bible. The Church had the whole of the Law and the Prophets and Psalms and other literature from its Jewish root; and new texts, from Paul, Peter, Luke, John, Matthew, and others, began to be received and read in the Church—at the liturgy, actually: this seems to have been the earliest use to which such writings were put. The Bible, as it came later to be known, was primarily the Church's book. It was not thought of as a bound volume whose principal use would be by the individual believer. Scripture was to be read *in the Church*; or, to put it somewhat differently, Scripture comes peculiarly into its own when it is read at the liturgy. This is its native context, so to speak. Here it is heard in all of its authority and plenitude. "Faith cometh by hearing", our Lord said. It has, from time to time in some sectors of Christendom, seemed as though this ought to be annotated to read "Faith cometh by reading."

To be Catholic is to be acutely conscious of the harmony that obtains between Scripture and the Magisterium. It is not, however, simply to be conscious of this harmony: it is to be deeply grateful for it.

Catholics see the tumult that rises from the contradictory readings of Scripture offered by rival groups in Christendom and wonder what the faithful are supposed to believe when there is no final voice or forum that has power to say, "*This* is what is to be believed, and *that* is heresy." It is, of course, widely imagined that we are now in an epoch that disallows any vocabulary as peremptory as "heresy", since to trot out such a word is to inflame things, for a start, to be "judgmental", and to roil the ecumenical waters. Nevertheless, however we may all wish to soften things, it remains true that not everything can be true. It cannot, for example, be the case that God is at the same time immutable and "in process". Nor can it be true simultaneously that the bread at Communion is only bread, to be used as an aid to memory, and that it is the Body of Christ in a fully sacramental sense. Either there is a hell or there is not. If John Calvin is correct about who may be saved, then John Wesley is wrong. If Christian believers are to be whisked away from danger at the end of time in a "secret rapture", then everyone who supposes that the Church will go through unexampled tribulation as the end approaches is mistaken. Not everything can be true.

The Church ran into questions, not only like these, but, more seriously, over the matter of just exactly who, or what, Jesus Christ was to be believed to be. An excellent man? A prophet filled with the Holy Ghost? A phantom? A creature begotten by God at some remote "point" in past eternity but not eternal as the Father is? These were the questions that vexed the early Church, and Scripture was adduced by all sides. The New Testament supplied everyone, heretic or orthodox, his ammunition. It took the Church in her councils of bishops to settle forever (they believed) such questions. We today believe what we believe about the Son of God because of the Councils at Nicaea, Chalcedon, Ephesus, and Constantinople. We are not left forever leafing back and forth through the New Testament, shoring up our various points of view.

To be Catholic is to appeal to this. When Catholics recite the Creed, for example, it is not as though here were an item to be located either ahead of or behind Scripture. What is being articulated is "the Faith", and this is authoritatively attested by Scripture and by the Church's apostolic teaching authority, and that authority is present, as it has been from the beginning, in the Roman Catholic Church.

4

Going to Church

To be Catholic is to attach immense importance to the re-
current, regular act of going to church.

If pressed, many good Christian people would find it
difficult to put forward compelling reasons for such an act. To
hear the Word preached, perhaps: this would be volunteered
by a great many. But of course one can hear the Word
preached via radio or television without going to the trouble
of dressing, driving, parking, and so forth. There must be
more to it than this.

Yes. We are not to forsake "the assembling of ourselves together", St. Paul tells us. We try to be obedient to that injunction. But of course there are all sorts of assemblings:
suppers, meetings for special prayer or fellowship, parish
business meetings. In what sense do St. Paul's words oblige
me to present myself most particularly for worship? I am
happy to come to any number of church-sponsored assemblies: but her worship occurs just when I have my best
chance to be with my family and to relax with tennis or golf.
And yet gathering for worship seems somehow to take priority.

There must be more to it than mere assembling. Christians
from the very first days after Pentecost have made it their

habit (1) to assemble (2) for worship. Both components in the matter—both the coming together as a group and its specific and limited purpose, namely, for worship—both components belong to the essence of the matter. One can, of course, worship as one walks alone on the beach, but this is not the specific activity known to Christians as the Church's worship, and it will not suffice even for the individual believer to make this solitary activity his characteristic worship. And no matter how busy an agenda of meetings a given parish has, the chief one—nay, the exclusively mandated one—is the meeting for worship.

To be Catholic is not only to have both components in mind; it is to see both as deriving from the very nature of God and man and, hence, as touching the very essence of what the Church is. Assembling. Worship. Why insist on things being just so?

To come at the answer to this we may hark back to Catholic theology itself, which is sacramental. That is, the Church, in keeping with the whole scriptural rendering of things, teaches that in the realm of salvation the physical world has not been huddled offstage, so to speak, but has been swept in, along with the whole creation, to the precincts of the holy, so that physical things (bread, wine, water) may become the very points at which the unseen and eternal touches the seen and temporal.

It is a natural religious tendency to huddle the physical offstage: hence the great appeal of all forms of gnosticism. We mortals like to think of ourselves as "spiritual", which of course we are; but in our eagerness to think thus, we often blithely jump out of our flesh-and-blood selves and talk as though we were pure spirits, disembodied. The poor flesh is left on one side both in our imaginings and in our religious exercises. For nonsacramentalist Christians, it is permitted to sit or stand perhaps, since how else shall we dispose ourselves for religious gatherings. We may speak and sing and listen, since these activities indicate what is in our thoughts and our hearts. But let us not kneel or bow or make physical gestures like the sign of the Cross, or sprinkle things with holy water and hail our olfactory nerve-endings with incense: all of that is too heavily physical, and we know that the physical has been set aside by the New Testament.

No, says the Church. No, says the Bible. No, says our humanity. The New Testament was inaugurated, not by the Word of God arriving through the ether, but by that very "Word" arriving and lodging in the womb of a woman. And then this coming of the Word to us proceeds on its way with a Visitation, when its cousin, also in the womb, leaps in recognition, and with a Circumcision, and hunger and fatigue and tears, and finally thorns and flogging and Crucifixion.

Very physical, this New Covenant. But of course *then* things rise to pure spirituality surely? Yes, if we mean by this that a New Creation is now inaugurated. But if we mean that all is now restricted to thoughts and spirits, and the human intellect and will, then no. A body comes back from the dead; whatever this body is, it is not a phantom. It has wounds, not illusionary wounds; and it can eat. And it is "taken up into heaven": again, the Bible and the Church speak of this as an actual event, not a mere idea. It is an event, however, that occurs on the frontier between the seen and the unseen, and between the temporal and the eternal. No one can plot out the trajectory of the Ascension or speak of acceleration and speed and distance in connection with this mystery: and yet it is all real, somehow—even literal, even physical. The very words real and physical and literal are "born again", so to speak, when they appear in this New Creation: but they are not empty metaphors. They summon us to the mystery that presides over this frontier between the seen, as we are accustomed to it, and the unseen, which reaches beyond our mortal imaginings.

And it is on this very frontier that Christian gathering for worship occurs. It matters that the people—embodied men and women and children—*show up*. It is not good enough that they remain at home, an invisible "church" connected by good will and a commonalty of belief. Even telephone hook-ups won't do. We must *all be here*, under this actual roof (or in this field, if that must be), in our bodies. Catholic theology, because it is wholly sacramental, has already set the stage for this physical assembling. Catholic theology has for its native turf this frontier land between the "physical" and the "spiritual" (again, the words themselves seem to overreach their commonplace significance), where the temporal touches the eternal and becomes the very vehicle of the eternal (a womb: an infant, blood, bread, wine, water). This is the very region of sacramentalism. It is the region in which we find ourselves when we have gone to the trouble to get ourselves up and out of our several houses across the city and have collected here in close juxtaposition with each other.

We are now more than a crowd. We are more, even, than an audience. We are a *congregatio*. This, said our Greek-speaking forerunners in the faith, is the *synaxis*—the gathering. It is a physical event and a physical presence that reaches far deeper than mere psychology, which might volunteer that it's *nice* to get together; togetherness achieves an ethos; we all find ourselves encouraged and stirred and revivified in such an ethos.

All of that, to be sure, says the Church. But that is thin gruel next to the Christian (sacramental) substance brought into actuality by the collecting together of these people in their bodies. What you have here is an epiphany, really: you see "the Church".

That might seem so painfully obvious as to be anticlimactic, after all of this sacramental build-up. But we will have failed to grasp the fully Christian meaning of things if we suppose that to say "the Church" here implies simply these believers who happen to constitute this chance crowd, come together to sing, pray, and hear the Word, since that is their custom.

Again, all that is certainly the case. But again the Catholic Church teaches that in this particular gathering (as opposed to the same people assembled for fellowship, a conference, or a supper) the Church herself appears. For in the liturgy—the Mass, that is: the act of worship as understood by Catholic Christians—the eternal Church, Spouse of Christ, is constituted, here, in this place, at this hour, by this gathering. The eternal, that is, has appeared in time and place, under sacramental species. We *are* "the Church".

But then what of the ten thousand times ten thousand others who surely must be included in any talk of "the Church"? Millions have gone before us through death, for one thing: and millions are scattered all over the globe, not here. We cannot call this little company "the Church".

Yes, we can, says the Church. For in the liturgy the scrim that divides the seen from the unseen is drawn back in more than a merely psychological way, and the whole Church in heaven and on earth is here, just as the whole of the Godhead was there in the manger even though the Holy Trinity was also "in heaven" and "omnipresent". No diagrams will help here. The riddle (Christians call these things mysteries, and *sacrament* is the Latin word for the Greek *mysterion*) outrages all that is calculating and rational in us. Nevertheless, it is so, says Christian faith.

The whole Church is here. We may see nothing but some bent and doddering figure in threadbare vestments at the altar and one old man in a pew. Behold the Church! says the Church. Angels and archangels and all the company of heaven are present, literally—and again, "literal" outstrips its ordinary suggestion of the tangible, the visible, and the spatial: those are qualities that belong to the physical world, and that world is only one ingredient, so to speak, in any sacramental situation, which embraces the whole fabric of creation, the physical and the transphysical.

The priest and the old man; the straggling noonday gathering of shoppers and tourists at St. Patrick's on Fifth Avenue; the troops bobbing in the LST en route to Normandy Beach; or the half million in St. Peter's Square with the Bishop of Rome himself at the altar in front of that gigantic façade: here and at any Mass in Peoria, Billings, or Cape Horn we may see the Church.

In this sense Catholics do indeed differ from their fellow Christians who also "go to church" but who would scarcely see anything mystical, much less sacramental, in the crowd they form when they have settled into their pews. A Catholic is (or ought to be) acutely conscious of crossing a metaphysical line, as it were, when he goes to church. He sees himself as both summoned and invited: summoned to appear before the Sapphire Throne and at the same time invited to a Supper.

To this extent, of course, any Christian, Catholic or not, may share the profound sense of occasion that broods over such a summons from such a king and such an invitation from such a host. And on the surface of things, we must admit, Catholics do not differ very much from their Protestant fellow believers: both tend to arrive in church somewhat distracted, chatting, looking around to see who is there, and generally only very poorly disposed in the inner man.

But Catholic custom plucks us by the sleeve, we may say. There is a holy-water stoup just inside the door, for a start. When non-Catholics see Catholics dab their finger at the water and make a hasty gesture that may or may not touch forehead, breast, and both shoulders, they conclude that this is merely a bit of mumbo-jumbo that is part of one's being Catholic. The little ritual is, to be sure, part of one's being Catholic, but it is neither "merely" nor mumbo-jumbo, if by mumbo-jumbo we mean meaningless superstition. To touch oneself with holy water in the form of a cross is to acknowledge, on the deepest possible level, that one wishes to be found among the company of the holy—the angels, saints, and all the redeemed—and that one is thereby aware of his own need both for cleansing and also for being specially set apart for service in the Holy of Holies. The water, which has itself been "blessed", that is, set apart for use in connection with holy things, speaks to him of his baptism, in which the stain of original sin was washed away and which he must daily recall so that he may order his life, day by day, in the light of this washing. It reminds him of the washing so scrupulously observed by the priests of the Old Testament when they readied themselves to offer sacrifice in the Tabernacle, since he is himself a member of the priestly people set apart to offer sacrifice in the holy place where Jesus Christ's own self-offering has superseded all the Old Testament sacrifices. And the sign of the Cross he makes, having dipped his finger in the water, announces, first to himself, then to all of heaven, earth, and hell that he enters this holy service only insofar as he is found "under" the Cross of Jesus Christ, to which he clings for salvation. There is no other refuge. Apart from this Cross, he is an outcast. This alone is the sign and the reality to which he must bind himself if he is to be numbered among those bidden into these precincts.

It will have been noticed long since that it is physical matter (water) and a physical gesture (the sign of the Cross, entailing one's hand and arm) that bear this immense freight of significance. Nothing is more natural to a Catholic, supported as he is by the Church's teaching on sacrament: of course the physical—matter and gesture—is to be brought into play in the service of what is true. Non-Catholic Christians often find it difficult to grant to any mode other than words this task of bearing significance. Gestures begin to look like magic: such is often the suspicion. A Catholic, if he is taxed on the issue, can readily point to all the other human situations in which we call upon gesture rather than mere words to be the carrier of significance: nods, waves, kisses, embraces. We are verbal creatures, to be sure. But we are not *only* verbal creatures. It is the gnostics, not the Christians, who wish we were.

So: Catholic custom assists us as we come to church. It plucks us by the sleeve with, "Pause. Recollect. Remember where you are and what you are about to do. You come to the Throne, and to the Altar, and to the Supper."

But there are two further customs traditionally observed by Catholics that also help in this connection. As we move from the doorway, with its holy water stoup, along the aisle to where we will sit, we drop onto our right knee before we take our seat. Again, to a non-Catholic, the movement may look perfunctory. (His opinion in the matter may, alas, have formed itself on the evidence to be drawn from the egregiously perfunctory manner in which many Catholics make the move.)

This is called genuflecting. Most Catholics become so accustomed to genuflecting that the matter sinks into their semiconsciousness. They would have to stop and make a conscious decision if they were to omit it. They would feel vaguely uneasy merely to saunter in and plop into a seat.

But again, this action, so routine, occurs precisely on the frontier between the seen and the unseen, and to miss it, or to look upon it as frivolous, is to fail seriously in discernment.

For what is at stake here is nothing less than my mortal approach to the precincts of the holy. On the surface it is only I—Jane or Bill—getting seated, and it is only this unspectacular building on this random street, and it is 10:57 on the morning of October 5, shall we say. The statistics suggest that what we have at stake is almost nothing at all. Nobody, arriving at no particular church, on no particular day of history. Pure routine. Entirely humdrum.

No. The statistics always miss everything. A drab village in a drab province, on a night like all other nights in a year not to be distinguished from any other year that has dragged on time out of mind in a stable behind an inn not listed in Michelin. Nothing here. Only God being born, and angels singing *Gloria*.

The eternal does this. It attires itself in the routine, the inauspicious, the anonymous. It does this because it reserves itself (it is so holy) for the pure eye of faith. The little pig eyes that leer at things with concupiscence, the glaring eyes that challenge, or the haughty eyes that annihilate cannot see it. The eye of faith alone can pierce the surface and see Reality.

That is why Catholics genuflect when they come to church. They know that this is a holy place, and to be found on one's knee is a very good posture in such precincts. It says, ceremonially, not verbally, "I am a creature, and thou art my Creator. I am thy child and thou art my Father. I am a subject and thou art my Sovereign. And, alas, I am a sinner, and thou art holy." To kneel, only briefly, in this fashion is to order one's body as well as one's mind to what is true. A Catholic has difficulty in grasping what it is that non-Catholics espouse that precludes this act. Surely we are not mere minds? Surely all of us bring physical gesture to bear on all situations (a wave, a nod, a kiss). Why is the physical excluded here? Surely to exclude it here and here alone is to imply a gnostic (disembodied), not a Christian (incarnational) state of affairs?

There is also, and preeminently, a particular significance to the act of genuflecting. It is not simply to acknowledge the generally holy. Catholics follow the early Church in taking the Lord's teaching in the sixth chapter of John altogether soberly. He spoke of immense mysteries there—of the bread that comes down from heaven and of his giving his flesh for the world and of this bread being his flesh. Very difficult matter, not to be approached, much less dismissed, by common sense, or even by gigantic intellectual prowess, least of all by myopic exegesis. The apostolic Church, to a man, understood him to mean that this bread, when it is taken and spoken over as he did in the Upper Room, *is* (not recalls) his Body. To perceive a miracle here, and not simply a memorial, is to be at one with the ancient Church.[1] To think otherwise

---

[1] Ignatius of Antioch (A.D. 35–107): "But consider those who are of a different opinion with respect to the grace of Christ which has come unto us, how opposed they are to the will of God. . . . They abstain from the Eucharist and from prayer, because they confess not the Eucharist to be the flesh of our Saviour Jesus Christ, which suffered for our sins . . ." (*Epistle to the Smyraeans*, VI, VII; in *The Ante-Nicene Fathers*, vol. 1 [Grand Rapids: William B. Eerdmans Publishing, 1979], 89).

Justin Martyr (A.D. 100–165): "For not as common bread and common drink do we receive these; but in like manner as Jesus Christ our Saviour, having been made flesh by the Word of God, had both flesh and blood for our salvation, so likewise have we been taught that the food which is blessed by the prayer of His word, and from which our blood and flesh by transmutation

is to dissociate oneself from that lineage and to choose a view appearing very late in time.

Because the bread offered in the Mass is, mysteriously (sacramentally), the Body of the Lord, the Church has always treated the consecrated species with the reverence due the Lord if he were present in the flesh. (If? No, since. This is the belief of the Church from the beginning.) Since this is the case, then the Lord may be said to be "there" (again, space and time stagger) on the altar, in the tabernacle, where the consecrated species are kept. It is all, as we have admitted, nonsense to common sense. The mystery that the Church acknowledges, "pinpointed" there in the tabernacle, rebuffs all efforts to come at it with the powers native to us mortals. Science, logic, and magic all stagger here. Only faith assists us across the threshold into the holy place where the Church gathers and kneels, in obedience to the summons.

This brings us to the third action customary among Catholics as they enter the church and prepare themselves to celebrate the sacred mysteries (the other two being, as we have seen, the signing of ourselves with holy water and genuflecting). Visitors will notice that everyone, having found his chair or his place in the pew, thereupon kneels again. The first order of business at this point is not the arranging of one's

are nourished, is the flesh and blood of that Jesus who was made flesh" (*The First Apology*, LXVI; in *The Ante-Nicene Fathers*, vol. 1 [Grand Rapids: William B. Eerdmans Publishing, 1979], 185).

Irenaeus (A.D. 130-200): "When, therefore, the mingled cup and the manufactured bread receives the Word of God, and the Eucharist of the blood and the body of Christ is made, from which things the substance of our flesh is increased and supported, how can they affirm that the flesh is incapable of receiving the gift of God, which is life eternal, which is nourished from the body and blood of the Lord, and is a member of Him?" (*Against Heresies*, II; in *The Ante-Nicene Fathers*, vol. 1 [Grand Rapids: William B. Eerdmans Publishing, 1979], 528).

purse or coat or greeting one's acquaintances in the nearby pews. It is to pray.

What else are we mortals to do at such a point? Adam and Eve hid themselves when they heard the voice of the Lord God. Noah built an altar. Abraham did likewise. Isaiah cried out, Woe is me! The shepherds were sore afraid. St. John the Divine on Patmos fell down as one dead. Every one of these exhibited the response proper to us mortals in the presence of the Most High. They all showed that they had been well schooled: this is what you do if you are a true man when the Deity draws near. And in so doing, you show, to all of heaven, earth, and hell, the great dignity with which we men are crowned.

Dignity? Surely such groveling betrays the dread of thralls and helots before a tyrant?

Dread, yes: groveling, no. There is a paradox here. We might speak of a salutary dread, that is, the acute awareness on the part of the creature, sheltered as he is in ordinary circumstances by all that pertains to the familiar, that suddenly immensity has opened out before him. The familiar, the domestic, and the near-at-hand have suddenly fled, as heaven and earth are said to flee away from the presence of the Most High. He finds himself hailed with—with what? How shall we find words for what faith sees? Blinding Glory. Thunderous majesty. Searing purity. Unfiltered light. Such splendor that sapphire itself scarcely suffices to suggest it. If the seraphim cover their faces, what are we to do? What is the protocol in these precincts? How is one to dispose himself?

We, mortals that we are, can only take our cue from the venerable figures of Adam and Abraham and St. John. In them we may see how mortality disposes itself in the presence of the Ever-living One.

And of course what we see is this paradox: somehow the

thing that is clearly evinced in the attitudes these figures adopt when they find themselves at the holy place turns out to be, not groveling servitude, but rather the capacity, immensely noble, to recognize and to adore that Glory from which the lesser glory that crowns our own species proceeds. Far from recalling thralls and helots, what we witness here recalls, rather, the noble solemnity apparent when a great prince doffs his coronet and bows before the greater nobility of his sovereign. In that bow, somehow, we see the mark of greatness. It is your popinjay and your cock-o'-the-walk who strut and puff and miss all the cues. St. John: the seraphim: the prince: this is the company among which I would wish, at last, to be found.

No such picture, of course, ordinarily presents itself as we kneel briefly before Mass. Most of the time it is only the very modest business of trying to dragoon one's thoughts and to achieve some rag of collectedness and focus as we arrive yet again to offer the sacrifice in the presence of the Divine Majesty and to sup at his table.

It is not always easy to know exactly what to say when we kneel to offer a prayer before Mass. In the days when there were all sorts of devotional books full of prayers for every possible juncture in the Catholic's day, the faithful had at their finger-tips all the prayers anyone could possibly want. Now, when it is widely supposed that people do better to consult their own resources when it comes to prayer, we may find ourselves either casting about for words or offering an Our Father or simply remaining in a kneeling posture for what seems a creditable lapse of time with nothing more occurring in the inner man than, "Hmm. What is one to say at a moment like this? I never have anything very apt to offer. Alas."

The following prayer, from the Chaldean Liturgy, gives

expression to one way of disposing oneself as one approaches the sacred mysteries. On the other hand, it raises a question to which there is no altogether satisfying answer. Here is the prayer:

> Before the glorious seat of Thy Majesty, O Lord, and the exalted throne of Thine honor and the awful judgment seat of Thy burning love and the absolving altar which Thy command hath set up, and the place where Thy glory dwelleth, we, Thy people and the sheep of Thy fold, do kneel with thousands of the cherubim singing Alleluia, and many times ten thousand seraphim and archangels acclaiming Thine holiness, worshipping, confessing, and praising Thee at all times, O Lord of All.

The question is, does this language come to us from such a remote distance in time and in sentiment that it is unusable? Nothing in us, we may protest, ever soars to those empyrean arches. We live in a much more humdrum world. We moderns don't incline toward awful judgment seats and burning love and ten thousand seraphim. That is not our language. I just want God (or, as many Catholics say, "the Man Upstairs") to know I'm here at Mass. Our Father, who art. . . .

Yes. Such a demurral in the face of that Chaldean acclamation is not to be scoffed at. Those sentiments are very far from being native to us. But, if we press our point here, two considerations might help us to see things in a greater light.

First, *ought* those remote Chaldean sentiments to remain quite so remote for us? Our forerunners in the faith, for thousands of years, thought of God in such terms: Will we put forward the tiny scrap of time known as the "modern world" by way of dissociating ourselves utterly from such notions? The language would not have seemed odd to our Hebrew fathers in the faith; and our own Christian lineage, from St. John, through St. John Chrysostom, Augustine, Benedict, Bernard, and Francis, has found such expressions to be apt. Surely we cannot suppose that the very small circumference drawn around our own vocabulary and sentiments by "modernity" is a circumference worth defending?

Second, as it happens, we *do* approach such lofty regions every time we open our mouths at all to pray. "Lord, help me!" Or, "O God, forgive me!" What have we invoked here? Lord? What Lord? Certainly not the local mayor or the governor or the President. Who? Who? It is Jesus, whose name means Savior. The one sought by seers and prophets and wise men, by the blood of Abel crying out from the ground, and by Hagar in her dereliction, and by all widows, orphans, and dispossessed people from the beginning. Lord, help me. *Exaudi orationem meam.* The cry goes up from every page of history. By framing such a request at all we have at once placed ourselves in that innumerable and immemorial lineage of supplicants who have called upon the name of the Lord.

Or again, perhaps we rattle from time to time, "Hail Mary, full of grace. . . ." Here we sweep back at one stroke the curtain that hangs between the little daily world (Nazareth; late-twentieth-century America) and the eternal. What do we come upon with these words? *Angelus Domini nuntiavit Mariae.* Heaven has broken through to Nazareth—to us all.

We cannot so much as say one Hail Mary without bringing down the whole of glory onto our heads. Our great task, of course, is so to dispose ourselves, day by day, that we will become increasingly the sort of person who can receive such annunciations from heaven.

The Chaldean acclamation may give us help here. It may hale us out of the dim backwater of the modern world, into the bright regions where Truth dwells. It may alarm us with

its language about awful judgment and burning love and thus
awaken us from the lethal torpor of self-absorption into
which our own epoch has lulled us with its soft crooning of
"You have to find yourself. You must be your own person.
Look inside yourself." It may astound us with its seraphim
and cherubim; and it will certainly supply us with a vocabulary, long lost to our impoverished argot, that we may bring
with us as we venture toward the glorious seat of that Majesty. (Majesty: not a category for us. But is it we or Majesty
that is under scrutiny when we point this out?)

So. We kneel for a moment before Mass. The Father who
has bidden us here is eager for whatever stuttering we can
manage. Lord, help thou mine unbelief. Lord, I am not worthy. Where dwellest thou? Who art thou, Lord? Surely the
Lord is in this place. *Miserere mei.* Our Father. Help me to
collect my thoughts here. Help me to forgive that one who
makes my life a nightmare. Lord, I never can think of anything very much to say.

The Chaldeans can help us here—or a thousand other
ready-made prayers, from old devotional books or from the
back cover of the newsprint missalette. Or, if we are the sort
from whose heart springs a great rush of spontaneous love
and joy and praise, without external helps, so much the better.

But one way or another, by the sign of the Cross, by
genuflecting, and by saying a prayer, Catholics make their
way *ad altare Dei*—up to the altar of God, to God who is the
joy of our youth, as was said at the beginning of the liturgy
for many centuries.

This is very much the picture when Catholics speak of
"going to church". They are not thinking of a meeting primarily—even a meeting for such salutary activities as singing,
testifying, enjoying Christian fellowship, or even hearing the
Word preached. None of these is the anchor point. The very

Word preached at Mass is one with the Word partaken in the sacrament of the altar. It is the Word spoken in Eden, given on Sinai, announced by prophets, incarnate in the womb of the Virgin, crucified, risen, ascended, and given to us, his people, by his promise, until he comes again.

When a Catholic "goes to church", these are the sacred mysteries among which he finds himself.

5

Eucharist

To be Catholic is to have a profoundly eucharistic notion of what the activity of worship is. To be sure, worship may go up to the Most High in various fashions: St. Francis' gladsome biddings to sun and moon and fire and water to praise God; the gigantic music of J. S. Bach's B Minor Mass; the spontaneous exclamation "Praise Jesus!"; the waving of charismatics' arms; the stillness in the choir of an abbey church; Southern Baptists singing "What a Friend We Have in Jesus"; or the murmur arising from the simultaneous prayers offered by Pentecostalists kneeling at their pews. To be Christian at all is to recognize, and extol, this great panoply of adoration with which all creation decks itself. It is to hear the praises of God in the soughing of the west wind, the soft fall of surf on pebbles, and the song of the winter wren, the hermit thrush, or the white-throated sparrow and even in the scream of jays and the cackle of crows.

But the still point at the center of it all, for a Catholic, is the Eucharist. The Mass. For it is here that the entire chorus is gathered and brought to a point, the point, that is, at which we (men and women, uniquely made "in the image of God") stand before the Most High as speaking for the whole creation. It is in *our* explicit, conscious, intelligent, and voluntary offering of the oblation of worship that the sea, the wind, and the thrushes find the exactness adumbrated in their own offerings. Catholics believe that God gave to Adam and Eve, in some deeply mysterious sense, the "vicariate", so to speak, over the creation: that they were to "stand for" the rest of creation before God and to speak, actually, to God for all creatures, with the godlike articulateness with which we alone are crowned. All of this implies that we are to be kind and good stewards of this creation and not plunder or rifle or rape.

But of course that is exactly what we have done, plunging the whole world into tragedy and ruin, by our own perfidious act when we stretched out our hands in Eden to seize a prerogative not vouchsafed to us, who are creatures. This act wrecked all and opened the gates of hell, from which sin, sorrow, and death rushed upon us.

The chorus of worship was suddenly drowned in sadness. This sadness is what we hear in the sighs of the oppressed and the poor, the whimpering of wounded animals and birds, the groans of the sick, and the cries from the depths of our own disfranchised hearts. *Kyrie eleison. Agnus Dei, qui tollis peccata mundi, miserere nobis!* we cry.

What is that? Lord, have mercy. O Lamb of God, you take away the sins of the world, have mercy on us!

How did we come to this from Eden? Alas, our own disobedience was our undoing, and the undoing of the whole creation. We, not the wind and sea and birds, are the villains. They have received their ruin from us. So it had to be one of us who restored the fabric. But who? Adam? No, he was the culprit and, in him, I. Then who will go for us? Who is worthy?

Thou shalt call his name Jesus, for he shall save his people from their sins.

Ah. The Savior. The Second Adam. The Lamb of God, offering himself to the Father in our behalf, in a sacrifice that redeems Adam and Eve, and you and me, and the whole creation stricken with our sin. The only way for the great chorus of adoration to be restored is through this offering. All praise flows now through this mystery—the mystery of the self-offering of the Son of God, unfurled at the table in the Upper Room and played out at Golgotha the next day.

There is no disjuncture in the Catholic mind between sacrifice and praise. They are not two separate activities, as though sacrifice were the grim part and praise the happy part. No. All true praise arises from sacrifice of some sort—from the "offering up" of what I have, "I" being the wind or the sea or the thrush or the man. It is I, bringing what I can offer and presenting it to the Giver. If he has given me a song, as he has the hermit thrush, then that is what I bring. If he has given me proud waves and foam and roaring, then that is what I bring. If he has given me might and wisdom and love, then that is what I, the seraph, offer.

But if he has made me in his own image, crowned me with a dignity belonging alone to the race of man, and put into my hands the awful mystery of free will, then the offering I bring is a unique one. But what is this offering to be? The words of my mouth, to be sure. The works of my hands, to be sure. But all of that must be caught up and ratified in the offering—the "sacrifice"—of myself. Self-offering. Self-donation. There is where the mystery of true praise lies.

By this time we seem to find ourselves in a region where sacrifice and praise and love itself run together (for is not love the name given to total self-donation in behalf of the other?).

To be Catholic is to believe that this region is, lo and behold, the Kingdom of Heaven; and that the Church is the "sacrament" of that Kingdom here on earth for as long as history lasts; and that the Church's quintessentially characteristic activity for as long as history lasts is to offer herself, day by day, in union with the One Offering that could save us, to the Father, from whom all self-donation proceeds. For the Father is One God with the Son and Holy Spirit, and in these Three, who are One, we discover the fountainhead of all self-donation, which spills over in its plenitude and sparkles all across the whole creation.

The place, or the act, rather, where all of this is made present to us mortals is the Mass. The Mass is the event in which we see most exactly, most clearly, and most plenteously the entire mystery of self-donation. God "gave" himself to us in creation, when he crowned us with his own image. He gave himself to us in all of his patience and forbearance with us through the aeons between Eden and Nazareth—in sending us Moses and the prophets and the law—even in supplying to us the very lambs and goats we needed for our offerings to him. But at Nazareth, then at Bethlehem, and then at Cana and Bethsaida and Capernaum, and finally at Jerusalem, he disclosed the true nature of this self-giving: in Jesus, his only begotten Son, who became obedient unto death, even the death of the Cross, he gave himself to the uttermost.

The mystery staggers us. It cannot be penetrated. It is inexhaustible. This is why no Catholic is troubled by what may look to outsiders as the unremitting *repetition* of the Mass: millions of Masses, everywhere, century after century, over and over and over. Is it not a treadmill? What about "vain repetition" such as marks heathendom and against which our Lord himself warns us?

The Mass is very far from being the mere repetition of something. Rather, in its action it takes us mortals across the

threshold that lies between time and eternity and locates us
in that Presence where there is no time and, hence, no repetition. In this Presence (it is called eternity), that which is
true appears in its perfection. There is neither before nor after. (We might try the word "perpetuity" here, except that,
like all human vocabulary, it too fails in these precincts, tied
as it is to the notion of "on and on and on".) There is only
Actuality, we might say. That which "was" ever true "is always" true: we even have to acknowledge with quotation
marks our awareness that the verb *to be* itself is insufficient for
the mystery.

This difficulty of locating just where in time we are in the
Mass suggests at least one aspect of the mystery that cloaks
Calvary and the Incarnation itself. Jesus Christ was "the
Lamb slain from the foundation of the world", and yet this
was not played out in our earthly time "until" he suffered *sub
Pontio Pilato*. But Christians, of all people, insist upon the reality of time, with its before and after. We are not transcendentalists, or even Platonists, who suspect that the terms of
our mortal existence are somehow illusionary. Time is a
component of the creation and, hence, real. Solid, we might
even venture. This is why that prepositional phrase *sub Pontio
Pilato* is so crucial in the Creed. The events that constitute
the gospel do not exist in some floating mode, attached only
very ambiguously to our own real history. (To read many
twentieth-century theologians, both Protestant and Catholic,
one would be led to suppose that the events to which the
kerygma—the preaching—of the early Church testified cannot quite be located on the same screen with the battles of
Marathon, Malplaquet, or Omaha Beach.) No, says the
Catholic Church: Jesus Christ, the "Second Adam", the Savior, God with us, was crucified by the Romans, and this mis-
erable miscarriage of justice, which can be dated and located,

was at the same time the eternal self-oblation of the Son to the Father in behalf of us sinners (including me and the Romans).

It is a mystery. Indeed, says the Church—and it is this very mystery into which we are drawn in the Mass. When Catholics go to church they are doing something they did yesterday, or last week, and doing it "again". But the "again" applies only to them, not to the mystery that is always taking place in the heavenly Mysteries, where our Great High Priest offers himself at the heavenly altar (the whole epistle of the Hebrews is about this). The Mass unites us with this offering. It is we who go and come. It is we who experience it as "again and again". The mystery is present. It is "always" present (we have to reach for an adverb of time), and to go to Mass is to return to the center. It is to corral the clutter of ourselves and our time and our distractions and perplexities and joys and sufferings and to bring them to the still point of the turning world.

To this extent, the Mass is very much like the events of the Gospel itself. That is, in those events we saw eternal mysteries appearing veiled under the inauspicious terms, not only of our world, but of the most unlikely crannies of our world. Nazareth: the ultimate small town. A stable: dung and straw for the child born to the purple. Crucifixion: the worst that our malice could arrange. And yet in all of these the eye of faith sees glory. It finds at these points what T. S. Eliot called "the point of intersection of the timeless with time".

Likewise with the Mass. To all intents and purposes, it is 8:00 A.M. on Tuesday, June 13, A.D. 304, or A.D. 1995, in Lyons or Peoria. But we have stepped, the way the shepherds did, into the precincts of the eternal. No straw, no dung, no braying ass, that does not belong here. Belong here? Surely the mystery is to be perceived *in spite of* all that noisome stuff?

No. Belongs here. This is where, and how, the Most High

prepared and set the scene for his advent. Let the straw stay; let the straw be acclaimed even, since in it all straw is touched with the dignity of proffering something to the Most High. If the asses are what they truly are, made by this Most High, then their very dung testifies to the odd and cyclic harmony that characterizes this creation. The Incarnate One will not draw fastidious skirts away from this that marks his beloved asses. No: he will be found, quite helpless, right here.

For this reason Catholics are not primarily concerned with the elegance of the setting for the Mass. Oh, God be thanked (they will admit) for great architecture, which is itself our mortal offering *ad maiorem Dei gloriam*. What could be more appropriate than the purity of the basilica, the immense height of the gothic, the ebullience of the baroque, or the modesty of Spanish adobe? Let us deck the holy place thus. Yes. But we all know that God did not shun a stable for farm beasts. Hence he may be found, in his sacramental presence, in all sorts of structures, from the Gesù in Rome to a prefabricated, jerry-built hall on Long Island. Whether it is marble, ceramic tile, linoleum, or straw underfoot is a matter of only the smallest significance (it is not significant at all to him: it is we who care and who do well, in fact, to offer the best that we can to him: if we can manage ceramic tile, so be it: if mud is the best we have, so be it).

And it is thus with everything with which we deck the Mass. Vestments: burlap or polyester will do as well as damask, if that is what we can manage. Decor: caramel and pink and mint green are possible colors for the plaster, as well as white. God will not carp. Music: chant and the polyphony of Allegri would seem to stand at a remote pole from some of the candied ditties heard now and again at a Mass. But a strange alchemy goes to work on the strains of our mortal music as it ascends to the Throne, and if it has been offered with humility, integrity, and wholeheartedness, it will be received by the One on the Throne as pure and just.

There is a separate topic in all of this, namely, the extent to which we mortals are, or are not, obliged somehow to welcome instruction in these matters and to test our local, tribal "taste" by the wisdom of history and the Church. We might discover, for example, that Gregorian chant, while it may not at all appeal to us at first, does have a unique capacity to bear us aloft, in a way not quite true of our favorite ditties. Or again, if we are humble enough to inquire into architectural matters, we may find our hasty local inclinations chastened and instructed by history and by the Church's strange and rich interaction with history. But none of this alters in the smallest degree the reality of what Catholics seek when they come to church.

"What Catholics seek when they come to church." That has, of course, been the topic occupying us for many pages now. But it may be worth pressing home a point that often troubles observers of Catholic worship and that certainly rises in the consciousness of Christians coming to the Mass having been nurtured in denominations where hearty fellowship and humming activity are the hallmarks of Sunday morning at church. It can be the case (not always: thousands of Catholic parishes are as convivial as the most tumultuous evangelical parish)—it can be the case, however, that one comes to Mass from the happy precincts of Evangelicalism, say, and goes away at the end with great sadness. "But I miss the fellowship!" he might say. "I didn't sense the eager atmosphere of glad attention and participation I knew in my former church."

This response from a newcomer touches on a matter very near the center of the mystery brooding over Christian worship. When a Roman Catholic "goes to church", he sees himself as *joining himself* to something that is already going on. He sets aside both the hurly-burly of his domestic or professional situation and any preoccupation he may have with such patently excellent concerns as fellowship or chat or even a certain vitality in the air. He has been summoned to the *unum necessarium*. He here takes his place—literally, he believes—with angels and archangels and with all the company of heaven, who *incessabili* laud and magnify the Holy Name of the Most High, as the *Te Deum* puts it. This is the Mass, he says to himself. This is the eucharistic mystery, in which there is presented, and enacted, everything that has flowed from the heart of the Father in our creation and redemption. There is no possible exhausting of this. Hence in this liturgy—this "work of the people"—I return to this center, descrying ever anew the amplitude of the Divine Love incarnate for us men and for our salvation in Jesus Christ, whose Table we now approach.

To speak of things in this way is to speak truthfully of what is (or should be) in the mind of every Catholic as he comes to church. But it is to leave unsaid a major aspect of what is at work here, namely, that our Catholic comes, not only to join himself to the heavenly worship, but also to join himself to fellow believers who have also come.

Worship is not a solitary activity. (It may be, of course: Antony in his cell in Egypt, or I as I walk my dog, or the old woman kneeling at the shrine over there.) Worship is most characteristically a corporate thing. It is what the whole creation does, of course, with stars and winds and marmosets all bringing their peculiar oblations. And it is what the great company, to which we, the Church, have been united in Christ, does. In the Latin Mass this company is spelled out for the ears of the faithful in the first eucharistic prayer: the Virgin Mary, *Genetrix Dei*, and then the blessed apostles and martyrs, *Petri et Pauli . . . Lini, Cleti, Clementis . . . Cosmae et Damiani . . .* and all the saints, with all the angelic hosts. And this company is not primarily chatting and greeting each other. The whole throng faces in one direction, like the congregation in the abbey when the monarch is crowned, or the multitude at Golgotha where that Man is being crucified. Our "togetherness" does not at this point take the form of demonstrative friendliness to each other. Rather, we are united, each to each, at a level infinitely deeper than chat. We face, and adore together, the *Mysterium Tremendium.*

We have fugitive glimpses of what it is like in Scripture. Isaiah had a fleeting view of it and was undone. St. John the Divine found himself at a point when "there was silence in heaven for the space of half an hour." Who will so much as shift his feet here?

It is this vision that arches over the Mass. The faithful have come together here, as is *dignum et justum.* But the quality of being together has now been mantled with a mantle heavier than conviviality. This mantle, we might venture, partakes of the same flesh the Savior wore in his Incarnation. We are his *Body.* What can this mean? It is mystery, not to be dissipated by helpful talk of "body" suggesting mere togetherness, as in a metaphor. We have risen above the reach of metaphor here, to the realm of sacrament, where metaphor finally drops away, and meaning touches the actuality that the metaphor hints. In these precincts bread *is* (not recalls) the Sacred Body. Wine *is* (not signifies) the Precious Blood. The *congregatio* is the body of which Jesus Christ is the Head. Oh, to be sure, like the bread that still lies there with all the modest properties of a baked wafer of wheat, we are still Tom, Dick, and Harry. But we are Tom, Dick, and Harry born anew and constituting the Body of Christ in a way not to be fully grasped until we finally break through this veil of time.

It is awe-ful. But it is true. Hence, when a Catholic comes
to church, he does well to remind himself of this and to dispose himself accordingly. And for the new Catholic, wistful
over all the happy tokens of togetherness he knew in his
former church, it is a daunting but joyous summons "farther
up and farther in", where *congregatio* takes on immense
weight and splendor.[1]

---

[1] What, then, are we to gather from the restlessness, scuffling, crying of
babies, and coming and going that mark many a Catholic Mass? Has everyone
lost sight utterly of the sacred mysteries that loom here?

No doubt many have done just that. We mortals are a scatterbrained lot,
and even when the Messiah is feeding us miraculously by Galilee, we are likely
to be found blowing our noses, chasing after our tots, nipping into the bushes
to relieve ourselves, or struggling to help our neighbor adjust his coat. We do
not do well when it comes to occasions. Unimportant, and even frivolous,
matters distract us.

The Most High is aware of this. He made us. Hence he is infinitely patient
with our efforts, intermittent and halfhearted though they may be, to present
ourselves before him. The reality at work in the occasion remains: the Infant
God is still there in the manger, notwithstanding the braying of asses to the
contrary. The loaves and fishes are still purveyed. The Mass still goes on.

For the man or woman who wishes most earnestly to remain collected and
focused in the presence of the mysteries, things may be trying indeed. But
grace, and the self-discipline that cooperates with grace, can assist us here.
Probably St. Francis was as happily lost in the liturgy with great tumult and
disorder all about as he was in the cool hush when only the brothers were
celebrating. Very few of us can even imagine this peaceful state of mind. Dis-
traction, irritation, and even fury beleaguer us. But we are summoned, alas, to
answer for ourselves here. If no practical arrangements can be made to allevi-
ate the chaotic situation, and the pastor seems as oblivious to it all as do the
other communicants, then indeed one has one's work cut out, so to speak.
The way of Charity opens before us. What does Charity do in such havoc? I
myself would have to be a wholly different person to be able to remain collected and devout here, I protest. Ah, that is what I am summoned to: to
become a wholly different person, finally. But at this point the writer must
take his own place at the very tag end of the pupils queuing up for this most
difficult lesson.

6

The Mass: Diagram of Glory

To be Catholic, then, is to have the Mass at the center of one's whole existence and consciousness. It is to be a "eucharistic" man or woman. It is to see the liturgy as one's greatest "work". It is to have taken one's place at the Lord's Table.

In just such brief comments as these we come upon a mother lode of significance. The various terms by which the Church has, over the centuries, referred to her worship are themselves rich with meaning. The Mass; the Eucharist; the liturgy; the Lord's Table; Holy Communion; the sacred mysteries: each of these terms indicates an aspect of Catholic worship.

The Mass, to begin with. The word stems from the Latin words with which the priest dismisses the people at the very end of the liturgy: *Ite, missa est*, ordinarily translated as meaning, "Go: the Mass is finished."

Go. That would seem to strike a somewhat peremptory note. Can we not tarry here in the presence of the Divine Love? Must we now go out into the world, back to monotony, routine, stress, and fatigue?

Yes, says the Church (and Yes, says the Divine Love). The whole point of what you have been doing here just now is that you be nourished and thus fortified by the sacrament.

Besides this, by the whole liturgy you have had your vision clarified. That is, every element of the Mass constitutes, in one sense, a touchstone by which you may test all that you do in the hours and days of your ordinary life. For example, the Mass greets you with the Name of the Trinity, as the superscript under which things are now to occur. Are you conscious that this superscript is written over the whole of every day during your week—or, shall we say, that you yourself are to affix it over those days so that all you do will be "in that Name"? In just such small (small?) ways as this, the Mass clarifies for us, and brings to bright focus, that which is (or should be) true of the whole fabric of our lives.

So when we refer to the Church's worship as the Mass, we remind ourselves that from it we must "go"—out, now, into the routines of the day, fortified by what we have received here and instructed, by every gesture, response, and act, in the ways of that Kingdom of which we are citizens. (One other "small" detail might augment this point for us: we make the sign of the Cross at various points in the liturgy. Does this sign mark all that we think, say, and do during all the hours that are *not* liturgical? Someone stupidly, I fancy, holds up the line at the post office when I am greatly pressed for time or cynically cuts me off in traffic: The Cross! The Cross! Jesus, Savior, help me to turn from my ire and pique and, through that Cross by which I am crucified with thee, and by which I have signed myself so often, to learn the virtues of patience and charity. The Cross is the gate by which I pass from hell to heaven, both of which are at my elbow hourly.)

This all seems like very big freight to load upon the one syllable of the word Mass, and yet, like all other aspects of Scripture and the whole Catholic faith, this syllable opens through onto immense vistas.

The Eucharist. This, too, is a common designation for Catholic worship. The word comes from the Greek for thanksgiving. Here we find ourselves caught up into the realm of the Divine Love itself, where obedience, even to the length of self-immolation and hence sacrifice, turns out to mingle with the offering of thanks. We see this in every detail of Jesus Christ's example: "I thank thee, Father . . ." seemed always on his lips. To "make Eucharist" is to offer thanks to the Father in this *particular* manner, disclosed to us by the Savior's own self-immolation for us, not merely of uttering the words of gratitude due to the Father for his infinite bounty to us all, but of identifying ourselves with the perfect thanks offered by the Son to the Father—thanks that always rose from his heart to his Father and that was finally revealed for what it was, namely, a total self-offering, at Calvary. It is into these precincts that Eucharist brings us who wish to be configured to Christ.

The liturgy. We have already spoken of this "work of the people", which is the particular point at which we mortals here on this earth gather to join with the whole company of saints and angels, and of the entire universe, in the only "work" there is, finally, namely, that of offering laud and blessing to God. All work is to participate in this: Adam and Eve's tasks in Eden were to be a continual act of adoration. Hence there was no liturgy as such in Eden. There did not need to be any special setting-apart of an act to which all the rest of their work might be brought, focused, and made into an oblation. They never ceased to do this.

Sin wrecked this diurnal rhythm, and now work has become drudgery, and we, heirs of that sin, must consciously "re-hallow" our work by bringing it, with our selves and our prayers and our adoration, to this act we call liturgy. This "work of the people" is the act in which we discover and enter into that which is true of all work in Eden, and in the City of God, and in our world, if we will hallow it thus.

The Lord's Table. "Love bade me welcome, yet my soul drew back", wrote George Herbert. All who come to this Table know this salutary hesitancy. "Lord, I am not worthy"—certainly not to sit with the very apostles in this closed room, at table with thee. But the bidding is there. "I am the Bread of life. . . . Ho, every one that thirsteth. . . . Take, eat. . . . Drink you all of it." Ah, *Domine Deus*. But speak the word only.

But it is more than the word, fathomlessly gracious as is that word. We have not accepted the invitation until we have actually partaken of the Food with which he has prepared his Table for us.

We would have done well, no doubt, to have hesitated a moment before swallowing the loaves and fishes, if we had been among the five thousand, or the fish baked on that open fire on the beach after the Resurrection. One doesn't snatch at God's gifts. But *these* gifts: my Body; my Blood. How can one do other than fall on one's face, demurring.

"You must sit down, says Love, and taste my meat: So I did sit and eat." Thus George Herbert. And thus all who wish to be numbered among the Christian faithful.

Holy Communion. This is the mystery into which we enter when we come to the Lord's Table. Because the food is what it is—the very Body and Blood of our Host—the fellowship that comes into being at this Table is a far more profound thing than the conviviality that sparkles at our own feasts and parties. That conviviality is a thing of great value, to be highly treasured as one of the loveliest attributes of our mortal life. But, like all the attributes of our mortal life, it scarcely hints at the reality that lies at the far end of all conviviality. *O Sacrum Convivium*. O Holy Banquet. The fellowship at this Table is to be, as St. Paul phrases it, "the fellowship of his sufferings".

Mysteriously, we the faithful are drawn into that fellowship. It is the deepest sort of fellowship, as we know from our own experience of suffering together with someone we love. But this "Holy Communion" is even more: it is to enter into our Host's very life, and death. "If you do not eat my flesh and drink my blood, you have no life in you", he says to us. This is the mystery, hidden in God from all eternity, and now revealed to us in the New Covenant—that we should become partakers of the Divine Life.

It is incomprehensible and unimaginable. One is left bemused. *We* (mortals; sinners; prodigal sons), to share the life of the Most Holy Trinity? Lord: be it far from thee to do this.

If you do not eat my flesh and drink my blood, you have no life in you. You are dead. And the only life I have to offer, says our Host, is my own life itself. That is what I offer. This is the communion I seek with you—which I sought when I went to my death at Calvary and descended into hell.

Amen. So be it. I wish to be found in this communion, with all who partake of the Divine Life—with Blessed Mary, ever Virgin, with St. Joseph, her most chaste spouse, with Holy John, Holy Peter and Paul, Linus and Cletus, Felicity and Perpetua, and Agatha and Augustine and Benedict and Albert.

All of this is what we refer to when we speak of the Mass, the Eucharist, the Lord's Table, Holy Communion. These are indeed the sacred mysteries. This is the Holy Sacrifice.

To be Catholic is to find oneself in these precincts.

The Mass may be said to be a diagram of what is true. That is, in each of its elements we find starkly drawn the very pattern of what is true in that region where God is acknowledged as King. We may observe this by touching briefly on those elements.

The first thing specified in the order for Mass is the Entrance Song, or Introit. This is sometimes said by the priest and people just as the priest arrives at the altar; or it may be sung by the choir if there is a procession. In this song we hear a scriptural text that we may take as a sort of ensign over what we are about to do. "He gave them bread to eat", or "The Lord is in his holy temple", or "Hear my prayer, O Lord": the text strikes the note that will be heard reverberating through all that we do in the coming period. This text, of course, speaks something that is true at all times, and we do well to remind ourselves of such texts from time to time as we go about our daily tasks. But we are distracted creatures; and we have many responsibilities that militate against keeping our minds focused at the point articulated by the text. So it is designated for us as we come to this hour that distills all our hours. What gets blurred for us in the confusion of ordinary life (the fact, for instance, that the Lord is in his holy temple) is here brought into stark focus. During this hour, which "carries" all our other hours, we find the truth announced.

We are then greeted by the celebrant in the Name of the Trinity, and we sign ourselves with the Cross of Jesus Christ as he offers this greeting.

It is a most solemn moment. There are a thousand other greetings that might occur to the priest: It's nice to see you all! Or, Hot weather we're having these days, eh? Or, Thanks for coming, everybody. But no. It is not now Jack Smith who greets us: it is the priest, who speaks in the stead of Jesus Christ himself in the midst of his Church, which is what we all are now. The solemn occasion finds itself in the presence of the Trinity and proceeds in that trifold Name.

"Amen", we say. So be it. We assent to being found here.

Then, as though immediately to reassure us who, if we have our wits about us at all, may well have trembled at the august Name, we may hear, "The grace of our Lord Jesus Christ and the love of God and the fellowship of the Holy Spirit be with you all." Ah. We are safe. What we find flowing from that ineffable Trinity is grace, love, and fellowship. We are welcomed, and received, and empowered. It is like arriving in heaven. (Indeed it is, says the Church: the liturgy is the clearest picture you will have on earth of how things appear in the City of God. And it is even more than mere picture: it is pledge [sacrament], that is, foretaste.)

"And also with you", we respond. This answering back and forth between celebrant and people is "antiphonal". Antiphons are responses, or even cries, we might say, which call back and forth from one to another. Heaven is like this, with the archangelic hosts crying aloud, "Holy!" and finding their cry echoed in myriad voices from the saints. The universe is like this, with day unto day uttering speech, and night unto night showing knowledge, and with fire answering to water, and mountain to valley, and sweet to sour, and silence to song. Antiphons. In the liturgy we are invited in to this state of affairs, which is true in that it is *like* heaven and the whole universe. God's glory is such that it evokes these glad cries, which themselves bid from us our own gladsome cry of assent.

So, here in the liturgy, as the celebrant greets us with the grace, love, and fellowship of the Holy Trinity, we find that this charity coming to us from the celebrant calls forth our own fervent wish that he, too, may know this grace, love, and fellowship.

Too much to extract from one little antiphon? No, says the Church. When we are in the presence of the Most High, every syllable is ennobled and glorified and amplified, over-flowing with more substance than its tiny stature might seem to suggest.

"To prepare ourselves to celebrate the sacred mysteries, let us call to mind our sins."

No. Surely that is too negative a note to strike just here? We have come, and we wish to be uplifted and made happy. Must you regale us with our sins?

Yes. Christian joy is not the flimsy and specious joy of "eat, drink, and be merry", which huddles all unpleasantness and doom under the rug and capers about in a mad oblivion. Christian joy is, specifically, the joy on the far side of sins forgiven, and there is no notion of us mortals worth a moment's notice that omits this bleak category of sin. All efforts to affirm ourselves and to gain uplift and to be positive are misbegotten if, in the interest of being "affirmative", they tiptoe past this mire in which the taproot of our human identity is so deeply rooted. "Against thee and thee only have I sinned" (David), or "Woe is me, for I am a man of unclean lips" (Isaiah), or "Depart from me, Lord, for I am a sinful man" (Peter)—these are the utterances that launch us on our way toward our true dignity and freedom; and only confusion, vanity, and fatuity await us if we refuse to take our own place among the men and women who from the beginning have approached the Most High with this on their lips.

The thing we approach when we "call to mind our sins", and confess them, in the presence of God, Blessed Mary ever Virgin, and all the angels and saints, which the *Confiteor* obliges us to do—that thing, namely, the forgiveness of our sins, is the prize that no friend, no spouse, no father or mother, no counselor, no therapist, and no psychiatrist can offer to us. All human love, earnest and well-meaning though it may be, stops short of this, which only the Divine Love (which is our Host here at the liturgy) can grant us. It was to open up this fount of forgiveness that Christ suffered for us on the Cross. He is the Lamb who taketh away the sins of the world. Not merely the missteps or failings of the world: it was our sins (Scripture uses harsh words: iniquities; transgressions; wickedness) that sent the Son of God to Calvary, not our limitations.

Jansenism? No: Catholic teaching. *Recordare, Jesu pie, quod sum causa tuae viae*: Remember, merciful Jesus, that *I* am the cause of thy coming hither. *Ingemisco, tamquam reus, Culpa rubet vultus meus*: I mourn, like a guilty man, and guilt reddens my face. Such stark words used to be on the lips of our forerunners in the faith, in centuries sturdier and more frank than our own.

Let us call to mind our sins. This is not a neurotic indulgence, the Church would say, nor an exercise in pathological self-loathing. It is the lucid and candid acknowledgment of the mere truth. "If we say that we have no sin, we deceive ourselves, and the truth is not in us", says St. John; and truth alone is the region where our authentic dignity and freedom lie.

And when we have done so, we hear the words of forgiveness—from Almighty God. It is not Bill, our priest, amiable and good-hearted though he may be, who speaks here. This is the Word of God, sounding through the liturgy, restoring us to our true place as his sons and heirs, "heirs of God, and joint-heirs with Christ", St. Paul goes so far as to say. By our sins we had forfeited this great inheritance. By the event we celebrate in this liturgy, namely, the life, death, and Resurrection of the Savior, that inheritance is restored to us. To attempt to palliate things by substituting mere "brokenness" or "mistakes" for the thing that occasioned the advent of the

Savior is to falsify the entire liturgy and to diminish the gospel itself.

Now: *Kyrie eleison!* we hear. Lord, have mercy. Christ, have mercy. Lord, have mercy.

Does this not suddenly plunge us all back into the darkness suffusing heathen temples, with the suppliants cringing and pawing at the sleeve of Moloch or Dagon or Zeus Pater? Surely this is not a Christian cry we hear? Our God *has* had mercy on us. "Let us therefore come boldly to the throne of grace", says the holy apostle. Why this uncertain note?

Because, says the Church, it is only by invoking this mercy that we have any standing at all, much less any footing for celebration. All is mercy. All is grace. All is gift. Any other notion is illusory. The liturgy here, as in every one of its elements, brings us into the precincts of stark truth. It is the Divine Mercy we invoke and in which we exult. So it is good for us to speak these words. They place us in the truth. It is not a matter of ruefully trying to placate a haughty deity: rather, in these words we announce, gladly, to heaven and hell, as it were (as it were? it will very likely turn out to have been literally the case), the warrant we have for being found at this liturgy in the first place.

There is another note in this sequence. *Kyrie!* was the cry in the ancient world with which the populace would greet the emperor. This was taken over by the Church as an acclamation to Christ, thereby testifying that Jesus Christ is Lord. This was very much the note struck in the first apostolic preaching: St. Peter rang the changes on this. This Jesus, whom you crucified, God has made both Lord and Christ. *Kyrie!*

Then: *Gloria in excelsis Deo!* What should we say, we might well ask ourselves anxiously as we cross the threshold into the presence of the Most High. Protocol dictated what you said (or did not say) when you approached the khan, the tsar, the sultan, or the king. No foolish talk here. (St. Peter tried to find helpful things to say when the princely glory of Jesus was fleetingly glimpsed on Mt. Tabor and was quickly hushed. No gabble here.)

What shall we say, then? Our own words clatter dismally.

Say *Gloria!* Take your script from the angels' acclamation to the Infant God at Bethlehem. *Laudamus te, benedicimus te, adoramus te, glorificamus te*: we praise thee, we bless thee, we worship thee, we glorify thee. *Quoniam tu solus sanctus, tu solus Dominus*: for thou only art holy; thou only art the Lord.

Worship, or adoration, is not an achievement easily gained by us distracted mortals. Our efforts, as often as not, trail off into bathos. The words supplied to us by ancient usage in such canticles as the *Gloria* (or in the *Te Deum*, now rarely heard) are an immense gift to us all, since they do for us what our own pitiable resources cannot do. They lift us up, out of the shallow puddle of those resources, and place us with the choirs of angels "who forever laud and magnify Thy glorious Name, evermore praising Thee and saying, Holy, Holy, Holy" (another one of the canticles that the liturgy invites us to join).

It is in such canticles that we encounter true solemnity. Here is how C. S. Lewis explained this rich and misunderstood word for his readers:

> [Solemnity] implies the opposite of what is familiar, free, and easy, or ordinary. But it does not suggest gloom, oppression, or austerity. The ball in the first act of Romeo and Juliet was a "solemnity". . . . A great mass by Mozart or Beethoven is as much a solemnity in its hilarious *gloria* as in its poignant *crucifixus est*. Feasts are, in this sense, *more* solemn than fasts. Easter is *solempne*, Good Friday is not. The *Solempne* is the festal which is also the stately and the ceremonial, the proper occasion for *pomp*—and the very fact that pompous is now

used only in a bad sense measures the degree to which we have lost the old idea of "solemnity". To recover it you must think of a court ball, or a coronation, or a victory march, as these things appear to people who *enjoy* them; in an age when every one puts on his oldest clothes to be happy in, you must reawake to the simpler state of mind in which people put on gold and scarlet to be happy in.[1]

The *Gloria* is not always sung or said at Mass. In Advent and during Lent it is omitted, in keeping with the austere, and even penitential, ethos of those seasons. But when it is used, Christian believers are given the occasion to join themselves to the very bliss of heaven.

After the *Gloria*, the Collect. This is the brief prayer, often consisting of one sentence only, that summons us and our thoughts and forms into a petition the particular theme that characterizes the liturgy for that day. On September 29, for example, when the Church celebrates the feast of the three archangels, Michael, Gabriel, and Raphael, we hear: "God our Father, in a wonderful way you guide the work of angels and men. May those who serve you constantly in heaven keep our lives safe from all harm on earth." Or again, on the First Sunday in Advent, which is the beginning of the Church's year, we pray: "All-powerful God, increase our strength of will for doing good that Christ may find an eager welcome at his coming and call us to his side in the kingdom of heaven. . . ." During "Ordinary Time", from Pentecost to Advent, and when no special feast or memorial is observed, the Collect may simply petition God for some grace for us or for diligence or faithfulness on our part.

The Collect is a significant element in the liturgy, if one may speak thus, when every element is profoundly signifi-

[1] C. S. Lewis, *A Preface to Paradise Lost* (London: Oxford University Press, 1970), 17.

cant. This prayer reminds us of the unity that binds us together—all who are here at this Mass, all Christians who are at Mass anywhere in the world today, all Christians who have ever constituted the Church, from Pentecost until now, and all the heavenly host of angels. That is, it is not merely a set of worthy sentiments that occur at the moment to the mind of our excellent pastor (such a prayer would be customary in many places of Christian assembly). Rather, because it is specified for all Masses all over the world on that day, it knits the praying Church together in a global fabric—or better, it acknowledges the seamless cloth into which all of us are joined at our baptism. The Church is not merely an immense aggregate of believing individuals. She is one—the Mystical Body. The Collect reminds us of this.

Now follow the readings from Scripture. On most Sundays we hear a reading from the Old Testament (sometimes it is from Acts), then a psalm, then a reading from one of the epistles or the Apocalypse, and then the Gospel. We *hear*: a point worth pondering. "Faith cometh by hearing", says St. Paul. We, literate age that we are, might incline to substitute, "Faith cometh by reading." And certainly faith can indeed come by reading. But the Bible is most characteristically itself when it appears in that context from which it sprang, namely, the Church. The ancient Church was keenly conscious of this, not simply because there were no printing presses and the faithful could not all have their own copies of Scripture. The matter was somewhat more substantial: the Word of God, written down in the text, comes alive in a unique and fitting way at the liturgy. For here is the whole picture. It is not just the solitary believer with the text in his lap. Here we find the Church, that is, the Body of Christ, gathered under her Head and High Priest, Jesus, attending to his Word. For all the words of Scripture, Old as well as New

Testaments, are to be received as the Word of God, in a way not true of the most exalted of human words (Plato, say, or Shakespeare). It was the people of God among whom that Word was spoken and who were chosen to write it down. It was *for* Israel and *for* the Church. It was the Church that wrote, recognized, collected, and ratified this Bible. No committee, no publisher, no university, and no institute of scholarly clerics was responsible. The Bible, always the Word of God, is most visibly, or audibly we should say, itself in that Church, that is, at the liturgy.

In the first reading, which is usually taken from the Old Testament, we encounter the Law, the Prophets, the history of Israel, and the Wisdom literature. "Whatsoever things were written aforetime were written for our learning, that we through patience and comfort of the scriptures might have hope", says St. Paul (Rom 15:4). The Church has always received the Hebrew scriptures as the record of God's purposes in creation and, then, in redemption. "When we fell into evil and death, you sent Jesus": the Old Testament is big with the anticipation of this event. From the skins prepared by God to cover the guilty Adam and Eve (blood was shed for those garments), on through the patriarchs, the prophets, the kings, and Israel's exile and return, we may see the *preparatio* for the Incarnation. So the Church usually offers us readings from this Testament at the liturgy. During the season of Easter this reading is from the Acts of the Apostles, St. Luke's account of what happened in the early days of the infant Church.

Then the "Responsorial Psalm". The psalms are the songs of Zion. In them we find the most acute probing of the human spirit ever achieved. The poetry of Goethe or Keats or Yeats, noble record of the human spirit though we may find there, seems obtuse next to the psalms. Here the depths of the human spirit are laid open. Every utterance is spoken to God or in the presence of God. Hence the "truth" of the psalms: utterance finds the purity toward which it strains when it is thus spoken. Joy, perplexity, fear, rage, melancholy, despair, trust, exultation, dereliction: every chamber of the human heart is probed. Nothing is lacking. There is no cry of mortal man that does not find itself perfectly articulated here.

The Church, very early on, saw that insofar as she kept herself daily suffused with psalmody, she would remain in the courts of the Most High. This is the reason for the monastic Office: all the psalms recited, in their entirety, day by day, in behalf of us all, by cloistered men and women who had consecrated themselves wholly to such service, at the cost of their entire lives. *Te decet hymnus, Deus, in Sion*: Unto thee shall songs be sung in Zion, O God. It is very meet, right, and our bounden duty that we should at all times, and in all places, give thanks unto thee, O Lord, Holy Father, Almighty and Ever-living God: these "all times and all places" are distilled in religious houses and also made present to us here in the liturgy. When we join ourselves to the psalm by responding antiphonally at this point in the liturgy, we find ourselves in the actuality of this ceaseless offering of song that ascends to God from the whole creation. These psalms are "our" cries, aspirations, and votive offerings to him. (Even the dismaying "imprecatory" psalms are true, not in the sense of recommending to us such attitudes, but rather of probing to the bottom our mortal, even hateful, capacity for resentment and vengefulness.)

The reading from one of the New Testament books other than the Gospels now follows, on Sundays and feast days at least (on other days there are only two readings, one from either the Old Testament *or* the New, and then the Gospel).

Here we find apostolic teaching that accords in some thematic way with what has been adumbrated in the first reading. We do well to attend here with all possible attention: these are our instructions or examples for our edification. We will be judged one fine day on the extent to which the word we have heard has "become flesh" in our own selves. For example, we hear the word, "Be ye kind, one to another, tenderhearted, forgiving one another." Those are words. Have they—or rather, has *it*: it is the Word of God—been received into my innermost being in faith and obedience, so that what is read from the ambo now becomes actual (incarnate) in my flesh, by my behavior toward everyone else? *Et verbum caro factum est*: we say those words referring to the Word that came to the Virgin and that became flesh in her flesh. Do all the words of God thus find in my soul that same "Be it done unto me according to thy word" that must precede any fructifying of word into tangible actuality in my being?

At the end of each of the readings so far, the liturgy asks us to respond, "Thanks be to God."

A crux. Gratitude may be the farthest thing from me upon hearing words as troublesome, say, as "Be ye kind." I might incline, rather, to pass it off with "Lovely sentiments to be sure", or, "Well, there are limits. Let's be realistic", or "Anon, anon."

Alas. "Thanks be to God" is what the liturgy waits to hear from me. It is not the mere shell of a formula. It is meaty, and I must bite down hard upon it. The "thanks be to God" may well have to be spoken from my will before it flowers in my feelings. Once again, I find myself hailed by sheer truth in the liturgy, the truth that illumines the whole City of God, whose citizen I hope one day to have learned how to be by thus thankfully receiving the Word.

So: whether the reading has held consolation for me, or

encouragement or challenge or instruction or rebuke, I am to say (and mean—or at least fully intend to mean), "Thanks be to God."

The reading of the Gospel is set apart with a certain amount of ceremony. In some churches and on some festal occasions, the Gospel Book is carried in procession down from the altar into the center aisle, with lights and incense. The point here is that we have Jesus Christ himself taking his place in the midst of his own people. The Gospel takes us directly into his life on earth and speaks directly to us with his words. We are, at this point, as close to the center as Scripture can bring us. If there is no procession, we will nonetheless still be awakened by what leads up to the reading. Alleluia! is repeated, and then a sentence from the Bible (the "Gradual"), with Alleluia! again, and "A reading from the Holy Gospel according to ———", at which point we all make the sign of the Cross on forehead, lips, and breast. Let my whole mind and my speech and all my affections be illumined and bound by this Gospel. Let all in me that is not "gospel" be crucified.

A solemn transaction, easily missed in its brevity, either because my mind has wandered for a moment or because I have grown used to responding with these small gestures. But if every hair of our head is numbered, and no sparrow falls without our Father knowing it, we may reckon that such gestures, too, are entered in the ledger that the recording angel keeps for us. *Liber scriptus proferetur, In quo totum continetur*: A book will be brought out, in which everything is contained: all these gestures by which I *said* I wanted to live the gospel as well as every cup of water I may have offered to some thirsty man.

When the Gospel is announced, we say, "Glory to you, Lord", and when it is finished, "Praise to you, Lord Jesus

Christ." We thus place ourselves with that company, the Virgin being foremost, who have only Glory! and Praise! on their lips and in their hearts, for all the Savior's words and doings.

The homily follows the Gospel. Here the Church appears, in the person of the preacher (usually it is the celebrant), opening up the Scripture and reflecting on it. If the homilist is able to link all three readings from Scripture by some theme, we are reminded of the seamlessness of revelation. No Levitical law, no skirmish with the Philistines, and no widow's last drop of oil but finds its place in the mighty plan of salvation. In the Catholic tradition, the homily is of one piece with the entire liturgy, unlike more recent Christian traditions, which have abandoned the ancient liturgy and have made the homily, or sermon, into the principal reason for coming to church. Catholics are often puzzled by this turn of events in the history of worship among various Christian groups.

At the conclusion of the homily, the congregation stands and repeats the Creed, usually the so-called Nicene Creed. On the surface of things, this might well appear to be a somewhat inert moment in the liturgy. We are asking for nothing particular here, and this iteration of events and beliefs, one after the other with almost triphammer-like rhythm, does not sound much like worship, and after all everyone present already knows all of this anyway. Why, exactly, does the Church wish us to repeat it all week by week, year after year?

The Creed, or "symbol" of faith, was incorporated into the liturgy very early in the Church. It has, for one thing, what we might call a pedagogical aspect to it. That is, we Christians are those who believe, for example, that the Almighty is the Creator of heaven and earth. Out the window at once flies all gnosticism and Manichaeism, which, in the interest of a lofty spirituality, abhors the solidity of the material world and hence attributes the material creation to a "demiurge"—some lesser, and probably filthy, deity who is not to be confused with the Spirit whom we invoke. That material world is good, says the Church, made as it was by God himself and pronounced good by him. This is the God we Christians acclaim in our gathering here.

"We believe in one Lord, Jesus Christ, the only Son of God, eternally begotten of the Father, God from God. . . . Suddenly we are aloft in the ether of high theology: surely this is quite remote from us householders, plumbers, and clerks? These phrases were wrought from the struggle (and even politics) of councils in the fourth and fifth centuries. We don't need these salvos now, surely?

This is where we find the Creed carrying us farther than mere pedagogy. To be sure, each one of the phrases that refer to Jesus (even single words—"Lord" and "Christ") teems with meaning and stands over against some error about him that had gained currency in the ranks of believers in those early years of the Church. But taken into the liturgy, these lines assume the character of acclamation. We exult, the Church seems to shout, in this God and his Christ, who for us men and for our salvation. . . .

The very iteration of the words takes us deeply into the mysteries we have gathered to mark. And in their very simplicity—monotony, even—they echo the simplicity, even monotony, that cloaked the coming of the Savior and all that he did for us. No fanfare. No triumphal arches, processions, and palms (well, yes, actually—palms once—but proffered by the ragtag and bobtail of the populace).

This distilling of the whole of redemption, from creation to Last Judgment and heaven, takes on the character of acclamation in the liturgy and echoes, as does the entire liturgy, the voices of heaven. (An awesome note is struck when we recall that when we mortals say "for us men", the seraphim themselves must fall silent; they cannot sing that part of the song. We find ourselves caparisoned with dread dignity when we recite the Creed.)

Then follow the Intercessions. We pray for the Church and for the world. In so doing, we unite ourselves with our High Priest, who gave himself for the Church and for the world and who "ever lives to make intercession" now. We take on corporately here in the liturgy the priestly ministry that each of us exercises in his private daily prayers, interceding for all men. And once again, what exists as a "form" turns out to be brimming with reality. To be Catholic is to believe that the Church's prayers—far from being exercises in futility, with pain and war and horror grinding on implacably in spite of our prayers—*really are*, literally, taken into the mystery of the Divine Mercy and put to work, so to speak. On the Catholic view, the prayers of the Church are joined with the mystery of Christ's intercession for us, which itself culminates in his total oblation of himself for us to the Father; and all of this is caught up into the region where the Mercy and Providence of God well up in their eternal superabundance and over-flow, inundating the world with redemption.

This region is still impenetrable by us mortals. "We see not yet all things put under thee." How the Mercy and Provi-dence of God will turn out to have been unfailingly sovereign in this world of sorrow, blight, cruelty, and disfranchisement is unimaginable to us. Just here is the sorest test to faith. The old dilemma, so often flung at Christian believers down through the ages, still leers: either God is good but not all-powerful; or he is all-powerful but cruel. That is, he either can't or won't set things straight here. So runs this conundrum.

To be Catholic is to be obliged to take one's place with all

the men and women of faith from the beginning. It has
rarely seemed otherwise than that God is very absent. Joseph
is sold into Egypt, and years of wrong go unredressed, it
seems. The Philistines seize the very Ark of God, and fire
does not strike them. Hannah lives, forlorn, crying out for a
son. The widow of Zarepta reaches her last handful of meal,
and no help is in sight. Jerusalem itself, finally, is sacked, and
the Chosen People are bundled off to slavery under an Eastern tyrant. *Domine! Exaudi orationem meam!* How long, O
Lord?

To be Catholic, we say, is to take one's place with the men
and women of faith from the beginning. All of them had to
wait. The salvation of the Lord did not come, and did not
come. Nevertheless they presented themselves at his altar, day
by day, year after bone-wearying year. Simeon and Anna
would be the archetypes here, wrinkled and old and faithful.
But heaven does not open. No divine thunder terrorizes
God's enemies.

Only a penurious young woman and her husband, bringing an infant to be presented in the temple one fine day—
and Lord, now lettest thou thy servant depart in peace; for
mine eyes have seen thy salvation, which thou hast prepared
before the face of all people.

What? What? Where? Do but tell us where.

Here.

But we want Herod toppled, and Caesar overthrown, and
our chains sundered, and Israel's dignity and liberty restored.

Indeed. And it is all of that which faith sees in this Infant.

This is the vision at work in the Church's intercessions.
We pray for the world, and famine, war, disease, and injustice crawl on their implacable way. We pray for the Church,
and disaffected religious, discontented priests, unfaithful
bishops, and baleful theologians drown out the voice of the

Magisterium. We pray for the sick and they die. Let us give over this farcical business.

But faith—the faith of the Church it is, not simply my own attempts to soldier on—takes its place with Simeon and Anna, and with the psalms, which are sure, in the face of all evidence to the contrary, that God is the champion of widows, orphans, and all the dispossessed and enfeebled.

In what sense *is* God such a champion, we want to demand of the tribunal.

It is all "eschatological", says the Church, meaning by that arcane word that the mystery of prayer, with its confidence in God's promises to all widows and orphans, pierces the scrim of all that seems present and obvious and stubborn (pain and death and injustice), and carries us, not merely to some future where all will be set right (that, too, of course: it is the dearest hope of Christians), but into the darkness of God himself, who did not vouchsafe any helpful equation to Job but simply pressed Job to fix his gaze on God. It is faith, not common sense or calculation or weighing of the evidence, that speaks in the Church's intercessions.

And yet once more we find that the liturgy has caught us into the precincts where the servants of God, angelic as well as human, attend at his throne. Attend: it is the expectant, obedient mind presiding among all this holy court.

So ends the first part of the liturgy, the so-called *synaxis* ("gathering"), or the Liturgy of the Word. Now we approach the Liturgy of the Eucharist.

Bread and wine are taken and made ready by offering them to the Lord, from whom we have received them in the first place. Water is mingled with the wine, signifying the mingling of Godhood and manhood in the Savior—and adumbrating the great mystery, hidden in God and now disclosed to us in Christ, that we, in truth, are to share in the

Divine Nature, as he shared in ours. Such immensities at stake in such a small rite.

The priest ritually washes his hands. "Lord, wash away my iniquity; cleanse me from my sin." The words, and the rite, take us back to the Tabernacle in the wilderness, where the priests attending on the altar had to be scrupulously clean for that service. We who now serve at the Altar of which that Jewish altar was only the foreshadowing are to be equally scrupulous. With the celebrant we can only serve here washed with the water of baptism and daily cleansed by the Holy Spirit. As he makes his ablutions we may join our own petition to the celebrant's: it is a salutary reminder that no sin—*no sin*—may appear in the holy place. I may not come to this Table stained with vanity or egoism or slovenliness, or with peevishness, greed, envy, lust, calumny, or anything else in the very long list of my own dispositions. Alas, how am I ever to gain admittance?

Lord, wash away my iniquity; cleanse me from my sin. That is how I, and you, my brothers and sisters, and the priest are to gain admittance.

Orate, fratres. Pray, brethren (or, as we may say now, brothers and sisters), that our sacrifice may be acceptable to God, the Almighty Father.

"May the Lord accept the sacrifice at your hands." Once again we find that the antiphonal calling back and forth of these matters is the very mode that speech in these precincts yearns for. It is the lively, even eager, attitude of Amen! Amen! So be it. We echo, with the gladness and generosity of the Divine Charity itself, what you ask.

Then follows the *Sanctus et Benedictus*, with its Preface. Here we are bidden to join the everlasting chorus of worship offered to the Father, in the light of the particular event brought to our attention in the Preface: Advent, Epiphany,

Lent, Easter; or, as is the case during most of Ordinary Time, in the light of our Lord's offering of himself for us. It is in the light of this, and in the strength of this, that we may sing *Holy!*
"Blessed is he who comes in the name of the Lord. Hosanna!"

Surely this is all wrong? That song belongs to the rabble who hailed the Lord thus on Palm Sunday but who were to be found, fickle as we all are, calling for his blood five days later.

No doubt many of the same people were to be found in the crowd on both days. But, says the liturgy, in spite of themselves, or at least scarcely beknownst to them in their zeal, they were absolutely correct to hail the Son of David with Hosanna! It is the shout of faith; and which of us, joining as we so habitually do in all sorts of acclamations to the Son of David in our liturgy, which of us does not quickly belie what we have said by "crucifying to ourselves afresh the Son of God", within minutes of our hosanna, by riding roughshod over someone's tender sensibilities, or by snapping at someone with a testy reply to a stupid question, or in a thousand other ways?

So: Holy, holy, holy. Hosanna. We are neither better nor worse, we hope, than the multitudes who from the beginning have wished, perhaps with only a fugitive and impulsive wish, to greet God.

There now follows what has traditionally been known as the Canon of the Mass. This is the great Eucharistic Prayer, and it shows up, in substance, in the earliest writings from the apostolic Church. Several forms of this prayer, of greater or lesser length, are offered to us by the Church in our own time. The prayer is addressed to the Father, and it "rehearses" what he has done for us in sending his Christ for our salvation. Presently it comes to the Consecration, which is the very focal point of the entire Christian liturgy. Here we are taken into the Upper Room and hear the words of the Lord himself as he takes bread and wine and offers it to his disciples with the calamitous words, "This is my Body. . . . This is my Blood."

Calamitous? Yes. Not in the sense of being disastrous: the words are salvific. But calamitous in the sense that all other reality flees away from them, as heaven and earth are said to do at the final coming of the Son of God.

To be Catholic is to understand this moment in a profoundly sacramental way. Here is no mere mnemonic device to assist us in recalling a long past event (many churches thus vitiate the Supper). Rather, we are, literally (the word does not help much here: it is too pale), to feed upon the Body and Blood of the Lord. To be Catholic is to take the Lord's words in John chapter 6 most solemnly. We can no more "sense" what is occurring than could the shepherds at the manger. No connection at all can be sustained by our senses, or by our reason, between the wafer and the cup, on the one hand, and the Body and Blood of Jesus Christ, any more than the Infant in the manger could be "imagined" to be the Second Person of the Holy Trinity.

At this moment, all the words we canvassed at the beginning of this chapter loom upon us: Mass; Eucharist; Lord's Table; Holy Communion; liturgy; the sacred mysteries. All is present here. It is a point of intensity not unlike the moment on Mt. Tabor when the Lord was transfigured, or when there was darkness over the whole land at the Crucifixion, or when in St. John's vision there was silence in heaven. Who is equal to the mystery?

For this reason, it has been traditional for centuries for the people to be kneeling during the Canon: What other posture is apt? On the other hand, it was the case in the early Church, and again in many places now, that the people stood. This posture is one of attentive and obedient readiness, as it were. If we wished to reproduce exactly the posture of the disciples when the Lord distributed the bread and wine to them, we would have to recline, and at this point the literal would clash with the liturgical, which is, we may remind ourselves, not an attempt to "reproduce" things literally, such as we find in drama, with realistic stage sets and actors recreating things with the greatest possible verisimilitude, but rather a patent "stylizing" of reality under the austere demands of ceremony attuned to the timeless rather than to the ephemeral.

The people are then bidden to voice the Church's faith, in the Memorial Acclamation. Christ has died! Christ is risen! Christ will come again! Hear, O earth! Hear, ye heavens! Let hell itself take note! Christ has died, is risen, and will come again. It is where we Christians take our stand. We exult in this; or, it may be, we hang for dear life on this when doubt and fatigue and adversity shout at us that it is all a farce! Or: Dying you destroyed our death, rising you restored our life: Lord Jesus, come in glory. O death, where is thy sting? O grave, where is thy victory? In the liturgy Catholics are, line by line, moment by moment, wholly in the presence of the mighty acts of God our Savior.

The Eucharistic Prayer continues now, recalling the whole Gospel and praying for the faithful, living and departed. It concludes "through him, with him, and in him. . . ." Three prepositions in which are contained the whole scope of re-demption.

The Communion Rite follows now, as we are bidden to pray the prayer Jesus taught us. It is the very paradigm of all prayer. All aspirations, all worship, and all petition and inter-cession are gathered up in this prayer. Hence the Church has kept this prayer immediately before our eyes from the beginning, strongly recommending it for solitary as well as liturgical use. If any Christian is ever at a loss as to how to frame his prayers, he may straightaway resort to this prayer and find that all that is in his heart has been borne to the Throne in its words. But it is also a liturgical prayer: it is for the whole Church when she assembles at Mass. In its seven petitions, and in its concluding words of acclamation, the Church speaks with perfect confidence, since the words are a gift from the Lord himself.

Then the Peace. The *Pax*. Only a brief action in the Mass. Yes, certainly—the peace of the Lord be with everybody—but we may, on some occasions, find ourselves asked to offer this peace to everybody *in the persons of* those immediately around us at the liturgy. Here is where our charity find itself tested. I would prefer to pick attractive specimens to greet with peace; but here is this bore next to me and that henwife behind me and that bugbear in front. Yes, says the liturgy (which is to say, the Divine Charity): to be at this Table is in very truth to greet all souls with peace. It is the very rehearsal for heaven. Hell slinks away with its luggage of snobbery, grudge, and malice.

At the *Agnus Dei*, which follows now, the Church joins St. John the Baptist in his acclamation to Jesus. It is faith that sees in him the Lamb of God who takes away the sins of the world. The priest now takes the Host, breaks it in the sight of all, and places a small piece of it in the chalice with the words, "May this mingling of the Body and Blood of our Lord Jesus Christ bring eternal life to us who receive it." (The Church teaches that the whole Christ is received in either species, the Body of Christ or the Precious Blood of Christ. Hence no one need feel disfranchised if only the Host is offered to the people, which is the practice in many parishes.) Then the priest raises the broken Host with the words "This is the Lamb of God. . . . Happy are those who are called to his supper." We respond with the words of the centurion when he found that the Lord was actually going to come all the way to his house: "Lord, I am not worthy to receive you, but only say the word and I shall be healed."

It is an exquisite protest, deeply moving in its aptness. How had this centurion's soul been schooled, that he perceived so accurately what was so profoundly true? We are not told: but from this man we may learn true *pietas*—the clarity of vision that results in a hesitation, even self-effacement, in the presence of a greater majesty. The Greeks called it *aidos*. To have learned it is to have taken great strides toward the true dignity with which the Most High crowns us and to have abandoned the strutting refusal to bow that marks the vain man.

There is another element in this response that may claim our attention. The centurion was correct: a mere word from Jesus would indeed have sufficed to heal. It was the centurion's servant in the particular instance recorded in the Gospel; but what he believed, correctly, about the power of a word from Jesus may be applied to us all: only a word will do. But the God who is invoked in the Christian liturgy is not a God of mere edicts. It is not *sola Scriptura*. He waits to give us his very flesh. He comes to us, as he came to the centurion's house, in his complete Godhood and Manhood. To be Catholic is to believe that his Presence is here. His Word alone would do: but his Mercy, in its superabundance, gives that Word *Incarnate*. Islam is the religion of the book: Christianity is the religion of the Word Incarnate.

It is with this realization that the faithful now make their Communion. To eat the Body of Jesus Christ and to drink his Blood—all that is reasonable, and all that is fastidious in us, resists. It is primitive, someone might venture. It is far more than primitive, says the Church: it is eternal. This is the Lamb slain from the foundation of the world. Primitive rites, insofar as they acknowledge the necessity of such a participation in the being of the god, are to that extent correct. It is modern man who has fumigated and tidied the holy precincts, rinsing the flesh and blood away and illumining all with the pallid fluorescence of mere Reason.

There is recited now the Communion Antiphon—once again, a text that stresses the mystery of what we have done here.

Then all of a sudden it is over. A brief prayer, then the blessing, and then Go.

But it is Go in peace. What peace? The euphoria that may hover about us from our having stolen away from the hurlyburly for an hour in this cool, quiet place? Or that may linger in us in the wake of noble sentiments? Or that may have flowed over us in the strains of the music?

Not really, says the Church. If any of that is the case, thank God. But the Church's peace is Christ's peace; it is that peace that was made "through the blood of his cross", as St. Paul phrases it (Col 1:20). It comes to us from the river of Life, not the drowsy current of Lethe. It is the true Peace that awakens us, not the false peace that lulls us.

And—Thanks be to God, we say. That is the word on our lips as we emerge into the world. Thanks. Eucharist.

7

Catholics and the Gospel

To be Catholic is to be a man or woman of the gospel.

The matter is not very often put in just that way. For one thing, it is sometimes supposed that "gospel" is a sort of specialty of store-front sects, television evangelists, and Appalachian stump-preachers. The cinema and the stage have reinforced this picture for us all, so that when the word "gospel" arises, we often imagine someone waving a placard announcing doom, or a street-corner scene with cornets, tambourines, treadle-organ, tracts, and testifying. Furthermore, Catholics themselves may be found demurring if you hail them with a question about the gospel. "What? Gospel? No—I'm a Catholic." Or, "I don't know—ask the priest."

At some removes from both that down-at-the-heel stereotype and this Catholic diffidence we find the Protestant Evangelicals. Catholics are not infrequently put off their stride by the jaunty confidence with which an evangelical Christian believer will speak of the gospel. Scripture texts pour out rapidly, linked one to the next with unnerving deftness, and various tags are much in evidence: "saved", "born again", and the question as to whether one has "accepted the Lord Jesus Christ as one's personal Savior". The note struck is so remote from anything the Catholic has ever come upon in his own milieu that the conclusion may be reached by both parties that there is no similarity at all in the two renderings of faith.

There is an irony here, since of course the Catholic Church is nothing at all if she is not evangelical, that is, *of the gospel*. Every mark of the Church—her antiquity, her unity, her authority, her Magisterium, her sacraments, her hierarchy, her piety, her mission—is wholly evangelical, since everything flows directly from that gospel.

To assert this, of course, is to dumbfound some hearers and to pique the curiosity of others. "We haven't been in the habit of thinking along exactly those lines", might be volunteered, or "Nonsense! The gospel has long since got lost in the sheer immensity of Catholicism", might also be heard.

To come at an answer to the questions implicit in these responses, we need to ask, What is the gospel? The question itself daunts us, since libraries have been written on the topic in the last two thousand years. How is one to give any sort of manageable answer here? But then we recall that the gospel was, and is, good news for ordinary people, so it must be possible to say something to the point, even though we are all acutely conscious that this gospel, touching our mortality so simply and so intimately, opens into the infinity of God himself and his eternal counsels.

The readiest place to begin, if a Catholic asks himself, or is asked, just what the gospel is, would be with his baptism. There are, to be sure, certain churches that have driven a wedge between baptism and the moment at which one is "saved". Baptism, in those churches, is an external detail—a matter of one's publicly confessing Christ as Savior and Lord—which affects one's salvation not a whit. The Catholic Church herself, of course, is aware that the Divine Mercy is such that where baptism is impossible for whatever reasons (sudden death, say), the "baptism of desire" comes into play (the person *would have* wished baptism, if he had known of it or if there had been time). The Church also speaks of the extreme case of the "baptism of blood"—where someone who confesses Christ but has not been baptized in water gives up his life as a martyr for the faith. His blood, in this instance, suffices for his baptism.

But the Church would stress, with the whole New Testament, that the matter of our salvation is not to be sundered from baptism. When the Lord, speaking to Nicodemus about being "born again", says, "Except a man be born of water and of the Spirit, he cannot enter into the kingdom of God", the Church takes the words at their full value. St. Peter, speaking in his First Epistle about Noah's Ark, says, "Baptism, which corresponds to this, now saves you. . . ." In commissioning his disciples, the Lord says, "He that believeth and is baptized shall be saved" (Mk 16:16). It is an immense topic, and vigorous controversy has often arisen in connection with it, especially since the Reformation. The *Catechism of the Catholic Church* puts the matter in this way:

> From the very day of Pentecost the Church has celebrated and administered holy Baptism. Indeed St. Peter declares to the crowd astounded by his preaching: "Repent, and be baptized every one of you in the name of Jesus Christ for the forgiveness of your sins; and you shall receive the gift of the Holy Spirit." The apostles and their collaborators offer Baptism to anyone who believed in Jesus: Jews, the God-fearing, pagans. Always, Baptism is seen as connected with faith: "Believe in the Lord Jesus, and you will be saved, you and your household," St. Paul declared to his jailer in Philippi. And the narrative continues, the jailer "was baptized at once, with all his family" (1226).

If, then, any Catholic wishes to clarify for himself just what the gospel is, he may recall his own baptism. In that rite the gospel springs up before us, as it were, in all its newness. "The Christian community welcomes you with great joy", says the celebrant to the child. "In its name I claim you for Christ our Savior by the sign of his cross." We pray that by the mystery of Christ's death and Resurrection, this child may be given the new life and that through baptism and confirmation he may be made Christ's faithful follower. At the blessing of the water, we hear the priest say, "May all who are buried with Christ in the death of baptism rise also with him to newness of life." The parents and godparents, speaking in the child's behalf, are charged to "reject sin; profess your faith in Christ Jesus", and to answer "I do", when asked if they believe the Creed. Here is the gospel, as simply rendered as it can be. And, lest there be any uncertainty lingering in our minds, we hear the priest say this after the baptism: "God the Father of our Lord Jesus Christ has freed you from sin, given you a new birth by water and the Holy Spirit, and welcomed you into his holy people."

Here is the gospel, and every Catholic has heard it proclaimed at baptism. If anyone protests, "But I was only a few days old, scarcely of an age to grasp all this", then we can only say to him, "You mean you have never gone back and read over what happened at your baptism? Then do so at once, for it is the gospel, and never again will you need to be in any confusion as to what that gospel is."

It might also turn out to be the case, upon my thus reading over what was said at my baptism, that I find myself flagged down, as it were. Was *this* said, to me, and over me, at that ceremony? But I have never paid much attention to all of that. And yet, would I wish to wave my baptism away as insignificant if I knew that today was my last day of earthly life? "Thou fool, this night thy soul shall be required of thee"—some such dire words, I seem to recall, were spoken to another man who was counting on a great may things besides the state of his soul. Alas! Help, Lord! What must I do to be saved?

Very excellent words, the very words of conversion itself. Words, it may be added, that are never, never lost in the vast gap between heaven and my little cries. There is no such gap, in any case, says the Divine Mercy. Before you call, I will answer, and while you are yet speaking, I will hear. For whosoever shall call upon the name of the Lord, shall be saved. There is joy in the presence of the angels of God over one sinner who repents. My anxious signal for help as I read over what was said at my baptism has been amplified and resounds all through the courts of heaven.

A fanciful scenario? Not really, if we recall that as Catholics we live every moment of our lives on the cusp between the seen and the unseen. We are people who really do suppose that not only the Mass itself but also our most halting and imperfect prayers occur at this cusp, or frontier, and that the ear of the Divine Mercy is bent closer to us than our most inaudible aspirations.

But it is in the familiar structure of the Mass itself that a Catholic not only encounters but finds himself received into the very gospel itself, day by day, year after year. There is, of course, something artificial about canvassing the Mass for points at which "the gospel" is specially articulated: the entire liturgy is a seamless gospel fabric, so to speak. It *is* the gospel, in public, ceremonial, ritual, explicit form. But on the other hand, because we all know that not every Catholic in our own time seems quite certain about just how he himself might phrase an answer to the question, "What is this gospel?" it is no doubt not a bad exercise for us to scrutinize the very familiar steps of the liturgy from this point of view in order to see how this "good news" (that is, gospel) is unfolded and enacted and blazoned. If we wish to compress the good news into a few handy words easy enough for anyone to remember, we can do no better than to echo St. Paul's words to Timothy, "that Christ Jesus came into the world to save sinners" (1 Tim 1:15). There, surely, is the nub of the good news. There is what my mortal and sinful ears need to hear. There are the tidings that the heart of man has yearned to hear, from the beginning, in his deepest aspirings.

We hear these tidings from the moment we first gather for the Eucharist. We are greeted with "The grace of our Lord Jesus Christ and the love of God", echoing St. Paul's words to the Christians in Corinth: "For ye know the grace of our Lord Jesus Christ, that though he was rich, yet he became poor, that ye through his poverty might be rich" (2 Cor 8:9). The same apostle's words to the Christians in Rome echo here: "But God commendeth his love towards us, that while we were yet sinners, Christ died for us" (Rom 5:8). There is the gospel—all of it—in the very greeting with which the priest greets us.

And in the Penitential Rite, what do we hear? "May Almighty God have mercy on us, forgive us our sins, and bring us to everlasting life." What a loud echo we have here of our Lord's own words to Nicodemus: "For God so loved the world that he gave his only-begotten Son, that whosoever believeth in him, should not perish but have everlasting life" (Jn 3:16).

In the *Kyrie* we call upon the mercy of the Lord, of whom St. Paul speaks to the Christians in Ephesus this way: "But God, who is rich in mercy, for his great love wherewith he loved us, even when we were dead in sins, hath quickened us together with Christ, (by grace ye are saved), and hath raised us up together, and made us sit together in heavenly places in Christ Jesus. . . . For by grace are ye saved, through faith, and that not of yourselves, it is the gift of God, not of works, lest any man should boast" (Eph 2:5ff.). Roman Catholics ought to be brimming with these tidings. They count upon this news every time they cry *Kyrie!*

In the *Gloria* we join the song that the angels sang when the gospel first appeared among us at Bethlehem, and we acclaim the Savior with the words that occur again in the *Agnus Dei*, as the Lamb of God who takes away the sin of the world. That is the gospel.

The Collects proclaim the gospel for us. Here is the Collect we hear on the Vigil of the Nativity: "God our Father, every year we rejoice as we look forward to this feast of our salvation. May we welcome Christ as our Redeemer, and meet him with confidence when he comes to be our judge." On Christmas Day we hear this: "Lord God, we praise you for creating man, and still more for restoring him in Christ. Your Son shared our weakness: may we share his glory. . . ." And on Good Friday we hear, "Lord, by shedding his blood for us, your Son, Jesus Christ, established the paschal mystery. In your goodness, make us holy and watch over us always."[1] The teaching opened up in these Collects is very rich. No Catholic need hesitate over just what the gospel is. He hears it in the Collects from week to week.

And he hears it in the Epistle. At the Midnight Mass of Christmas, we hear this:

> God's grace has been revealed, and it has made salvation possible for the whole human race and taught us that what we have to do is to give up everything that does not lead to God, and all our worldly ambitions; we must be self-restrained and live good and religious lives here in this present world, while

---

[1] These collects are taken from *Daily Roman Missal* (Princeton: Scepter Publishers, 1993), 87, 97, 339.

we are waiting in hope for the blessing which will come
with the Appearing of the glory of our great God and saviour Christ Jesus. He sacrificed himself for us in order to set
us free from all wickedness and to purify a people so that it
could be his very own (Titus 2:11–14).[2]

Or this reading, from the Mass at Dawn on Christmas:
"When the kindness and love of God our saviour for mankind were revealed, it was not because he was concerned
with any righteous actions we might have done ourselves; it
was for no reason except his own compassion that he saved
us, by means of the cleansing water of rebirth and by renewing us with the Holy Spirit which he has so generously
poured over us through Jesus Christ our saviour. He did this
so that we should be justified by his grace" (Titus 3:4–7).[3]

If there is any Catholic anywhere who is not sure that he
has ever heard the gospel (I am thinking of all the people
who say that they were Catholic until they were seventeen,
and then they met Jesus, or were saved), surely we can urge
such a person to listen to the living Word of God as it is read
at Mass. "Faith comes from hearing, and hearing by the Word
of God", says St. Paul (Rom 10:17).

A particularly solemn moment in the liturgy comes, as we
all know, when the Gospel is read. Here we are very close to
the center of revelation, and the Church has always marked
the public reading of the Gospel with great solemnity. Any
Catholic whose mind has not been wandering has heard this,
on the Second Sunday of Advent: "Repent, for the kingdom
of heaven is close at hand. . . . I baptise you in water for re-
pentance, but the one who follows me is more powerful than
I am, and I am not fit to carry his sandals; he will baptise you
with the Holy Spirit and fire" (Mt 3:2, 11; cf. Mk 1:7; Lk

[2] *Daily Roman Missal*, 92.
[3] Ibid., 95.

8:16; Jn 1:27).[4] Or this, on Christmas Day, speaking of our Lord Jesus Christ: "He came to his own domain and his own people did not accept him. But to all who did accept him he gave power to become children of God, to all who believe in the name of him who was born not out of human stock or urge of the flesh or will of man but of God himself. The Word was made flesh, he lived among us, and we saw his glory, the glory that is his as the only Son of the Father, full of grace and truth" (Jn 1:11–14).[5] If that is not gospel, there is no gospel.

(Again, it might be pointed out here that this is the text from which the Evangelicals draw their phraseology about "accepting Jesus as your personal Savior". St. John speaks in this Preface to his Gospel of people "accepting" the Word who came into the world to save us. Catholics are taken aback by someone who hails them with "Have you accepted Jesus as your Savior?", not entirely sure just what sort of transaction the interlocutor has in mind. But if we are truly Catholic, that is to say, biblical Christians, we will have no trouble replying, "Yes—most certainly I want to be numbered among those who have received him. I hope my whole life is a matter of increasingly accepting him—that is, of hearing and obeying his Word and of walking in the new life he brings. Yes, I have accepted Jesus as my personal Savior. Have you?")

In the homily that follows immediately upon the reading of the Gospel, ideally speaking we should hear that Gospel unfolded and linked with the other scriptural readings. It is not unknown in Catholic churches for the time for the homily to be preempted by various announcements, perhaps in connection with some effort in the parish to augment the

[4] *Daily Roman Missal*, 23.
[5] Ibid., 99.

ordinary offerings of money. If this is ever the case, then of course this element in the liturgy has not carried its gospel "weight", we might say. The congregation may, in such an instance, turn its attention then with redoubled zeal to the rest of the liturgy.

The Creed supplies us all with the very words by which our forerunners in the faith have confessed the gospel for more than fifteen centuries. "We believe in one God. . . . We believe in one Lord, Jesus Christ, the only Son of God. . . . For us men and for our salvation came down from heaven . . . he was crucified . . . on the third day he rose again from the dead." There is the very heart of the gospel, on every Catholic's lips.

It may be thought that in the Intercessions, which follow now, we do not find the gospel spelled out in so many words. This is, of course, true, if we are looking for succinct phrases. On the other hand, in this act of intercession, any Catholic is in the gospel, so to speak. He is drawing, in every petition, on the fountain of mercy that was opened up for all the world at Calvary, when the Savior offered himself in behalf of us all. It is to that mercy, and because of the merits of that Savior, that we bring the world and the Church and each other. There is not a line of the intercessions that does not proclaim "gospel!"

In the Preparation of the Gifts, we hear the great mystery of the gospel uttered in the fewest possible words. "By the mystery of this water and wine may we come to share in the divinity of Christ, who humbled himself to share in our humanity." This touches on one of the most unimaginable aspects of the gospel, that mystery which some of the Eastern Fathers of the Church have spoken of as the "deification" of man. It is not a topic to be canvassed frivolously, and most of us would do well to remain silent in the presence of such language. But we do know that God has willed us to share his life and that this great gift is brought about for us by our Lord's having shared our humanity. Here is matter for the most solemn of meditations.

Along with the Collects, the Prefaces to the *Sanctus* for the various seasons and feasts of the year are a great treasury of the gospel. Let us take only one, the Preface for the Feast of the Triumph of the Cross: "Father . . . you decreed that man should be saved through the wood of the cross. The tree of man's defeat became his tree of victory; where life was lost, there life has been restored through Christ our Lord." [6] Listen, from day to day, as the priest says these Prefaces: they are redolent of the gospel. No Catholic need ever be at a loss for words as to what is meant by the question, "What is the gospel?"

In the *Sanctus*, we greet the Savior, who comes to us now in the eucharistic mystery, as he came before to Jerusalem, to accomplish the work heralded in the good news, the gospel, namely, his offering of himself for our salvation.

In the Eucharistic Prayers we "rehearse" the gospel—that is, we call to mind what God has done, from the beginning, to bring us back to himself when we had fallen into sin and death. In the fullness of time he sent his only Son to be our Savior, says the Fourth Eucharistic Prayer. Here is the gospel, in words that any child can hear and remember.

In the course of the Eucharistic Prayer we are all called upon to proclaim the mystery of faith: "Christ has died, Christ is risen, Christ will come again." There is no readier summary of the gospel than that. Who is this "Christ?" It is Jesus of Nazareth, the One we sing about in all the Christmas carols. For unto you is born this day in the city of David a

---

[6] *Daily Roman Missal*, 637.

Savior. We all know those words. O come, let us adore him, Christ the Lord. Joy to the world, the Lord is come. O little town of Bethlehem . . . in thy dark street shineth, the everlasting Light. Holy Infant, so tender and mild: *He* is this savior, who is to die, rise from the grave, and come again. He is the One who for us men and for our salvation came down from heaven and was incarnate by the Holy Spirit of the Virgin Mary.

Every Catholic knows all these words. Hence, every Catholic knows the Gospel and, if he stops to think about it, has placed all his hopes on that gospel. "For there is no other name under heaven given among men by which we must be saved." Catholics hear this proclamation every year when St. Peter's first sermons are read at Mass during the days following Pentecost.

Or, "Dying you destroyed our death, Rising you restored our life: Lord Jesus, come in glory." There is the gospel, and every Catholic has it on the tip of his tongue. Death —the "wages of sin", St. Paul calls it—was destroyed by Jesus' death at Calvary (yes: it is an impenetrable mystery, and St. Thomas Aquinas himself would never claim to have done more than approach its outskirts, so no Catholic, or any other Christian, for that matter, need ever claim to be able to *explain* it). "Dying you destroyed our death." O death, where is thy sting? O grave, where is thy victory? Thanks be to God, who gives us the victory through our Lord Jesus Christ. The words come tumbling out faster than we can speak them. "Rising you restored our life." We, who were "dead in trespasses and sins" (Eph 2:1)—our life restored! The people that walked in darkness have seen a great light—so said Isaiah as he peered into the thick darkness of God's redeeming purposes, saying much more than he imagined. "Lord Jesus, come in glory." Even so, come, Lord Jesus: it is with that yearning that the

whole Scripture comes to a close, in the last phrase in St.
John's Apocalypse. We celebrate Eucharist "till he comes". It
is the blessed hope of Christians. Maranatha! Come, Lord
Jesus.

Or yet again, "When we eat this bread and drink this cup,
we proclaim your death, Lord Jesus, until you come in
glory." There is the whole sweep of the gospel. This bread—
what bread? "My flesh, which I will give for the life of the
world." *For the life of the world*: there is the gospel. Jesus died
for us. No apostle and no evangelist and no theologian can
put it more exactly than that. Nor can any apostle, evangelist, or theologian explain it. *How* this death—this willing
self-oblation—of Jesus Christ wins the forgiveness of sins
and eternal life for us lies in the heart of the Father. This
Cup: "this is the New Testament in my Blood." "The blood
of Jesus Christ his Son cleanses us from all sin" (1 Jn 1:9).
The Precious Blood, Catholics say. Why? The Church early
learned the phrase from St. Peter. "For as much as you know
that you were not redeemed with corruptible things, as silver
and gold . . . but with the precious Blood of Christ" (1 Pet
1:18). "You are bought with a price", says St. Paul (1 Cor
6:20). That priceless Blood is in this Cup that we drink at
Mass, Catholics believe. To be Catholic is to be a man or
woman of this gospel.

In the Lord's Prayer and in the Peace, we speak, as gospel
people, to our Father in heaven and to each other. It is into
these precincts of faith and peace that the gospel has brought
us. But it is not only precincts: we have been brought to his
very Table, his banquet.

In the Communion we reach the very center of the gospel, that mystery of which our Lord spoke in John 6 and
which so scandalized so many people. How can we eat the
flesh and drink the blood of the Son of God? Intellect and

imagination stagger: we approach this Table by faith, which, as St. Thomas' great eucharistic hymn reminds us, grasps realities that elude sight and understanding. Surely it is one of the central paradoxes of the gospel that the Angelic Doctor, the little child, and any of "the least of these my brethren" are all on exactly the same footing here. But is this not characteristic of the gospel? We are told to preach the gospel to "every creature", not merely to the brilliant intellects of this world. "Whosoever" is the word that St. Peter, quoting the prophet Joel, lays down as describing those invited by the gospel (Acts 2:21). It is a very wide and generous gospel.

To be Catholic, then, is to live one's whole life "in" the gospel. A Savior who is Christ the Lord. This is my Body given for you. Behold the Lamb of God who takes away the sins of the world. He came down from heaven for us men and for our salvation. Blessed is the fruit of thy womb, Jesus. These phrases ring in the ears of Catholics. The Church teaches that it is faith that grasps these words of gospel, and that it is grace that enables us to live as gospel people, that is, as Christians; that is, as Catholics.

8

Are Catholics Saved?

The foregoing discussion of Catholics and the gospel raises a topic that is to be found at the root of many an animated, not to say shrill, conversation.

Such conversations often follow upon some such a remark as, "I was a Catholic until I was seventeen, and then I got saved." Or, in a somewhat different rendering, "I was raised Catholic, but when I was eighteen I met Jesus." In an even more stark form, we may hear, "I was raised Catholic, but when I was in my early twenties I became a Christian."

Clearly we are in the presence here either of immense confusion or of a distinction so dire that to call it a matter of salvation and damnation is scarcely to exaggerate.

Many of the people volunteering testimonials such as these would, if pressed, venture that it is the latter of our two options that looms. Catholics aren't saved—or at least *I* wasn't saved until I left Catholicism (goes the account). It was all legalism and rote and obligations: I had no idea about the real gospel of salvation—that a person could know himself to be born again and hence a new creature in Christ. No one ever so much as mentioned Jesus Christ as Savior, or in any event not in a fashion that gripped my attention. It was not until my friend took me to the Baptist youth group that

I came upon people my age who explicitly (and joyously, I might say) thought of themselves as born-again Christians, and who talked about Jesus as someone not only alive, but alive in their very midst. So, if damnation is the alternative to salvation, then I suppose my own situation actually was a matter of my passing from the former into the latter.

Where are we here?

Everyone bustles onto the stage. There is no salvation outside the Church! It is Protestants who aren't saved! (This from many a zealous Catholic perhaps.) Or: There you have it! See, Catholics aren't saved! Our young friend here has just demonstrated this melancholy state of affairs! (This from many an earnest Evangelical, perhaps.) Or, Hold! Someone needs to define our terms here! (This from a judicious and benign presence anxious to be a bridge over troubled waters.)

So, the tumult is assuaged momentarily, the fever cools, and we gird our loins for a civil consideration of the matter.

But who will venture into the breach? Five hundred years of strife lie at the root of everything that has been said. The fabric of Christendom was torn with a sundering so violent that there may be no reknitting of it for as long as history lasts. Indeed, the sundering is such that many on either side will not grant that the other "side" is Church at all. It is apostasy. It is schism. It is idolatry. Heaven fend off the day of accommodation: that will be a day of infamy. There can be no concord between Christ and Belial.

Happily, this level of vituperation is heard only fitfully now, and the pyres have long since died down. But we still have our testimonial here from this earnest Christian believer who, looking back on his Catholic upbringing, cannot identify anything in it with salvation. In his own eyes, he was not saved as long as he was Catholic, and when he was saved he ceased being a Catholic. Can light be cast on the matter?

It would seem so. There are at least four aspects to things here that need to be brought into play.

First, all Christians have known from the beginning that to be Christian entails more than just a certain spiritual feeling. That is, one's whole inner being may be suffused with the sunshine of benevolence and good will: this is a state of affairs most sedulously to be prized; but it does not make one a Christian any more than it makes one a Muslim or a Zoroastrian. Or again, one may exude courtesy, gravity, and high-mindedness, as did early Boston and its stepchildren the Transcendentalists. Such traits are to be extolled: but they do not add up to one's being Christian. And yet again, one may pursue "spirituality" at a thousand spas and ashrams and monasteries: but one is not thereby necessarily Christian.

To be Christian is to assert that certain events occurred in our mortal history. *Believe* is actually the word used by Christians in this connection, taking their cue from apostolic preaching and, more to the point, from the Lord himself. He told his nocturnal visitor Nicodemus that a man had to "believe", but it was belief linked with a link of iron to *what* one had to believe. There was a popular radio program in the 1940s that offered to the public the voices of noted men and women retailing their most deeply felt convictions under the heading "This I Believe", intoned with all possible sonority. There was no connection, often, between these testimonials and Christian belief. It is a point worth stressing, since the invitation to Christian faith is at times offered as a matter of one's opening oneself up to "belief": one is free to fill in the blank at will after the word belief: Marx; Hermes Trismegistus; Xiang Hsi. But Jesus Christ told Nicodemus that a man had to believe in the Son of God. Peter rehearsed for the throng in Jerusalem what they had done to Jesus Christ in crucifying him, made the connection between that event and

the whole scheme of Law and Prophets that they all acknowledged, and then asserted that this Jesus *was* the Christ
and that this fact had been ratified by God's having raised
him from the grave. Repent and believe this gospel, he concluded.

Christians have always insisted upon this. "No creed but
Christ" sounds inexpugnable and has at times been attempted by one religious association or another. But the
Christian creed ("creed" = *credo*, I believe) spells things out.
The Christ in question is Jesus. He is the Lord. He came
down from heaven. He offered his life on the Cross for our
sins. His blood washes away our sins. He rose from the grave.
He ascended into heaven. He is coming again. If that is what
we mean by "Christ", then "No creed but Christ" might do.
But the Church, taking her cue from Jesus Christ himself,
and from his apostles and from the whole witness of the New
Testament, has not been in the habit of leaving the matter
with quite such an vague slogan, neat as it may sound.

So: to be Christian is to assert, or believe, that certain
events occurred in our mortal history. On this point Catholics and the Christians who wonder if Catholics are saved
concur. Both groups will stand tall and recite the Creed and
mean it. The most fiery evangelist will not fault Catholics
when it comes to believing *that* certain things are true. He
may not feel fully satisfied if he tries to extract an account of
this belief from a man singing and swaying his way home at
dawn from a pub, from a peasant woman in a shawl somewhere, or a Mafioso with his Packard car and machine gun.
But with a little persistence, he will find that such unlikely
types probably do, at bottom, share his creed. (This litmus test
might, alas, break down if our fiery friend were to catechize a
Catholic whose religious instruction had occurred in the
wake of the convulsions that were visited upon the West in

the decade or two during and after the Vietnam conflict and the rise of a new culture. Such a Catholic might possibly have been taught that the Catholic Church's gospel has to do with a generalized outlook known as "caring", and that one needs to focus on unjust economic systems, United States big business, and the preservation of the saw-whet owl, insofar as one wishes to think of oneself as a modern Christian. The difficulty with this line of catechesis is that, worthy as all of its concerns indeed are, it somehow contrives never to come at the nub where we find that Christ has died, Christ is risen, Christ will come again. There are to be found some Catholics whose grasp of this nub is tenuous.)

This brings us to the second aspect of things at stake when we speak of what it is to be a Christian believer, Catholic or otherwise. There is, first of all, an assent to, and belief in, the Lord Jesus Christ.

But can one merely believe the story? The devils believe, St. James tells us, and much good it does them. The response, then, that Christians identify by their word "believe" seems to entail a wholeheartedness: authenticity; commitment; obedience. All of this is at stake when Christians, Catholic or otherwise, speak of believing the gospel. The gospel is not flat data, so to speak, that may be assessed and passed over, the way one might pass over statistics about soy bean production in the environs of Oskaloosa. The events call for my response. Indifference leaves me where I was before I heard about these events. But insofar as I hear about them, open myself to them, and receive (or "accept") them, then I am on the way to becoming what has always been known as a Christian.

A Christian believer reading this account will wish to adjust the vocabulary very slightly. It is only a matter of a pronoun, really. Let us say *him* rather than *it*, our reader will suggest. The invitation implicit in the gospel is that we accept *him*—Jesus Christ. *He* receives *us*, at our baptism, as we saw in the previous chapter. At that point, says the Church, we are "incorporated" into the Church, that is, into Christ. (Interestingly enough, to see the rite of baptism as the point at which we mortals are thus incorporated is not really a Catholic/Protestant point of discussion: the Orthodox, the Anglicans, the Lutherans, the Presbyterians, and the Methodists all look on this rite as in some sense marking our passage from "out" to "in"; it would be the Baptist and Anabaptist and free-church sectors of Christendom that wish to limit its significance to a public confession of Christ as Savior and Lord, and no more.)

But all would agree that the gospel holds out to us mortals the challenge to assent *to* the narrative about Jesus Christ and the invitation to receive him, in the sense of acknowledging him to be my Savior and my Lord. No Christian profession at all would wish to skirt this minimum. (Onlookers sometimes charge that Catholics think you are saved magically, simply by the rite of baptism. Not so. To be sure, grace is truly operative there, says the Church, and God accounts the baptized child as his own—"in Christ", that is. But if faith and obedience never arise to ratify what was done for me at my baptism, then it is the last folly for me to frolic through life counting on the external rite to get me "in". That is to turn the sacrament of baptism into a rabbit's foot, which it is not.)

So on these first two aspects of our original question of whether Catholics are saved, we find that all parties to the discussion concur: the Christian gospel calls for belief in something (upon which we all agree: Who will wish to edit Peter's sermon at Pentecost?); and it calls upon us to "accept", or receive, or commit ourselves to the Lord revealed in that gospel.

138 On Being Catholic

On this point I may introduce a somewhat fanciful vignette that has often presented itself to my imagination as exhibiting the difficulty arising when Catholic and non-Catholic Christians stumble into a discussion of who is "saved".

At the time when I was received into the Catholic Church, I came to know an old woman named Sarah who came to daily Mass. At that same time, my octogenarian mother was living at our house. My mother, being a Protestant Evangelical who spent many hours with her Bible open in her lap, might have wondered about the sense in which it could be urged that Sarah was saved, not that my mother would have doubted Sarah's humility and sincerity (the two women never met: I am only fancying the following vignette). But Sarah would have done poorly with a certain set of questions my mother might have put to her. "Are you saved?" Blank. "Well—are you born again?" Confusion. "Right. Have you accepted the Lord Jesus Christ as your personal Savior?" Consternation.

Just as my mother is concluding that her long-held fears about Catholics seem indeed to be well-grounded, I interfere. I lead the two ladies over to a crucifix on the wall, and in my mother's hearing, I ask Sarah who that is. Jesus. Who is he? The Son of God. What is he doing? Suffering death. Why? For our sins.

And suddenly my mother has heard Sarah make a confession that qualifies Sarah for the category "saved". Sarah has believed all of this all along, and her trust is in this gospel, just as is my mother's. But left to themselves, the two ladies might have gone off deeply perplexed about each other's Christian credentials.

This brings us to the third aspect of the question arising from our young friend's claim that he became a Christian, or was saved, only after he had left the Catholic Church, since he had never, if we will credit his own account of his experience, been challenged by the Christian gospel in any sense that arrested him and called for a response from him. Indeed, he might well insist, I never heard the gospel at all. I never had the smallest notion of what the Mass was about. And the religious instruction in my parish never once spelled out for us just what this matter of "knowing Jesus" might be, of which our Lord and the apostles spoke so urgently.

What is at stake here (besides the melancholy possibility that our friend's account is too true and that he has, in fact, been allowed to grope in darkness) is what might be called a matter of *style*.

To introduce such a word into such weighty topics will seem at once to be frivolous. Style? Come: we are speaking of substance here, not style. Christian belief, and the matter of one's salvation, can scarcely be treated as a question of style.

D'accord. The question itself is as weighty and substantial as the earth. But the way we apprehend it may be said to entail this apparently trivial category of style.

To illustrate this, we may turn to what non-Catholic Christians are referring to, often, when they ask whether I am saved or not. Among millions of non-Catholic believers the question of one's being saved attaches to an explicit, conscious, volitional experience. That is, one is trundling along through life when all of a sudden he hears Billy Graham preach, finds himself deeply affected by the message (which is, let us keep recalling, "Jesus died for you"), and "accepts Christ as his personal Savior". He believes himself to be, at that very point, saved. "Believe on the Lord Jesus Christ and thou shalt be saved", said St. Paul to the frantic jailer. Millions of Christians will point to precisely this moment of personal decision as the point at which they were saved.

There are, of course, a thousand variations on the theme. In Southern Baptist circles, and all across the world in Evangelical circles, the setting may have been one's own local church where, having grown up under the sound of the gospel, one finds oneself particularly flagged down one day at the age of ten (or fourteen, or twenty) and "accepts Jesus". Or again, thousands of high-school and university young people have encountered this gospel at the hands of Christian groups on their campus and will date their conversion to a specific point, perhaps in private prayer, at which they gave themselves to Christ. All of those, including many Catholics for whom the moment has turned out to be a genuine watershed, will urge that indeed this moment of decision was coterminous with their being saved.

Well, someone might interject here: Do you wish to locate such experiences under the heading of "style"?

No. The faith that was exercised in those decisions grasped a substance more lasting than the very universe itself, which will turn to ashes one fine day, as we know, while faith carries the faithful through the conflagration into the City whose builder and maker is God.

But we may juxtapose with these testimonials another sketch, which will perhaps make clear what we mean by style. In the first years of the apostolic and patristic Church, if I had been a pagan shopkeeper in Smyrna, say, and had been watching you, my Christian neighbor, for some time and had concluded that you Christians had something that I wanted, I might have approached you with, "Um—I'd like to be a Christian."

If you had been an Evangelical of the school that has arisen in the modern world under the preaching of John Wesley, George Whitefield, Jonathan Edwards, D. L. Moody, and Billy Graham, you might well have said, "Praise the

Lord! Here—here's John 3:16. See that? Do you believe that? Wonderful. Let's just bow our heads here, and you can repeat after me: 'Lord Jesus, I believe that you are the Savior—my Savior—and I want to accept you into my life right here and to confess you as Lord. Forgive my sins, I pray, and make me your own.' "

But of course you weren't a modern Evangelical. You were a Christian in Smyrna. So you would have said in response to my overture, "What? You want to be a Christian? Ah. Well, now—it's an immense business, really. You'll have to turn around and head 180 degrees in the opposite direction. But if you're serious—and you can mull it over for a while if you wish—I'll take you to Polycarp, our bishop here, and he will no doubt talk to you and then turn you over to some of the elders in our Christian assembly, and they will take you in hand and instruct you and bring you to our weekly liturgy (you'll have to leave half-way through, though: they won't let you stay for the Lord's Supper); and if, over a period of months, everyone, and most especially Polycarp, is satisfied that you are wholehearted in your desire to be a Christian, and that you understand all that it will entail, then Polycarp will baptize you at the liturgy, and you will then be a Christian."

The distance between these two pictures—the one depicting you and me with John 3:16, and the one from Smyrna—blazons for us all something of the vast breakdown that may mar things when we try to talk about who is saved. Both pictures show us a man grasped by the saving gospel of Christ. In the one, he steps across a line, as it were, just now, in his heart, with perhaps only one witness (or none). It is an interior transaction. It is intelligent, willed, conscious. In the other, it is also intelligent, willed, conscious: but it all appears to be under the auspices of the Church. The notion of a purely private and interior transaction is unthinkable, except, of course, in some extreme case where a jailer finds the walls and bars collapsing about him and cries out *in extremis*, so to speak. Even our Smyrnean bishop would have said that the Divine Mercy hears and honors such a cry. Of course. But that hasty scenario is not the blueprint for the quotidian life of the Church as she moves along her slow way through history. What you saw us doing here in Smyrna—that is the paradigm. Salvation, while personal, is not private. To be incorporated into Christ is to be incorporated into his Church. You cannot sunder the two: it is not two in any case. It is one thing. There is no such thing as an independent Christian to the extent that the Church *is* Christ's Body here on earth. You can't be "incorporated" into him and not into his Body, and that Body, far from being a loose aggregate of people connected only by the wispy filaments of coordinate belief, may be found here in Smyrna, and in Antioch under their bishop Ignatius, and in Jerusalem under their bishop James.

So: Who is saved? The conscious and interior transaction, punctiliar, that stamps a man with the identity "saved"? The Catholic (and, it may be observed, the Orthodox, the Anglican, and, to a certain extent, the Lutheran and the Calvinist) think of the category as inseparably linked to a man's being found in the Church, and this identity is stamped upon him at his baptism.

It will have been noticed by everyone by this time that we have omitted perhaps the most numerous category of people who would wish to be a party to any discussion of who is saved. We are speaking, of course, of all the Christians who were baptized as infants and who neither responded for the first time as adults to the preaching of the gospel nor, also as adults, passed through a process of catechesis analogous to our Smyrnean situation.

Are they saved?

The two poles between which the answer to that question finds itself stretched would be, on the one hand, the view that baptism is an external rite that actually effects nothing. It is strictly, and only, an ordinance we observe because the Lord commands it. It plays no actual role in determining our spiritual state. For that determination, we consult faith alone. At the other pole will be the view that baptism by itself does the whole trick: if I am baptized, I am safe forever. This latter pole, it will be immediately observed, is the frivolous misstating of the Church's view that baptism is a sacrament and that here, as with all sacraments, we come upon a real nexus between the superficial (the visible; the physical; the immediate) and the substantial (the unseen; the spiritual; the eternal). We really do see the principle *ex opere operato* at work: from the act itself the thing is effected. That is, the water of baptism does wash away the stain of sin with which we, as children of Adam, are stained. The soul is, at this point, "regencrate".

Those are the two poles. There is no topic at all, in heaven and earth, that has stirred up more zeal, not to say tumult. It is appropriate in the context of this present study only to point out that all the churches, including the Roman Catholic, the Orthodox, the Anglican, the Lutheran, and the Calvinist, that attach some actual, "covenantal" weight to the rite of baptism (not all of these, by any means, will allow that *ex opere operato* is at work) will insist, along with all Baptists and free-churchmen, that baptism is not magic. A soul's destiny is not sealed irrevocably with the water. What has occurred in the rite is both a present seal *and* a harbinger, so to speak, of the faith and obedience that must spring up sooner or later in this soul and ratify the rite.

So, in this third aspect of the question between our two

interlocutors of who is saved—the aspect, that is, of "style",
or how we visualize the entry into faith—we find that despite such enormous differences in practice and vocabulary,
no Christian has any hesitation about who the Savior might
be. That is Jesus Christ. They have all heard the angel tell
Joseph, "Thou shalt call his name Jesus, for he shall save his
people from their sins." To be Catholic is to rely wholly on
this Savior.

There is one further aspect of things, a fourth and, in this
case minor, point, to be sure, that marks this question of one's
being "saved". To a Protestant Evangelical, to be saved is ordinarily to have taken on vigorously forthcoming habits of
speech about the faith. One is, characteristically, ready at a
moment's notice to testify in keeping with St. Peter's injunction that we be ready always to give an answer to every man
that asks us a reason for the hope that is in us (1 Pet 3:15).
Evangelical believers take that at its face value: it constitutes
the warrant for the loquacity, we might say, that so unnerves
Catholics, Orthodox, and even Lutheran and Calvinist
Christians, none of whom, ordinarily, incline to quite this
chattiness when it comes to speaking of matters religious.
Hence evangelical Christians are often stumped when they
encounter the muteness sometimes evinced by Catholics:
"You ask them if they're saved, and all you get is an embar-
rassed mutter."

This is very often true. But one or two qualities of the
Catholic mind need to be stressed here. For one thing, one's
Catholic identity attaches not so much to a punctiliar experience of accepting Christ as Savior, about which one may or
may not wish to speak, as to the entire fabric, we might venture, of Catholic life. The Church, the sacraments, the Magisterium, prayer, the liturgy: it is in these precincts that one's
Catholic (and hence Christian) identity rests. "I am *all of*

that", a Catholic might volunteer as his contribution to the testimonials flying about. And if it seems, in this connection, that the Catholic Church has muddied the waters of faith, which seem to gush with sparkling clarity from evangelical springs, by introducing such immense machinery into the pure streambed of faith, we may consult our early forerunners in that faith. They had no Scriptures to quote so quickly; and they were conscious of having been incorporated into "the Church of the living God", with her apostolic authority and her weekly liturgy, prayers, and her moral demands (they had to take on a mode of life starkly to be distinguished from that of their pagan neighbors). "I am a Christian", they would have replied; and, soon enough, "I am a Catholic", by way of distinguishing themselves from the eager and febrile quasi-Christian groups springing up all over under the preaching of heretics. To be Catholic was (and is) to be identified with *that*. With what? With that company of men and women and children gathered in the name of Jesus Christ, under the presidency of the bishop, who himself is in obedient and unqualified unity with the apostles, around the eucharistic banquet instituted by the Lord in Jerusalem.

For reasons harking back to such a matrix, Roman Catholics do not appear so sprightly as their evangelical brothers when it comes to speaking up about the faith. Furthermore, if a Catholic has been well instructed—but alas: here we must admit that the "if" is a very loud subordinate conjunction: the world is full of Catholics who, like the men of Nineveh, scarcely know their right hand from their left; only the Divine Mercy can assess what, lurking in the mixture of piety, ignorance, and even superstition, may be taken as true faith, and we may be very sure that this Mercy is infinitely merciful and will account any smallest hint of response in the human soul as the faith spoken of in Scripture as saving us.

But *if* a Catholic has been well instructed, he holds the ancient faith as a fabric into which his whole life has been woven seamlessly. Tags and phrases and Scripture texts do not festoon that fabric ordinarily. He is, in all likelihood, not quoting to himself, "Cast all your care upon him for he careth for you", or "In everything by prayer and supplication let your requests be made known unto God", or "Thou wilt keep him in perfect peace whose mind is stayed on thee", as he goes about his daily tasks. Because his is a sacramental piety, there is no stark frontier between the physical and the immaterial worlds. He is accustomed, that is, to a world in which water is pressed into the service of eternity (baptism), and in which bread and wine are transubstantiated. Hence his entire grasp of his identity as a man of faith (he would perhaps scarcely recognize such a phrase) may rarely come to the point of articulateness, we might say. He has been assumed, so to speak, into the immense Catholic fabric, and things do not stand or fall with his ability to be explicit. Hence the characteristic Catholic's shaky performance under the drill of evangelical inquiries about his faith.

And we may also recall in this connection that there are almost one billion Roman Catholics in the world. What percentage of this billion is literate, much less trained in the muscular discourse so characteristic of northern Europe and its Reformation, would be difficult to track down. How the Divine Mercy assesses the faith at work in our muttering Sicilian crone, relative to the faith of a Mt. Holyoke undergraduate leading a crackling Bible study in her dormitory, is a piquant question. Since the whole point of faith is that we mortals be drawn ever more into configuration to Charity ("the measure of the stature of the fullness of Christ", St. Paul calls it), we find ourselves obliged to leave on one side all tests of how articulate, or scripturally adept, a given soul is and to address ourselves, rather, to the far more daunting question of how we are all doing in the school of Charity.

This is a sword that cuts both ways, of course. The world's most biblically adroit Evangelical, for his part, may have to stop in his busy tracks and ask what, exactly, he is about; and the local Catholic, fiercely loyal to his ethnic and cultural religion, may need to inquire about what, exactly, *he* is about. There is only one agenda for all of us Christians, namely, our growing into conformity to Jesus Christ, that is to say, our being made perfect in Charity. We must all appear before the judgment seat of Christ, and at that tribunal there is not one test for Protestants and another for Catholics. All of us have arrived there by grace, and all of us are "washed in the Blood of the Lamb", and all of us are to have been configured to Christ. *Juste judex ultionis, Donum fac remissionis,* we will all want to call out: O righteous Judge, grant us remission of our sins. And, *Recordare, Jesu pie, quod sum causa tuae viae:* Remember, kind Jesus, that I am the reason for your coming to earth. The crone and the Mt. Holyoke woman will both want to plead thus.

Are Catholics saved? If they are, it is on the basis of God's grace in Christ the Savior, as it is for the Evangelicals. Again, for his part, the Evangelical may need to ask whether he has taken this "so great salvation" and pocketed it like a laminated card, expecting that the door of heaven will buzz open when he arrives. "Oh, I'm saved: I accepted Jesus as my Savior on March 10, 1984." Yes: but is your lamp trimmed? How have you been doing in the "inasmuch as you have done it unto the least of these" sweepstakes? Have you forgiven your brother as I have forgiven you? Remember, that decision of yours on March 10 was the opening sentence in the story. Where has that story gone now? And, for his part, the Catholic will need to ask whether all of his faithful obedi-

ence to the commandments of the Church—Mass, holy days
of obligation, confession—whether all of that has been the
fruit of faith in him or whether he has supposed that it has all
been a matter of accruing as much merit as he can stockpile
for his account at the Judgment, hoping that it will add up to
an acquittal.

To be Catholic is to rest one's case in the pierced hands of
Christ Jesus the Savior, as the apostles taught our first forerunners in the faith to do. If the saving grace that was
vouchsafed to me at my baptism has indeed fructified in my
life, and if faith and obedience have sprung up from that
heavenly seed, then, when I am asked whether I am "saved",
I may say Yes.

My Catholic "Yes" will have, however, a ring to it that is
somewhat different from the ring heard in my evangelical
brother's Yes. For him it refers to a fixed status: I *am* saved.
My status as saved was fixed at the point when I accepted
Christ as my Savior. Of one thing I am certain: I will get into
heaven. That, really, is the thrust of my assertion that I am
saved. I will get into heaven. Nothing I do, or fail to do, will
in the least qualify that certitude. My eternal safety is as sure
as God himself, resting as it does on his promise and "the
finished work of Christ".

This way of looking on the topic of one's own salvation
derives from the teaching of Martin Luther, with his emphasis on God's unfailing grace vouchsafed to us in Christ, and
on Christ's "finished" work at the Cross, grasped solely by
faith on my part. It also has elements in it of John Calvin's
teaching on "the perseverance of the saints", by which he
meant that the elect will, all hell to the contrary notwithstanding, persevere to the end. Their souls' safety may not for
one moment be called into question. The modern derivative,
among the Evangelicals, of Calvin's teaching on this point is

ordinarily called "assurance of salvation", or "eternal security". It is this that rings in the heartiness of an Evangelical's Yes! upon being asked if he is saved.

The Catholic Church speaks rather of the blessed *hope*. Hope, not certitude, is the note struck all the way through the New Testament, the Church would urge. It is not the forlorn hope of a modestly endowed child wondering if there is any remote chance that he will be picked for the team or promoted to the next grade. It is the "hope which is laid up for you in heaven" of which St. Paul speaks to the Colossians. It is "the hope of his calling" of which he speaks to the Ephesians. It is the hope by which we are saved of which he speaks to the Romans. It is the helmet of salvation of which he speaks to the Thessalonians. It is the hope we have as an anchor of the soul of which the letter to the Hebrews speaks. It is the lively hope of which St. Peter speaks. It is the hope that makes us purify ourselves of which St. John speaks.

The Roman Catholic Church has always drawn her teaching about our salvation from this theme lacing the pages of the New Testament. Its vocabulary is one of hope. It is keenly aware of the dire thrust of the warnings, iterated so remorselessly by the Savior himself, against those who, looking upon themselves as safely among the righteous, will be startled one fine day to hear "Depart from me" read out after their name—not, it may be ventured here, for perpetrating murder and licentiousness, but for having failed to see Jesus Christ in the filthy outcast in the gutter.

The note struck in the Catholic Church on this question of one's being saved is also profoundly influenced by her whole understanding of what salvation is, when we are speaking of the individual Christian soul. One *was* saved by God's grace hidden in the bosom of the Father from all eternity. One *was* saved when Jesus Christ called out *Consummatum est!* on the Cross. One *was* saved when he rose from the grave putting death and sin to flight. One *was* saved at one's baptism, that being "born of water and the Spirit" of which our Lord speaks to Nicodemus.

But one is *in the Way*, as the early Church phrased it. *One is being saved*, insofar as one is to be found among those who name the Name of Christ, and insofar as one is to be found at his Table, and insofar as one is walking in that obedience which alone is the test of our love for him and is producing the fruit that appears on a branch that is alive, referred to by the Lord in John 15, and has the works to show without which faith is a mockery, as St. James so solemnly teaches. In this sense, one is being saved. One is in the School of Charity, whose tutelage fits us eventually to receive the crown of God's "Well done" in heaven.

And one *will be saved*, if one is found among the faithful, at the resurrection, until which time, says St. Paul, our salvation is not complete. It is not until then that one may quite say I *am* saved, with the ring of utter finality.

To be Catholic is to understand the answer to the question of whether one is saved in terms such as these.

9

Catholics at Prayer

To be Catholic is to think of oneself as having been adopted into "the whole family in heaven and earth", as St. Paul teaches. Naturally, all Christian believers see themselves thus: but to be Catholic is not only to have an especially vivid sense of being in this family; it is to carry on one's entire life of faith, and hence of one's prayers, in no other context at all.

This view of things issues, often, in forms that may set on edge the teeth of non-Catholic believers. Hail, Mary, full of grace: everyone knows that salutation. To Catholics it is as natural as greeting one's own mother. To many Christians it looks like idolatry: this charge is sometimes made by zealots who perhaps have not paused long enough, ever, to find out just what this mode of address might mean among Christ's faithful.

Or again, a non-Catholic may have heard (even, alas, as an expletive) some quick reference to Jesus, Mary, and Joseph. This may arouse in him the suspicion that the Catholic Church has introduced onto the stage two additional figures by way of edging the Lord himself ever so slightly off center and of diluting his exclusive honor with an honor spread out between two nondivine figures.

And yet again, what is a Christian to suppose when he

overhears a group of Catholics saying in chorus, "Holy Michael, pray for us. Holy Raphael, pray for us. Holy Agatha, pray for us"? Fie. Don't Catholics know that we may "come boldly to the throne of grace", and that we are to "let our requests be made known unto God", and that there is only "one Mediator between God and man, the man Christ Jesus"? Why this circuitous route? Why this multitude through which Catholics seem obliged to force their way in order to come to that Throne with their prayers?

No doubt the most colorful, and even jolting, way in which non-Catholic Christians come upon this Catholic exultation in the whole family in heaven and on earth presents itself in the images that may be found in many Catholic churches.

To be sure, thousands of parish churches were stripped of their images in the wake of the Second Vatican Council; and it is therefore not unusual for a Methodist or Baptist to find very little to offend him as he steps inside a Catholic church. "Why, this could be our church!" might even be heard, although a closer look will reveal a certain arrangement of furniture, with an altar at the center of focus, that may not fit comfortably with non-Catholic categories.

On the other hand, especially in Austria, Bavaria, and the Latin countries of the world, one is likely to find oneself having stumbled into a dizzying panoply of statuary and painting as one enters a Catholic church. Anyone who has ever visited one of the great cathedrals in France or England will, of course, have found statuary: but in the gothic cathedrals, the statuary is unpainted and made of the same gray stone as the rest of the building. Indeed, the figures probably form unobtrusive elements in the pillars, the doors, or the tympanum. Somehow this twelfth-, thirteenth-, and fourteenth-century display seems restrained. Protestant sensibilities are not rudely smitten, although many a tourist, lost in admiration in a gothic cathedral, has perhaps had to cope with a small voice at his elbow reminding him of the commandment in Exodus interdicting graven images. Heigh ho: Must we jettison all of this serene and regal display? It looks as though we must, but it is all so noble, so beautiful. . .

But in Austria or Spain a crowded universe leaps upon one's sensibilities when one comes into a church. Riotously painted plaster ceilings and walls and pillars, with—can it be?—figures who sail far too near the pagan wind for orthodox comfort, capering among the painted and billowing clouds. Or polychrome statues of the Virgin and saints with their eyes cast soulfully up into the ozone. Or worse, crucifixes that go so far as to hail us with horribly gaunt, twisted, hacked, and bloodied figures of the Savior in agony. And, introducing a note of the macabre into it all, perhaps a glass coffin with a recumbent and desiccated figure visible or, as it may be, a skeleton grinning there.

This itinerary seems to have brought us a very long distance from our topic of Catholics at prayer. But what one sees under these startling auspices in such churches is merely the unfurling of the interior vision that the faith of every Catholic presents to him.

The vision may be adumbrated in the following manner: in our own history here on this earth, we have become familiar with the figures of the great kings. They themselves are crowned with gold and robed in purple and ermine. The orb and scepter are in their hands. The throne upon which they sit is of damask and gold. Gems adorn everything. Nothing seems too costly to be brought into the service of expressing the majesty of these kings.

But—are they alone in their majesty? Do they sit, solitary, surrounded by empty space? No. They are surrounded by their court, and on their right hand is the queen in vesture of gold, as the psalms will have it. Ducal coronets glitter, and the great earls and barons stand in attendance with their insignia of rank.

Rank. Perhaps that is the word that may supply the clue necessary to open up the Catholic vision of God's majesty to non-Catholics who worry that the ancient Church has stolen away the exclusive glory of God and has distributed it among a great multitude of interlopers.

The "rank" of the noble men and women who throng the earthly king's court is, of course, derived from him. The duke's dignity not only does not subtract one farthing from the king's majesty: it augments that majesty, as though to say, "See, see what nobility this sovereign bestows. See how he raises his servants to share his glory." The awe that comes over us upon the entrance of one of the great barons into the presence glances immediately from his armor straight to the figure on the throne. The great ladies of the court, so serene in their fathomless dignity, decked with the vesture that, even in its richness, is scarcely adequate to the nobility that crowns them—they gaze on our awe with eyes that say, "To him. To him be all honor and majesty and might and blessing."

This is the Catholic vision of God's majesty. He is not a niggardly sovereign, sitting upon his riches like a dragon on a hoard, sullen and wary lest anyone snatch the smallest coin from the heap, thereby subtracting that sum from his exclusive prerogative. There are, alas, widely espoused theologies that talk of God's glory as though this were the picture and that grudge any spilling-over of that glory onto any creature. To listen to such theologies is to conjure the spectacle of a great king, solitary in his splendor and served by thralls, sycophants, and helots, forever groveling, forever scourged by their masters with, "Give *him* the glory! Be careful to give *him* the glory!"

It is an ironic refrain, of course, since the whole point of the splendid assembly of nobles is that indeed the sovereign receive the glory. To that extent the slave-driving master's refrain is technically true. But there is something parsimonious about it all. Give him the glory, as though any remnant of cloth on me that is not a filthy rag somehow calls in question that glory.

But the grimmest khans, sultans, and pharaohs in their tyranny have not grudged their glory thus. The greater their retinue, the greater their splendor.

It is thus, says the Roman Catholic Church, with God's glory. He is a God who crowns us with glory and honor (see Psalm 8). He is a God who has raised us and made us to reign with his own Son. He is a God who exults in ennobling his servants and who has made them his own kin, brought them into his banqueting house, and unfurled the banner of love over their heads.

This is what his bounty purposes for all who will receive him. "As many as received him, to them gave he the power to become the sons of God." *Sons of God*? Lord: I am not worthy that you should come under my roof. Make me as one of your hired servants. Let me hunt with the dogs for the crumbs that fall from your table.

You are to sit at my royal table, says his bounty to us all. You were indeed poor and wretched and blind and naked, and so covered with wounds and bruises and putrefying sores that there was no remedy for your condition—no remedy, that is, but my grace. But now you are washed, you are healed, you are clothed with the righteousness of my own Son, the Prince of Glory. Your tunic, your armor and spurs and robe and the very diadem that glitters on your brow:

these you have from me, because I love my only begotten Son and wish to present him with this guerdon for his suffering. He shall see of the travail of his soul and shall be satisfied. I have adopted you and made you coheirs with him of all my glory.

This is the picture of things that we find in Scripture and that is kept so vibrantly alive in Catholic vision and piety. All of us are heirs with Christ. But in a great many of us, the first inklings of the glory that attaches to that inheritance are scarcely visible yet. On the other hand, there are figures among his followers who do exhibit to us all, in the ardor, purity, and zeal of their obedience to him, just what that glory is going to look like. From among this number of the faithful, the Church has named many to be designated "saints". Of course that title may be applied to all who are in Christ Jesus: St. Paul often uses the term when referring to the Christians in such and such a city. But in the particular usage at work when the Catholic Church speaks of the roster of saints, the notion is that in these figures we may see in a particularly clear and splendid fashion just what the Divine Charity looks like when it is wholly embraced by one of us.

These "saints" who have gone before us are there, in the heavens and in the Roman "martyrology" (the roster of all of these saints, whether or not they were martyred); but they are not mere decorations in the heavenly temple: they are, says the Church, living members with us, the Church here in pilgrimage through history, in the one single Mystical Body of Christ. The Resurrection of Jesus overthrew death's sovereignty, and so we Christians deny that we are separated from those who have gone before us by the impassable abyss of death. No: we, with them, are one, living, interceding company of the redeemed.

Interceding? How interceding?

The answer to this query, and hence to the question non-Catholics have about the role the saints play in Catholic prayer, lies again in the Resurrection of Jesus Christ. When he arose from the grave, he not only overthrew the kingdom of death: he arose to pursue his office as our Great High Priest (see Hebrews 2:27, 3:1, 4:14, 5:10, passim). We are the priestly Body of which he is the Head. A priest's office is to offer sacrifice and to intercede for the people. Jesus Christ has offered that Sacrifice for us all, and it is forever present on the heavenly altar. We, his priestly Body, share in that ministry. With him, and with all those who are his, from the patriarchs and John the Baptist on down, we stand offering intercessions for all men. The picture of the Head alone interceding, with his Mystical Body banished from that which the Head is doing, is grotesque, in the Catholic view. God in his superabundant mercy has drawn us—*us!*—into the life of his Son, not merely (as some theologies seem to imply) in a juridical way, or not merely in some technical "status". No. As is always the case with the Divine Mercy, it is an actual state of affairs into which we, the beneficiaries of that Mercy, are drawn. We are to join Jesus Christ in his intercessory ministry in behalf of the Church and the whole world.

This "we" includes the saints as well as us here on earth. Or let us put it the other way around and thus gain a more exact picture: *they* are there, with the High Priest, made one with that ministry; and we, too, also begin, during our pilgrimage here, to enter into that ministry.

To be Catholic is to grasp, and reckon on, this great web of intercession, binding heaven and earth. Prayers go up before the Throne of the Most High like the smoke of incense, continually, from the High Priest and from all his priestly people, or, in the other metaphor, from the Head and his Body. All of us, here below and those gone before, are one, living, praying company.

Hence, says the Church, to ask St. Joseph or St. Anthony for his prayers is no more odd than to ask my brother here on earth for his prayers. If I ask you for your prayers for me, you do not say, "Why are you asking me? *I'm* not a comediator. There is one God and one Mediator between God and man, the man Christ Jesus. Take your prayer requests to him. To ask me to pray for you is to interfere with the exclusive prerogative of Jesus. It is to weasel a human comediator between you and the one Mediator."

All Christians—Orthodox, Brethren, Mennonites, and Methodists—would deprecate this parsimonious line of thought. We are *supposed* to pray for one another, we would protest. That sole mediatorship of Jesus, far from banning us in the interest of his exclusive prerogative, draws us in and makes us full participants.

Indeed, says the Catholic Church. That is why Catholics understand the saints to be full participants in the mediatorship of Jesus. Their participation no more subtracts from his ministry than the glory that shines upon them subtracts from his glory. It is all his, forsooth. There is one fountainhead from which we all have drunk and from which we bear refreshment to parched souls. SS. Joachim and Anne, pray for me. SS. Simeon and Anna, pray for us, that we may also be fortified in patience, as you were through your long decades of waiting for the promise of Israel. St. Ignatius Loyola, pray for us that our hearts may burn as yours with zeal for Christ's gospel. St. Francis de Sales, pray for me, that I may be spurred to follow the way of holiness as you taught it.

But we have no reason to suppose that the saints who have gone before us can hear us, or even that they are aware of our existence: thus the protest from many non-Catholic believers.

The Letter to the Hebrews calls them "witnesses" (12:1), a Catholic might answer; and a witness is someone who is watching something. Oh (the rejoinder might run), that simply means that their lives and martyrs' deaths witness to God's faithfulness by way of example to us. That too, our Catholic might reply: but take care with your adverbs there. "Simply" is a perilous word to bring into play on the divine mysteries. You are sure, are you, that the text *simply* means that? The difficulty there is that you have the whole tradition of the ancient Church seeing things otherwise. Don't be too punctilious with your private exegesis.

To ask one of the saints for his prayers is of one seamless piece with our asking each other to pray for us. The precincts of the Divine mercy cannot be parceled out with addition and subtraction, with my siphoning off this bit of Jesus' priesthood when I venture to pray for you, and you pocketing that much of his merit when you lay down your life for me with such generosity day after day (one is thinking of one's spouse here). There is only gushing superabundance here, immersing us all, filling us all, and sweeping us along in the tide of that amplitude overflowing from the Father himself.

But what about these *images* before which I see Catholics kneeling from time to time when I peer into a church in Mexico or Italy? That, surely, violates the Second Commandment: we are not to make any graven image.

The Catholic Church hears that Commandment, as all of Israel heard it, and as the Reformation heard it. What was being forbidden there? we may ask. If it is a blanket prohibition of all "representing" of things in heaven or on earth, as Islam has it, then of course we will all have to jettison not only our icons and statues but also our Hummel and Meissen figurines and the little carved ships that sit on our mantel-pieces: we must also get rid of our children's stuffed animals and their porcelain dolls. These are not, of course, all "graven": but they are all "likenesses". What can it mean?

The Hebrews, the very recipients of that law, then went on, under explicit instructions of the God who issued the prohibition in the first place, to make golden bells and pomegranates for the hem of their high priest's garment, and the figures of golden cherubim for the mercy seat in their Tabernacle. In the wilderness God commanded Moses to make a bronze serpent (Nb 21:8–9). Solomon's temple, erected under divine instructions, displayed twelve oxen holding up the immense basin for washing. Was this all in violation of the Commandment?

No, the Jews would say. And No says the Church. The command prohibits the *worship* of such images. "Thou shalt not bow down to them or serve them." There is the distinction.

If a child in a Christian household brings home from his art class a small soapstone penguin graven in a first halting attempt at sculpture, the Christian parents do not smash the figure in an effort to be faithful to the Ten Commandments. Probably the penguin will be set in a place of honor in the house. Trouble would arise, however, if they were to come upon their child saying his prayers to the penguin. "Dear penguin, please help Papa to take me to the beach on Saturday." Gentle expostulations would be put forward to the effect that this sort of thing won't quite do, and that prayer . . . , etc., etc., etc.

But there is precisely my point, urges our non-Catholic tourist. I see people *kneeling* in front of statues and lighting candles. That is worship, pure and simple. Catholics worship statues.

It is indeed true, the Church might reply here, that multitudes of poorly instructed Catholic faithful have not altogether grasped the distinction between what they are doing at this image of St. Anthony or St. Lucy and what they do when they kneel in the Lord's presence. Here they are asking for help, and for this saint's intercession, as any Christian will ask a fellow Christian for help or intercession. And we find our Catholic kneeling since that is the customary attitude of Christian prayer. All prayer ascends to the Father: it does not stop at St. Anthony. He, like your fellow Christian here on earth, with whom you share your burdens, is a "mediator" in precisely that sense: he is a personal, interested presence, we might say, exhibiting to us, and bringing to us, in his own unique fashion, Christ's priestly presence.

It may be recalled in this connection that such a counting upon the prayers of those who have finished their earthly race is not a "late" custom: non-Catholics often suppose that all sorts of questionable practices were introduced into the Church in the Dark Ages of Merovingian France, or in the high Middle Ages, when most Christians in Europe were illiterate peasants upon whom almost any fraud could be perpetrated quite handily. Who can deny that abuses of faith were indeed thus perpetrated: but this drawing upon the prayers of the saints is not one of them. Very early in the Church, the Christians were in the habit of seeking the help and intercession of those, especially the martyrs, who had won their crown and who stood in the presence of the High Priest himself.

Further in this connection, we may remind ourselves of the ancient maxim *abusus non tollit usus*: the abuse of a thing does not annul its right usage. A confused peasantry that has only the dimmest notions of the differing attitudes (asking for help or worshipping) at work when we kneel in prayer does not nullify the validity of our asking the saints for their help or prayers, any more than global lechery nullifies the proper usage of the marriage bed. If anyone wishes to cry out in protest against what he sees at the various shrines crowding the Catholic churches of the world, his cry should be only "Dear Church! Instruct your people!", not, "Down with this custom!" And even here, reticence ought no doubt to guard one's zeal for putting things straight: the piety of simple souls—of all souls, actually—is a fragile and secret thing, and for me to rush busily upon the prayers of the crone as she unburdens her heart to St. Lucy is to put myself in the gravest peril of sacrilege. Unless I am in the office of shepherd to that soul—bishop, pastor, or spiritual director— the warning to me will probably be "Stay clear."

All of this brings us back to our original assertion: to be Catholic is to think of oneself as having been adopted into "the whole family in heaven and earth". Or, if the vocabulary of adoption is not on the tip of our tongue, then say that Catholics see the realm of prayer as including that whole family. It is not just me, an isolated petitioner, venturing into the precincts of the Throne, although the lavish invitation from that very Throne to "come boldly" does indeed ring across the threshold as I approach. But to be Catholic is to see the precincts as thronged, not merely with my fellows in the redeemed hosts forming, as it were, a decorative assembly attending on the Majesty: it is to see them all eagerly sharing in the welcome that Grace holds out to me and eager to unite their ceaseless intercessions with my agenda of requests.

But where, exactly (a non-Catholic might want to know), is your warrant in Scripture for such a vision? It is appealing, to be sure: but is it not merely fanciful?

The Catholic reply would perhaps be twofold here. First, though there may not be a passage in the New Testament where the details here envisioned are spelled out, we may bring to bear all that the New Testament teaches about how God's grace not only saves us but draws us into its own operations, so to speak, so that we become joint heirs with the Son of God and are called a nation of priests, sent out, like apostles, as bearers of the news of that grace (God could do this by himself if he chose, but he does not thus choose), and, beyond all telling, actually draws us into the deepest mystery of all, namely, the suffering of Christ himself. "I am crucified with Christ", says St. Paul; and "I fill up that which is behind of the suffering of Christ." Not to mention the ceaseless injunctions in the New Testament that we pray for each other, when surely Jesus Christ's prayers alone are a thousandfold sufficient for the needs of the entire universe. And not to mention the glimpses, vouchsafed to us as the curtain on eternity is drawn back here and there in St. John's Apocalypse, of the throngs of saints and angels around the Throne. We hear them call out their exultation now, as the victory over death and the devil and hell unfurls, and we seem to hear them as having shared, up to the point of this victory, the intercessory prayers of the Son of God as he prays until all these things are accomplished.

"We seem to hear them." Is that a flaw? The text does not spell out for us the doctrine that the saints in heaven pray for us. This, then, brings us to the second of the elements in a Catholic's reply to one who wondered whether this picture of the interceding saints might not be a tissue of fancy. Here the Catholic draws on the Church's tradition. The apostles told the Christians to hold fast to the traditions handed down to them. Not all of those traditions were spelled out on the leaves of the writings that eventually came to be recognized in the Church as the "New Testament". The apostolic Church knew nothing of Luther's *sola*. *Sola Scriptura*? Why do you say that? St. Paul calls *the Church* "the pillar and ground of truth" (1 Tim 3:15). The fact that the Church, from very early on, has, in her liturgy and in her piety and in her teaching, held fast to the courage to be drawn from this awareness of the saints' prayers is the footing upon which Catholic and Orthodox (and many Anglican) Christians rest their practice in this connection. To ask for St. Lucy's help, or for the prayers of St. Anthony, is to take one's place in an immensely ancient lineage of Christians who have also done so.

10

Tradition in Prayer

When a Catholic prays he is deeply aware, as is any Christian, of the mystery presiding over what he is doing. He knows himself to be mortal, for a start, and for a mortal to step across the line circumscribing the precincts of the Ineffable is an act fraught with imponderables. Who am I to do this? And *how* am I to do this? And do I suppose that anything is actually occurring here beyond my own subjectivity? Is there any encouraging word from the other side? Is it all presumption or, worse, nonsense?

Such questions, flung at him from an unbelieving civilization, may find an echo in his own innermost being, and he will recognize this echo as, in one profound sense, not altogether misbegotten. A mortal should indeed be exquisitely aware of his mortality and, hence, of his shocking inadequacy to sustain what comes into play when he ventures across the line. It is not a bad attitude. It is probably a necessary ingredient in true *pietas*.

On the other hand, most mortals, quite rightly, are not thus paralyzed when they pray. "Lord, help me", we say, or "Thank you, God", and in saying this, we know that we are joined by the whole race of men, kings and peasants, philosophers and dunderheads, boulevardiers and rustics. It belongs to our humanity.

And not only this. We feel—we know, really—that *whatever* we pray, and however we say it, will be heard and received, insofar as the smallest rag of integrity spurs us to pray thus. The Most High does not sit as critic or arbiter of taste in the matter of human prayer.

On the other hand, we also know that we find ourselves helped insofar as we can call upon traditional forms of prayer. Far from fettering us, we discover that the already set form very frequently liberates us. It hands to us the very thing we wish we could say if we could find the words. It gives us our prayer, in fact. We have already, in earlier chapters, noted this paradox in connection with the liturgy: how fixed forms, far from constituting a grid locking us in, supply the grid by which we may find our way in the daunting landscape of worship.

To be Catholic is to exult in traditional forms of prayer. It is to look on the immense deposit of fixed prayers as a treasury, a treasury with no door locked. All may enter and help themselves, all the time.

First and foremost, of course, is the Lord's Prayer, usually known among Catholics as the Our Father. In this brief address to God, the whole mystery of God and man is opened to us. Father. *Our* Father. Who art in heaven. Hallowed. Every word opens onto the whole vista. And the seven petitions place upon our very tongues all that a mortal should be saying on the long itinerary from his conception, stained by original sin, to the fruition of his journey in the Beatific Vision. It is a prayer to be said constantly, for insofar as I say it, investing myself in it with all earnestness, it will configure me to Christ.

It is also a prayer that may be brought into play when I am

at a loss altogether about what to say. "Our Father, who art in heaven": Catholics resort to this utterance in time of great perplexity, or of fear, or of grief, or of a hundred other taxing situations. One scarcely knows what words to frame: the Our Father supplies one's need.

There is even a sense among Catholics, not altogether discouraged by the Church, that the Our Father may be repeated as a sort of "omniprayer", that is, that one may pray this prayer with a particular intention in mind—say, for one's son, that he may be defended from harm and sin, or for one's daughter, that God's angel will overshadow her, or for someone sick. To pray the Lord's Prayer in this context is to acknowledge that, in a mystery, its seven petitions gather up all possible intentions and requests and that the posture before the Throne of Grace that it imposes on us is a right one. Once I saw a Catholic mother gather her two teenage children to her at the edge of her husband's grave after his (Protestant) burial. The three repeated the Lord's Prayer. One could hear in the hurried mumble her supplications for her husband, her sorrow, her prayers for her fatherless children, and her hope that somehow a "Catholic" seal might crown what had occurred at the burial. One knew that all of this was borne up to the Throne, infinitely enhanced, by the words of the Our Father.

Without any doubt at all, the second most resorted-to traditional prayer among Roman Catholics is the Hail Mary.

This is a prayer virtually incomprehensible to non-Catholics. For a start, it sounds mind-numbing in its repetitiveness. How, it may be asked by earnest inquirers, does this sort of thing differ from pagan prayer—from Tibetans turning their prayer wheels, say?

The answer to this question lies in the notion that the prayers of the Rosary, with its many repetitions, are not so much—not at all, actually—a matter of one's plucking at the sleeve of the Most High until he vouchsafes to turn his attention to one, like the judge in the Gospel who was nettled into acting on the woman's behalf by her sheer persistence, but rather are a matter of "tarrying" in a certain place. One's lips are continually forming words acutely appropriate for any believer in any possible situation, and this assists one's mind to tarry in this place, along with the one, namely, the Virgin Mary, who, among us mortals, exhibited the perfect response to the will of God, namely, the *Ecce*, and *Fiat*, which we have already pondered in an earlier chapter.

The idea is, insofar as I will place my whole being here, in my present situation, with Mary, I will to that extent have ordered my soul to wholehearted obedience and purity vis-à-vis the Word of the Lord that is announced to me by this immediate circumstance. That is, just as Mary's response to the angel, whose word broke unexpectedly into her life and forever altered that life utterly, was one of obedience and readiness to be at the service of whatever was being asked of her, so I, when I hail her, place my own soul in the place of admiration for that obedience and of extolling that obedience. It is an excellent place to be, indeed, a salvific place to be. I will never come to the joy of the City of God until my entire being has long since learned, in every thread of its fabric, to say, like Mary, *Ecce*; *Fiat*. The word in her case, to which she responded obediently, was that she would be the mother of the Savior. The word in my case, on this particular morning, may be that I sit in a traffic jam for an hour or lose my spouse, or my health, or my life. Faith hears in every circumstance, no matter how chaotic, taxing, or untoward, the voice of the Lord: it is a lesson of such difficulty that most of us will scarcely have begun in that school by the time we reach our own hour of death. If my habit has been, day by day, to place myself in the company of the Virgin in her obedience, to oblige all that is in me to hail her, as did the angel, and to laud her response, then it may be that I will find help in my ordeal by myself saying *Ecce* and *Fiat* to the messenger of God. The fruit of Mary's innermost being, because of her obedience, was Jesus. Incarnate Love. Will mine be vexation, despair, or rage? Alas. By praying the Rosary, one is consciously, daily, placing oneself in the precincts of obedience, so that, as the Holy Spirit overshadows one as he did the Virgin, that which is born from one's innermost being will increasingly be Jesus himself.

The address to Mary rather than to her Son is also a stumbling block to non-Catholics. Aren't we enjoined to make our requests known to God himself? Is not Christ Jesus the one Mediator between God and man? Are not, then, all the prayers of the Rosary misdirected?

The answer to these questions lies in the notion of the communion of saints, which again we have pondered in connection with the Virgin's title as "Mediatrix". It is a matter of the priesthood of our Lord being, not a solitary or exclusive priesthood that leaves us all inert spectators, but rather a priesthood that brims and flows over upon all who constitute his Body. Hence we all pray for each other, even though we know that his prayers for us are sufficient by themselves ten thousand times over. In doing so, we evince our profound participation in the intercessory ministry of the High Priest. Mary, of course, is first among us, with her *Ecce* and *Fiat*, and also because she was drawn into the mystery of God in a way no patriarch, prophet, or apostle ever knew. And this communion of saints spans the abyss of death: we in pilgrimage here on earth are, because of the victory over death won by our Lord, as much one in the priestly communion with those who have gone before us as we are with those around us for whose prayers we ask day by day. Hence it is that the Hail Mary is addressed to Mary. It does not call Christ's supreme and sole and sufficient priesthood into question: it utters itself *within* that priesthood.

The Hail Mary, like the Lord's Prayer, is very often prayed, even as a brief exclamation, in some situation where what one might wish to say, given perfect utterance, eludes one. This prayer "gathers in", so to speak, any supplications we may have. To outsiders it may look as though Catholics rattle off the Hail Mary at some public occasion or in time of distress (in the Gulag or Auschwitz), because they don't know how to pray and must resort to a rote form. The truth, at bottom, is rather that to be Catholic is to have entered into the "Marian mystery", as it were, and to have found in this context a particularly pure region of prayer, a region that stretches beyond the place where each word is strapped to one specific meaning ("O Lord, give us strength here in our hour of trouble"), and where the words themselves ("Hail, Mary, full of grace") bear the heavy freight of *all* that we would like to say. Both forms of prayer are crucial; neither may be pitted against the other. Neither is preferable to the other. Both testify to the manifold, and mysterious, nature of the things that surround us every time we approach the Throne.

The Rosary, however, is not primarily a vehicle for intercession. It is a traditional devotion that places the believer, day by day, in the presence of the Gospel mysteries as *they were experienced by* the one of us who was most completely disposed to receive them, namely, the Virgin Mary. One moves, step by step, along the path that our salvation took when God came to us as Savior. Or rather, one *tarries* at each step, fixing his gaze on the tableau and desiring to be wholly receptive to all that is there. The repetitions are not unlike the "Ah ... ah ... " one might hear from someone over-whelmed by a sunset or by the flight of a swallow; or again, they are not unlike the "Amen ... amen ... " or even the "Praise you, Jesus" one hears murmured as a sort of continuo in charismatic communal prayer.

To be Catholic is to draw heavily on tradition in one's prayers. The Lord's Prayer is a scriptural text, taken up by tradition and placed at the center of all the Church's prayer; and the Hail Mary is a prayer drawn from Dominican and Cistercian tradition and also placed near the center of Christian prayer.

The tradition of prayer is, of course, immense. The *Gloria Patri*, wholly consonant with Scripture although not an actual scriptural text itself, is a case in point: just a brief exclamation, but gathering up in itself all that worship strives to say. The formula *In nomine*—"In the name of the Father, and of the Son, and of the Holy Spirit"—is another: brief, scriptural, and appropriate to a thousand situations, reminding one as it does that not only our conscious acts of worship but also every task and every motion of our hearts should proceed under this ensign. The *Magnificat*, sung by the Virgin herself, has been taken up by the Church's tradition and placed in the mouth of every one of the redeemed. Indeed, God has regarded the lowliness of his handmaiden (me). Indeed, he has done great things for me. He has filled the hungry with good things. The tradition supplies the believer with words to say that, left to his own devices, he might not think of saying, and certainly not so succinctly. The *Nunc Dimittis*—"Lord, now lettest thou thy servant depart in peace"—likewise has been borrowed by tradition from Simeon and offered by the Church to all of us. Can I say, at the end of the day, that mine eyes have seen his salvation today? Am I at peace? Am I ready to depart? They are searching questions.

The *Phos hilaron* ("O gladsome Light") and the *Te lucis ante terminum* ("To Thee before the light fades"), both evening hymns, supply us with traditional words that far, far exceed our own halting attempts to frame our evening addresses to the Most High.

In this connection, of course, we find ourselves at the doorstep of the psalter. The psalms. Here we have, once more, the fruitful union of Scripture and tradition. The songs themselves are Scripture; but it was tradition that took them up and placed them at the core of the Church's very life. For centuries they have been chanted, morning, noon, and night, in the Church. No one who has ever attempted Christian prayer on any sustained terms will have been able to go very far without the psalms. *Beatus vir*; *In exitu Israel*; *Miserere mei, Deus*; *Ecce quam bonum*; *Quemadmodum desiderat cervus*: the very phrases strike joy unbounded into the heart of the Christian.

The psalms: it is not for nothing that the Church offers them to us, not only daily, but repeatedly for each day. The voice speaking in them is the voice of the psalmist, of the King, of Israel, and, in a mystery, of Christ and of the Church, and, thence, of the man whose life is lived *in conspectu Dei*. His aspirations, his exultations, his rages and terrors and discouragements and despair: all is spread out immediately in the sight of God. In these songs we hear what it is like to live life in complete transparency before God. We encounter, and are brought into, the attitude of the man for whom God is everything. And when we reflect on this, we realize that this is, in fact, the very blueprint for our humanity: there is no being human at all without direct and unremitting reference to God in whose image we are formed. The existence, life, and consciousness of an atheist, ironically, draws upon God for its source, sustenance, and purpose. In the psalms we find the songs that define us mortals, we might say. They constitute a touchstone by which we may test, day by day, whether we are heading toward fatuity and perdition or toward authenticity and joy. Insofar as my innermost being is configured to the psalms, it is in good health. (Even the imprecatory psalms, as C. S. Lewis has pointed out, can at least show me what I, if *I* exist as "the wicked" to some other soul, can do to that soul by way of thrusting it toward this terrible rage and vindictiveness. It is a solemn warning.)

To be Catholic, and thus to be daily under the scrutiny of the psalms, is to live one's life in the presence of this touchstone, which judges one's attitudes: my fears, joys, triumphs, wrath, hopes, disappointments, and despondency, as well as my artfulness in finding pretexts for my sins—all is brought to the test in these songs. Indeed, for a Catholic, there is a profound sense in which the psalms take priority over all philosophy, poetry, song, and psychology; for what we have here is infallible. We bring our efforts (philosophy, poetry, and so on) to this touchstone to see whether we are still living and functioning in the precincts of the True.

Furthermore, to be Catholic is to have at one's fingertips, so to speak, an immense tradition of hymnody. All Christian traditions, of course, depend heavily on hymnody, and a Catholic will find delight in coming upon the great Lutheran deposit of hymns or, perhaps even more, the Anglican. (Ironically, it is the Anglicans who keep alive, in translations of great dignity by the nineteenth-century scholar J. M. Neale, many of the hymns from antiquity and the Middle Ages. One hears the work of Venantius Fortunatus and St. Joseph the Hymnographer, of Rabanus Maurus and Adam of St. Victor and Bernard and Thomas. It is a part of the treasury to be rediscovered by Catholics.)

The great eucharistic hymns of Thomas, still very much in use in the Catholic Church, draw us close to the mysteries of which they speak, and to which our own resources are so inadequate: *Tantum ergo, Pange Lingua, O Salutaris Hostia*, and *Lauda Sion*. To be Christian and innocent of these texts is to be greatly deprived. Thomas' austere lines assist us as we approach the cusp where eternity meets time, that is, where faith is asked to see in human flesh the eternal Son, and in the appearance of bread and wine the Body and Blood of that Son. It is a task to which we are not equal: to be Catholic is to be in grateful debt to Thomas, again and again.

There is one aspect of Catholic prayer that seems very odd indeed to non-Catholics. I speak of pilgrimages.

To be human at all is to be familiar with the general idea here, since of course nearly everyone wants, not only to hear about Washington at Valley Forge or the pilgrims' landing at Plymouth or Paul Revere's ride, but to go to the places where these events occurred. Enormous expense and time and inconvenience are poured into the effort to get ourselves to places that seem hallowed, somehow, by what has happened there. Gettysburg; Concord; the Tower of London; Normandy Beach; Jerusalem.

Jerusalem. We seem to have passed a delicate frontier here. Certainly Normandy Beach, for example, is "holy" in the sense that we find ourselves reduced, eventually, to silence here as somehow the only response possible in this acreage of death. Death here or at Treblinka or at Gettysburg—that is, death suffered, in some sense, *for* the rest of us—seems to hover and brood and pall. It will not submit to the category "a mere fact of past history". Somehow it *is* here, still. Our humanity itself testifies that this impression that comes over us in such places is a true one. Logic and pragmatism and common sense must themselves bow here. We will make our pilgrimage thither and stand, silent.

But in Jerusalem there is more. This is a city holy to three religions: Judaism, Islam, and Christianity; so the notion of pilgrimage thither is familiar to half the world.

Where is the line between a tour and a pilgrimage? Am I a tourist or a pilgrim? For most of us, most of the time, the former word obtains in connection with our travels back and forth. But if it should happen that on a day during my tour of France I visit Lourdes, then I seem to find myself mantled with a mantle somewhat more sobering than the tourist's T-shirt and shorts. What is here? Why does one come here? The scenery can be bested at a thousand locations in Europe. And hordes of people is not what one seeks out on one's holiday. Why come here?

You come, if there is anything deeper than impertinence at work in you, as a pilgrim. Prayer is made here. The air seems clarified with holiness. (This seems to be the testimony of everyone, both believer and nonbeliever, about Lourdes.) I come here in order to locate myself in physical proximity to events that themselves seem redolent of holiness. I come, perhaps, to bring my own insufficiency, physical or spiritual, and to offer it in particularly auspicious precincts, as an oblation. I come in order to benefit from whatever the man of faith may encounter here.

Thus Jerusalem. Thus pilgrimage. Canterbury, Walsingham, Tepeyac, Fatima, Assisi, Capernaum, Mt. Athos, La Grande Chartreuse: to be Christian at all is to be aware of these as more than dots on the folded map. This "more" is a sacramental more, and to be Catholic is to be profoundly rooted in the awareness, so vibrantly at work in such places, that the meeting point of the physical and the transphysical is not only significant but also, as it may be, salutary. It matters that St. Thomas Becket was murdered *here*. That spot there in the floor. It matters that our Lady is said to have vouchsafed an appearance there, right in that grotto there. It matters that

St. Francis lived and worked here, or that monastic prayer has gone up from these walls for centuries, or that God himself walked here in the days of his flesh. I may pray anywhere, to be sure: but, being a creature of flesh and blood, who has his existence in time and place, I find that actual proximity to the holy event or the holy figure yields not only a quickened inner awareness of the holy but also a benefit that can be said to be at work only in the place itself, quite apart from my own good will and ardor. Non-Catholics, whose piety does not run commonly to pilgrimages, will testify to a man that to be in Galilee or at Caesarea Philippi is an experience not to be attributed merely to feelings worked to a pitch of fervor by one's own devotion. It matters that I am now *here*. Not to be here is not the same thing. The only true response that my mortality can offer here is to kneel and pray. The clicking camera, while perhaps inevitable, does not seem to exhaust the reasons for one's having come hither.

To be Catholic is to understand pilgrimage as being of the very warp and woof of faith. Of course one goes on pilgrimage if one can: it is a joyous and health-giving thing, and it belongs to our humanity so to do.

Pilgrimage brings us, then, to the tradition of preserving and honoring relics. To be Catholic is to be at home with the practice, whereas to the non-Catholic eye the business may seem to sail too near the wind of superstition and idolatry. Come: this bit of bone here: it won't do. It is probably specious for a start; and even if it is what it is claimed to be, it has no virtuous properties.

The Catholic's response to misgivings like this is of a piece with his response when taxed about anything at all to do with the sacramental, namely, that it is not magic—but neither is it nothing. Neither chemistry nor logic will yield up the secrets here. The strictures spring, often, from genuine candor and good will and by no means need to imply a cavalier, much less sacrilegious, approach. To certain species of Christian faith, the notion that any efficacy, or even much interest, attaches to a fragment of someone's garment, say, or to a bone splinter is scandalous.

Once again, as in the matter of pilgrimages, a Catholic may point to common human experience for analogies. The lover with the lock of his beloved's hair; the snapshot, all faded and creased; the pressed flower; the figurine bought long ago in Venice when we were so happy together: we are clearly creatures for whom such artifacts are beyond valuing. And of course we all peer, round-eyed, across the velvet cord into Marie Antoinette's boudoir to see the chaplet or missal she used on her last night before the arrest. We squint at Washington's false teeth and Jefferson's little spectacles on the desk.

What does it all signify?

Physical continuity. The description in the textbook won't altogether satisfy. The abstract fact in one's mind won't either. Oddly, the *thing* matters. It seems to preserve in itself something of the personhood in question. A manuscript by Handel is infinitely more difficult to decipher than the published sheet of the same music; but that his very hand rested on this paper, pressed this paper, and that the notes are inked with ink dipped from the inkwell by the nib in his own fingers: this we will keep in the British Museum. For this we will pay ten thousand dollars.

Physical continuity. To be Catholic is to be a Christian whose piety has not been sundered from the physical, as though the only proper locale for religion is in the will. The Christians of the very first centuries went to pains to retrieve the bones of their martyr, and to keep them, to pray where they were kept. For them, the dead bodies of those martyrs were not nothing. The body is the epiphany of the very personhood, they believed, because they believed in the Incarnation. The body is not nothing. The women came to the Tomb bringing spices. They wept when it seemed that the Body had been taken hence. The body was not nothing, dead or alive. To be Catholic is to have one's piety deeply rooted in these matters.

Hence relics. To read of George Washington is to be impressed. To see (but probably not to touch: there are warning signs all about) his hat and cloak is, somehow, to be brought nearer to him—and hence to the thing Washington embodies and figures forth for us all. To read of St. Polycarp is to be impressed. To see, and perhaps to touch, that which was his own is, somehow, to be brought nearer to him and hence to the thing Polycarp embodies and figures forth for us all.

It is also to be physically "in touch" (remember our mementi and snapshots) with Polycarp, who, Catholics believe, is praying for us; and at this point we have come back around to our earlier picture of prayer, and indeed of faith itself, as binding us to "the whole family in heaven and earth".

11

The Virgin Mary

No talk of Catholic prayer can advance very far without coming upon the topic of the Virgin Mary And there is no topic, not the papacy, nor the Mass itself, that arouses greater consternation, not to say scandal, among non-Catholics. Where, pray (goes the question), did the Catholic Church get all of this about the Virgin? Surely, continues the inquiry, what we witness in our trips to traditionally Catholic countries can only be called Mariolatry? *La Virgen! Vive la Vièrge! Die Jüngfrau! Salve, Regina!* And what is this we hear linked to her cult: Mediatrix? Coredemptrix? Need we go any farther? The truth is out: Rome has, clearly, no less an agenda than to replace the unique mediatorship of Jesus Christ, the one Redeemer of man, with that of the woman.

Five hundred years of tempest cannot be lulled with a few paragraphs. But our task here is to reflect on what it is to be Catholic, to reflect *as* Catholics first of all on what we do hold and, in the course of doing this, perhaps to clarify things enough so that our interlocutors find themselves addressing what the Church actually teaches.

To be Catholic, then, is to hold the figure of the Virgin Mary in immensely high esteem. This esteem is so high, in fact, that there is a word applied to it in order to distinguish it from the worship that is due to the Godhead alone. Divine worship is referred to in the word *latria*, from the Greek. Such veneration may be given to no creature, not the burning seraphim themselves, much less to one of us mortals. It is reserved for God alone. At the other end of things we find *dulia*, which refers to the honor we mortals justly pay to those among us who should be honored: monarchs; heads of state; our elders; our parents; our teachers; heroes; and so forth. Such honor, it may be remarked here, can take on lavish proportions and yet stay clear of idolatry. We need only recall the golden state coach, Windsor grays, arches, plumes, guards, trumpets, ermine, gems, and gold that are brought out to honor the monarch of England; or the ticker-tape parades through Wall Street for astronauts and other heroes; or the rites and observances brought into play in connection with the memory of, say, Martin Luther King or John F. Kennedy. Mere *dulia*, then, often rises to sumptuous heights: but we do not call it idolatry, even though foolish people may indeed "idolize" such venerable figures. But the display itself is just and fitting, we claim.

Between *latria*, the worship of God, and *dulia*, the honor we pay to honorable men, we find a category, *hyperdulia*, applied to the honor that belongs, says the Catholic Church, to the one among us mortals whose glory is unique. Hail! said an angel from heaven. Highly exalted! Blessed! said Elizabeth. All generations shall call me blessed! says this one herself. She is, says the Orthodox Church, "beyond compare more glorious than the seraphim".

How so? She is only a lowly maiden. These ancient churches have made too much of her. Scripture itself leaves her in humble obscurity.

Not altogether, says the Church. There is a great vision in the Apocalypse of a woman clothed with the sun, with the moon under her feet, and with a crown of stars on her head. Like all of St. John's apocalyptic visions, this one has manifold significance, and the Church sees here both the Bride of Christ, in the sense of the Church herself, and also the figure of the woman whose particular role in the drama of redemption is extolled there. Is it Eve? Is it Sarah? Miriam? Deborah? Anna?

Who? There is so patently only one candidate here that the point needs no laboring. For of course all those women bore witness to the Word, as did Abel and Noah and Abraham and Moses and all the kings, patriarchs, prophets, and apostles. They all bore witness to the Word. This woman *bore the Word*.

No other creature in heaven or earth has ever been drawn into the mystery of God himself as has this woman. No seraph has ever borne offspring to the Holy Ghost. No archangel has ever suckled the Second Person of the Trinity. No heavenly grandee has reared the Messiah. This participation in, and cooperation with, the most secret reaches of the mystery of redemption is reserved for one among all creatures in heaven and earth.

The eye of faith sees in the young woman of Nazareth that figure. Christian faith grows ardent when it begins to contemplate the role given to this woman by the Most High. There are theologies, and forms of Christian piety, that demur here. This woman, they urge, was the merest vehicle, expendable forthwith, by which necessary details of the Incarnation were to be accommodated. Let us speak no more of her. Her modest role was finished, really, as of that night in the stable—or, if we wish to stretch things a bit farther, let us allow that she, with her husband, looked after the growing boy until he was twelve, at which point he seems in any case to have declared his independence of all that

Nazareth could bring to the matter. We wish to remain
faithful to Scripture alone, say such theologies. The woman
has very, very few lines in the script. She is seldom on stage:
only brief glimpses; and in every case, she is clearly in a subordinate role.

It may, paradoxically, be in this very subordination that
Catholic vision sees the particular glory that attaches to Mary
in the mystery of human redemption. It is worth pondering
the matter, since great confusion over the role, and hence the
dignity, of this woman arises frequently when the matter has
not been given sufficient attention.

What word better catches the true relation between the
Most High and the whole of his creation than the word
subordination? Ordered under; arranged, destined, appointed
under. Therein lies the dignity of the creature. The mightiest
powers in creation, the seraphim, hide their faces and cover
their feet as they *incessabili voce proclamant* Holy! before the
Most High. For us mortals, the word subordinate often seems
stained with the tincture of slavery, obsequiousness, and sy-
cophancy. We hear only with great difficulty how it rings in
the heavens with joy and honor. Subordination down here in
this vale of tears is freighted with the sad freight of the curse:
toil; burdens; bondage. But heaven unfurls the reality of
which our worldly notion is a poor travesty. It knows that
there is no dignity so inestimable as the dignity of the creature—angel, man, or woman—who can bow and offer his
particular dignity at the footstool of the Living One from
whom all dignity flows.

One creature demurred on the point and fell like lightning
from heaven. Lucifer, the Light-bearer himself, despised this
august subordination and ruined the universe. We, in thrall
here on earth, in the realm of this Prince of Darkness, find
ourselves also inclined to demur. *Non serviam*: I will not

serve. I am the master of my fate, I am the captain of my soul. So say we in our folly.

But this woman—the Second Eve, according to the early Church—what will she say? *Fiat mihi.* Be it done unto me according to thy word. And in that utterance we glimpse the true dignity of the creature in comparison with which the strutting and preening of popinjays and egoists of all sorts (I, alas, among them) clatter dismally. In her *Fiat* we may find the particular and authentic dignity that attaches to the creature. The creature, and in this case the woman, is exalted by the Divine Munificence insofar as she receives the divine approach with these words. All other honor is a fraud. All other dignity is specious. The strutting and preening find their origin in hell, and like hell they are a travesty of what is true.

In the Incarnate Word himself we find the principle of subordination also at work. How can this be? He is God and no creature. There is nothing in heaven or earth before which he must bow.

Nevertheless, "he made himself of no reputation . . . and became obedient unto death" and cried out, "Not my will but thine be done." Therefore "God has highly exalted him, and given him a name which is above every name, that at the name of Jesus every knee should bow, of things in heaven, and things on earth, and things under the earth."

In the very Holy Trinity itself, then, we may contemplate, over against all common sense, and against all of our poor vanity, this mystery of subordination. The Son, while equal with the Father, is nevertheless, in a mystery that eludes us, "subordinate" to the Father. It is at that fountainhead that the Church draws her awareness of the great paradox of honor-from-subordination. In the obedience the Son of God exhibited in his life among us here on earth, faith sees a mystery that reaches much deeper than to the merely sociological details of his having been born to an obscure and indigent peasant couple in a Judaea subservient to Caesar. What we see is a true glimpse into the life of the Trinity. Father, Son, and Holy Ghost: it is not a precarious triumvirate, like Caesar, Crassus, and Pompey, eyeing each other nervously lest any one of the three begin to inch ahead of the other two. Rather, we find ourselves at the eternal Source from which the great river of Love rushes, where primacy and subordination, and the bond uniting the two, dwell in living bliss. It has nothing, nothing at all, to do with the drab and gritty accounts kept by politics and logic.

All of this appears to have taken us far afield from the topic of the Virgin Mary. But the Church would refer us to this source in the trinitarian mystery itself, from which Love proceeds, in answer to our scandalized inquiry as to how this lowly young woman can possibly have found a place of such glittering honor. That is how it *is*, the Church would urge. That is the law of the City of God. God has highly exalted his Son "because" (see Phil 1:16) of his Son's humility and obedience. And all of those "in Christ", the Virgin Mary most expressly, are to have a share in that exaltation. What else does the Divine Love do with our mortal obedience but to stretch out its hand and say Arise!

But you are reading too much into the biblical account, a non-Catholic might volunteer at this point. You seem to be deriving an entire Mariology from silence.

The protest brings us yet one step nearer the center of the Marian mystery. Silence. She has been called "a woman wrapped in silence". Not a syllable is heard from her lips after the wedding at Cana. We glimpse her in two or three tableaux. But Scripture only nods briefly in her direction, it seems. Certainly there would seem to be little trace of an inchoate Mariology in its pages.

It would seem so—unless. Unless this silence is itself the veil shrouding a mystery worth guarding from profane eyes.

To be Catholic is to be acquainted already with the realm of faith, in which events of great consequence may find themselves wrapped in obscurity. To foresee a great nation when all we have is the dried loins of an old man would be one such instance: but Abraham's faith and ours relies on the promise, against all plausibility. Or again, that the Infant in this obscure straw here is to be believed to be God defies all credibility: but faith kneels with the shepherds. And yet again, to count on the raggle-taggle in this Upper Room as the cadre that will override the Caesars soon enough would seem madness; but once more, faith is at home with such a reckoning.

It is thus, for Catholics, with this woman. The written account of her is scant, but the vision that, over the centuries, has come to behold such plenitude adumbrated in the scant outlines in the Gospel finds an early spokesman in Ignatius, bishop in Antioch and himself a disciple of John the Apostle. On the very point before us, here is his comment: "Mary's virginity and giving birth, and even the Lord's death escaped the notice of the prince of this world: these three mysteries worthy of proclamation were accomplished in God's silence" (CCC 498).

This is an avenue not frequently explored in non-Catholic theologies. But to be Catholic is to suppose that the silence that guards so much of what God does in the mystery of redemption is not a less teeming silence than the silence that seems to prevail among the stars. Who has ears to hear?

The Church reflects slowly on the Gospel mysteries. First she had the apostles' preaching and teaching, then the apostolic letters, then the Gospels themselves. But even when the written record had been completed, her grasp had scarcely encompassed it all. It took several centuries, for example, for her to spell out explicitly the mystery of the Holy and Undivided Trinity, and of the two natures of our Lord Jesus Christ, even though he was worshipped from the first as Son of God and Son of Man. What corresponding wealth of meaning might be guarded by the silence that surrounds the figure of the Mother of the Lord was something that the Church grasped only gradually.

One thing was clear: Mary was unique among all creatures in that she alone had been chosen for a cooperation with the Most High that went far beyond bearing witness to the Word, as had been the office of the patriarchs, the law-giver Moses, and the Prophets. She was to bear the Word. The narrative of the Annunciation is simple: but in those few lines lies a mystery far exceeding the whole of the Old Covenant. It is a thing worth pondering, said the Church. What might it mean, that this woman was chosen to be *Theotokos*, the God-bearer? This is a title not often heard in non-Catholic and non-Orthodox circles: but it goes back to the Council of Ephesus (A.D. 431), when, by way of securing a clear notion of the deity of Jesus Christ, the Church said that it is appropriate to speak of his Mother as "Mother of God", not by way of implying that she is a universal sky-mother who spawned God the Father at some point, as some Middle Eastern religions might have it, but rather of asserting that that which was born of her was God, and not merely a most excellent man or prophet or even a demi-god.

If this seems to exalt her too highly, the Church would remind us that Mary herself, speaking prophetically, said, "He that is mighty hath magnified me", and that Gabriel had hailed her as "highly exalted". It is Scripture, in its record of her own words and those of Gabriel, that is the fountainhead of the exaltation of the Virgin Mary. To be Catholic is to have one's piety suffused with this vision.

Again, to be Catholic is to hear the Virgin's *Fiat* as a word uttered, in a mystery, in behalf of us all. "In a mystery": the phrase is not an idle one. Wherein lies the solidarity of us mortals? How are we "in" Adam and Eve in their sin? The mystery of our very humanity itself seems rooted in this solidarity. And, said the Church in her reflection on the Gospel, there came a Second Eve, as there came a Second Adam, and, as our first mother opened the gate to death for us all, so this second mother opened the gate to life, the first one by her disobedience, the second by her obedience. An aspect of the matter may be put this way: Mary's Son is the Redeemer: Mary is the type of the redeemed humanity. We are "in" her insofar as we share with her the dignity of having been created in the image of God but, beyond this, in that her obedience is the obedience asked, eventually, of all of us if we are to receive the approach of the Divine Mercy and be saved. God "needed", as it were, her *Fiat* in order to inaugurate the great event of the Incarnation and, thus, of our salvation.

God needed. No. That is carrying things too far. He needs nothing. Who hath been his helper? Where were you when I laid the foundations of the earth? The objection is apt, if what we are trying to do is to guard God's sovereignty and omnipotence. No one may share his exclusive and unique glory. . . .

Or may they? This sovereign and omnipotent Lord has crowned us mortals with glory and honor, says the psalmist. We are heirs of God and joint heirs with his Son, says St. Paul. We will be given praise, honor, and glory when our redemption is complete. We have been made kings and priests unto God.

No one, of course, may step in and siphon off for himself

some quantity of the divine glory. Lucifer tried. On the other hand, it seems to be a property of that glory, not only to share itself by glorifying the objects of its love, but also to place itself "in debt to" its creatures—to "need" our participation. We may recall Noah and the Ark here: God could have saved the remnant by his own *Fiat*, but he was pleased to draw Noah into the scheme and to require a boat at Noah's hands, a boat that God could have cobbled up with a word. Or again, we may recall Moses and Joshua and Rahab and Deborah and Barak and Saul (even Saul) and Elijah and the whole host of the faithful in Israel: there was nothing that any one of them did that could not have been done with infinitely greater dispatch by a simple word from the Sapphire Throne. The covenant unfolded slowly, almost imperceptibly, and even agonizingly, because of this peculiar property of the Divine Munificence, that it not only gives itself but places itself in the hands of its servants, so to speak.

The supreme case in point of this sort of "instrumentality", if we may marshal such a cold word, is, of course, the Messiah's own "Lo, I come: in the volume of the book it is written of me, to do thy will, O God." And linked intimately with that "Lo" is the Virgin's *Fiat*. Why it should be that the Omnipotence should carry things forward in such an apparently circuitous, and even vulnerable, way is an aspect of the mystery of his Will that we can only contemplate but scarcely grasp. The Virgin Mary is the icon, from among us mortals, of this strange property of the Divine Will, that it chooses to place itself in our debt. In her case, we may say that the incarnate Word received human flesh, the very agent of the redemption, from his Mother. And this was made possible— again, always acknowledging the mystery—by her *Fiat*. And further, it is insofar as the rest of us make ourselves one with her *Fiat* that we begin to participate in salvation. The Will of

God will not override my will. The august mystery of freedom with which we mortals have been mantled means that the Omnipotence waits to hear my *Fiat*. If *Non serviam* is what I reply, then I place myself outside the pale of joy.

This line of reflection brings us to a point that is perhaps the most alarming of all for non-Catholics when it comes to the topic of the Blessed Virgin. They hear the Church speaking of her as "Coredemptrix" and as "Mediatrix of all graces". Surely Rome has, as we suspected, subtly edged the one Mediator between God and man, the man Christ Jesus, over to one side and has juxtaposed the figure of his Mother there with him.

No. Jesus Christ alone is the Savior. He is not "Coredeemer". He, and he alone, is the one looked for with such yearning by patriarchs and prophets. Peter says, "you were redeemed . . . with the precious blood of Christ" (1 Pet 18–19). No one, not even the great Mother of the Lord herself, may claim to add something to the efficacy of that Precious Blood. It is his blood alone of which we drink at the Eucharist, not the blood of the martyrs, for example. The blood that gilds the Cross is his. Scripture and the Church have never for one moment allowed the smallest notion to be put forward to the effect that the blood of Jesus was not quite sufficient for our salvation and that hence we must look about for added merit. This is very far from being implied in speaking of the Virgin as "Coredemptrix".

What is implied in that title is, rather, the notion that we have already been pursuing in these pages, namely, the profound sense in which Grace draws its objects into its work. All is gift: that is patent. And part of that gift is this drawing-in. Only Jesus can save: but the blood of the martyrs, for example, turns out to be precious in its heroic testimony to the Savior and, by that testimony, to be, in God's will, instrumental in drawing many to the Cross. Shed blood: it is as though God says to the martyrs, and to us all: I will save you, not by a mere edict, nor yet by a legal fiction by which I see you "in" Christ when really you are wholly outside of him. No. It is my will, not merely to see you by a legal fiction "in Christ", but to *place* you in him, to plant you in him, to unite you with him, in his death, Resurrection, Ascension, and glory. These are not juridical fictions. We are speaking of the life of God imparted to man here.

But where does this bring us in our consideration of the question as to the title "Coredemptrix" for the Virgin? To be Catholic is to hear that title as referring to the fact that her "contribution" to the mystery of salvation, namely, the very flesh of that Body that was broken for our salvation—that that contribution was real and not empty. It is not, says the Church, as though God said, "Here: we'll have to have a body for this enterprise, so let us get on with it as expeditiously as possible and then set that gynecological detail behind us." Even to fabricate such an idea brings us too close to blasphemy, we feel. The mysteries of our salvation, including certainly the great mystery of the Incarnation, are not nettlesome details to be got through and then sequestered. At every single point we find ourselves hailed with yet another spectacle that thunders over us with significances that our mortal frame cannot sustain.

The title "Coredemptrix" touches on this aspect of things. Mary's participation in the whole drama of redemption was not only real: it was inestimably significant. The Church ponders this when she ventures to speak of her as Coredemptrix. Once more, the *merit* won for us was won by Christ alone—and his Mother was one of the beneficiaries of that merit of his. But the Savior "owed" his flesh to the gift of his Mother, just as she, for her part, owed to grace the very response that enabled her to offer that gift. Her obedience was gift. The flashing back and forth, so to speak, of gift and response itself hints, not only at the bliss that illumines the City of God, but, beyond that, at the mystery of the Trinity, in which the Three Persons know nothing but mutual gift, if we may speak of God as "knowing nothing but". (We ourselves are vouchsafed a glimpse of this order of things in marriage: the "giving" of the one spouse is gift both given and received; the husband gives himself to his lady and in so doing finds himself to be the beneficiary, and so forth, literally *ad infinitum*.)

If the Most High himself does not stint to place himself thus "in debt" to his creature the Virgin Mother, who, then, are we to stint in acknowledging our indebtedness to her? None of us has trouble acknowledging his debt to St. Paul or to St. Augustine. But Paul's and Augustine's gifts to us pale when we recall the immeasurably greater gift we owe to the woman who, by her obedience, gave us the Savior.

It is this of which the Church speaks when she speaks of the Mother of the Lord as Coredemptrix. The prefix "Co" does not suggest a certain quantity, by which a portion of merit must be subtracted from Christ's work and attached to that of his Mother, although many non-Catholics fear that just some such arithmetic is indeed at work in the Catholic vision, and no doubt many an ill-instructed peasant supposes that Mary somehow is more approachable than is her Son. Rather, the prefix "Co" points to the great mystery whereby Grace draws us—and most notably, and uniquely, the Virgin—into its munificence and grants us a true share in the work.

By some extravagant extension of things, all of those who are in Christ might be said to be "coredeemers", in that every one is appointed to be a partaker of Christ and his saving work; but this would be to extend the term so broadly as to make it too diffuse. The title Coredemptrix is wisely applied only to the one of us whose share in redemption was absolutely unique: in her womb was formed and nourished, from her very body, the Body that was offered for our salvation.

To be Catholic is to see all of this, and no more, in the title Coredemptrix.

But then, what about Mediatrix? Again, surely we may not introduce a second figure in priestly garments next to the Savior, who, as High Priest, forever pleads for us before the Sapphire Throne? But we, the Church, do enter into the sufferings of Christ, which are always salvific, for ourselves and, in a mystery, with him in behalf of others. This is the "fellowship" of which St. Paul speaks in Philippians 3:10.

Mary is the first among those who thus participate. A sword will pierce your soul, predicted Simeon at the Presentation in the Temple. The Mother of the Lord stood by the Cross all during her Son's agony, "pierced" with sorrows unimaginable to us. We may be sure that her sorrows were not wholly occupied with her own loss here but that they were, like her Son's (and like all Christian suffering), *for* something. There are no cul-de-sacs in the economy of the Divine Mercy. One is never a mere recipient. One is also a conduit. My sorrow must, eventually, flow on out from me to the Church and to the world. My salvation does not stop dead with me: I am saved in order then to be a conduit of the Divine Mercy to others. I am not saved and then set on one side, among the mere statistics of the saved. I am baptized into Christ's death and raised from the water with him, not solely for my own soul's benefit, but so that I may join the Body of which he is the Head and do his work (his work: the offering of himself for others: this becomes my work).

To this extent it may be said that all of us are "mediators" with Christ. He is *the* Mediator: but insofar as I—or Billy Graham or Mother Teresa or some obscure old woman praying for us all in the solitude of her room in the nursing home—become a conduit of salvation to others, I participate in Christ's mediatorial office. We do not preempt that office, and we do not diminish that office, and we do not add to that office. But we do share in it.

To be Catholic is to see the Virgin Mary as "Mediatrix" in the sense that her self-oblation (*Fiat mihi*) gave us the Savior. That is her gift, and her only gift, to us. She was chosen by God to give us Jesus, the Savior. She is there in the pattern of the mystery of Grace, in her unique and irreplaceable role. (It is no good putting forward the notion that God "could have done things" without her. That is idle talk and meaningless. The only script we have is the one in which a woman called Mary has this role to play.)

12

Our Humanity

"And in the sixth month the angel Gabriel was sent . . . to a virgin."

It would seem gratuitous to point out that the virgin was a woman. What else?

On the other hand, to be Catholic is to be wholly at home with meditation, that is, with the activity in which the Christian believer places himself at the disposal of a text, as it were, and allows that text to draw him along an itinerary of thought in which he finds himself encountering, one after another, aspects of the truth that might perhaps escape cursory notice. Such meditation is no doubt as old as piety itself. We find it already mature in the psalms: When I consider thy heavens . . . what is man? Or, speaking of the godly man: His delight is in the law of the Lord, and in his law doth he meditate day and night.

The saints, and all the so-called masters of the spiritual life, teach us about such meditation. Take note of every word in the text. Allow no detail to escape you. Permit your imagination to move into the region surrounding the text. It is a salutary exercise, and your soul will benefit. St. Ignatius Loyola, in his *Spiritual Exercises*, brought the activity to perhaps as high a point of elaboration as it has been brought.

We may permit ourselves, then, to pause over the womanhood of this figure chosen by God for the highest honor ever conferred on a mortal.

Worldly honors have tended to collect on the brow of men rather than of women. The effort to summon women's names from the crannies of history in order to redress the imbalance in the roster of notables is pyrrhic. The bare record is there, whether we applaud or deplore it. The conquerors, the explorers, the scientists and philosophers and poets and composers, the monarchs and statesmen and scholars: the number of men in the list dwarfs the number of women, mightily as we try to balance the score.

Scandal, frustration, and sometimes rage mark the attitude of our own time when it is obliged to acknowledge the data here. Hence we have witnessed the attempt, as colossal, energetic, and sudden an attempt as has ever been launched in the history of man, to achieve parity for women, if not by rewriting history, which seems to bite back at us, then by taking history into our own hands now and recasting its terms.

It is impossible to be awake at all in our own epoch and miss the fruits of this attempt. Within two decades women have appeared in their millions in the work force. And not only that: the upper echelons, traditionally the province of men alone, find that women have forced the door and will no longer settle for a spindly typist's chair in the outer office. Attaché cases, horn-rimmed spectacles, vocabulary, and a posture and demeanor that announce No Longer Subservient—these replace aprons, soapsuds, chapped hands, and perambulators in the iconography of woman offered by the late twentieth century.

All of this occurs in the public realm. That is to say, this is all the stuff of history. Events occur; movements arise; trends eddy along; sensibilities ebb and flow. These supply the data that make up the history texts.

But to what extent does all of this exhibit fidelity to our humanity, we want to ask from time to time? That is, do the events and trends constitute progress and good health for this creature Man? Or is a disservice being rendered to what we *are*, say, by the Enlightenment or by the invention of the internal combustion engine or the splitting of the atom? These things occur; do they thereby bear the stamp Well Done? How can we tell what is salubrious, and what calamitous?

To be Catholic is to find oneself asking this question about the great shifts of sensibility and public order that have occurred in our own time with respect to the matter of femininity. A Catholic might wish to ask, that is, about the *image* of woman. Is the "new woman" of the late twentieth century a figure who may be seen to be in direct descent from womanhood as that has been understood in Christian tradition over the centuries? Or do we see a wholly new shaping of the image, a new image, really?

Ironically, the two answers called out from the two profoundly differing viewpoints on that latter question may be identical. Yes! We hear from those who applaud what is happening—Yes, and let us have more! And, Yes! From those who view the topic with somber misgivings—Yes, and womanhood is being betrayed!

The topic has been canvassed widely. We are speaking here of the Virgin, attempting to order our thinking to the great mystery that Catholic faith perceives in the figure of this woman who is there, with God himself, as it were, at the center.

Catholic vision does not pass lightly over the immense datum that this one, unique and highly favored from among the whole race of men, is a woman, not a man. As we noted earlier, it is men, out of all proportion to women, who seem chosen for great roles: the patriarchs, kings, prophets, apostles, evangelists, bishops, and doctors of the Church are, over-whelmingly, men. But then we find that it is a woman to whom is vouchsafed the dignity next to which the dignity attaching to the offices assigned to all of these men must take an inferior place. They all bore witness *to* the Word: she bore the Word. There is no comparison.

What does it mean? To contemplate this mystery is to be brought near to the other mystery, hinted at in nearly all my-thologies and religions, namely, that in some profound sense, all of us mortals—men and women—are "feminine", if we are speaking of ourselves in relation to the approach of the gods to us. Ouranos (the sky) pours energy into Gaea (the earth), just as (hint the myths) the male pours energy into the woman. "He" does the initiating: "she" receives.

There is no fructifying if you leave the male alone. Some-how there must be the collaboration of sky and earth, of god and mortal, of male and female, for the thing to occur.

Thus the myths. But we need not linger in such a lush matrix. Language itself seems to testify to some such notion. *Psyche*: *anima*: the soul. All feminine. Feminine vis-à-vis what, we might inquire. And this inquiry in its turn brings us to that sense which lies as deeply at the center of the human mystery as any other, namely, our sense that we are addressed by the god at the profound depths of our identity. It is called the religious sense, and to be Catholic is to attach great weight to this. Catholicism is not a "secular" view of man, as though to say we sprouted, who knows how or when, some-how autonomously and impersonally, into being and some-how crawled toward our present physical and psychological stature. No, says Catholicism: Thou hast made us for thyself, and our hearts are restless until they rest in thee. The Church takes up St. Augustine's great utterance. And, Who art thou: that is the religious question, with its imperative corollary, What wilt thou have me to do?

It was the woman in the Christian story of redemption who responded to the Deity in that way. And Catholicism, being a sacramentalist understanding of the gospel, sees the physical as bound to the spiritual in a more-than-random way. Just as bread (and not rice) is to be the sacrament of Christ's Body in the liturgy, and the Church (made up of humans, not angels) is to be the sacrament of Christ's presence in the world, and as the man Jesus is, in a perfect sense, the sacrament of God with us, so Mary, in her womanhood, is a similarly apt embodying of all who will say, with her, *Fiat mihi* in response to the approach of the Deity.

Her womanhood. Here is the crux of the topic before us.

To be Catholic is to pause before the quiet fact that this woman achieved the highest dignity ever achieved by a mortal *with no fanfare*. The Virgin Mary girded on no sword, summoned no army; she did not sail to the Antipodes or scan the stars in order to gain the eminence that Catholic vision sees as her proper rank. Those are the tactics brought into play characteristically by men in order to win eminence, which is not to say that a woman cannot commandeer a ship or wield a sword: Penthesilia, queen of the Amazons, was a great warrior, as was Boadicea, the British queen. Our own time has seen at least three immensely powerful and successful women as prime ministers.

The question is not whether a woman can do this or that. When it comes to the activities that constitute history, few would argue very shrilly that a woman *can* not do the job as well as a man. Scientist, artist, monarch, conqueror: the sweepstakes seem open to both sexes, if we are speaking of the ability to do the thing.

But we want to probe further and ask, not so much what a man or a woman can *do* as what he or she *is*. Again, the question has been widely, and loudly, canvassed in our own time.

To be Catholic is to suppose, first of all, that the fact lying at the very root of our humanity, namely, that we appear as man and woman, is itself the great clue as to what we are. Made in the image of God, we are told: male and female he created them. Somehow in this antiphonality we are to constitute that image. It is not good for man to be alone: this "lack" is there before the fall and the curse. The *imago Dei* must appear under these two modalities of man and woman, and the two must then, in mutual self-donation, achieve the unity that testifies to, or constitutes, that image. Catholic vision perceives in this protohistoric maleness and femaleness the great ontological cue, so to speak, that hints at what we *are*.

What is it to "be" a man? Is it to hunt mastodons with a club or sail a ship or build a tower? Indeed, such activities do seem, somehow, to attach themselves to the notion of man. But of course the woman can do all that, if she is so disposed. What can the man do that the woman cannot do?

He can be a husband. He can sire offspring. He can be a father.

Here there is no interchange or role-switching or parity. These perquisites are reserved strictly to the man, and no political movement can make the smallest dent in the scheme. These roles and activities, for good or ill, attach to the male, forever.

What is it to "be" a woman? Is it to stir the pot and rock the cradle and keep the house? Indeed, such activities do seem, somehow, to attach themselves to the notion of woman. But, of course, the man can do all that, if he is so disposed. What can the woman do that the man cannot do?

She can be a wife. She can bear seed. She can be a mother. And she can suckle her young.

Here there is no interchange or role-switching or parity. These perquisites are reserved strictly to the woman, and no political movement can make the smallest dent in the scheme. These roles and activities, for good or ill, attach to the female, forever.

These "roles", if we may borrow such a frigid word from the behavioral sciences, are witnessed to in the very anatomy of the woman and the man. The roles seem inscribed in their very form. Their bodies say "woman" or "man". The female body "receives" the man's questing body. He goes "out" from himself, as it were, in the rite wherein they most exactly constitute the unity that encompasses their two beings, body and soul, and she receives him "in". That which leaves the man must come to rest and fructify in the depths of the woman.

Who does the giving here? It is an empty question. The man and the woman both know, in this unity they constitute, that to give is to receive, and vice-versa. Mutual self-donation.

Sacramental vision perceives in all of this an icon—a sacrament, even—of what is true. That which presents itself under physical aspects—the female body and the male body—is the epiphany of that which transcends the physical. It reaches to the very identity, the personhood, of each. The man does not merely enact the office of father: he *is* "father", somehow, in the depths of his being. The woman does not merely play the role of mother: she *is* "mother", somehow, in the depths of her being. (This is why the vocabulary of roles and of "parenting" clanks so dully in the ears of a sacramentalist. Sacramentalism does not live and move and have its being solely in the region of what things *do*: it wants to know what they *are*. Bread does not "play the role" of the Body of Christ in the liturgy: it *is* that Body, in a mystery that will forever madden the one who approaches it with logic, common sense, experiment, or magic; and rice or oats can never enjoy this privilege, which is reserved strictly to wheat.)

The woman, then, in this accounting of things, *is* mother, in some profound sense that reaches to her identity as woman. The man *is* father similarly.

What, then, of the unnumbered women who have lived and died barren? Have they been disfranchised? No, says this line of thought: the woman may, alas, have to sustain the loss entailed in the denial of physical offspring to her; but she is nonetheless mother, in a mystery. This paradox, of course, is seen with great clarity in the figures of women religious who have consecrated their virginity to God. No child has opened their womb; but they bring to the life of service and prayer that is their vocation something that no man can quite bring. This is a *woman* religious: she is an icon of the Church herself, in a way that is not quite true of the man; and, by virtue of her womanhood, she participates profoundly in the aspect of the gospel mystery opened to us in the figure of the Blessed Mother. The Church would urge that the Pope himself is not as "close to the center", if we may so speak, as a woman whose womanhood is consecrated to God. He is Pope, yes; and as such he is Peter and Supreme Pontiff and Vicar of Christ. He is *servus servorum Dei*, servant of the servants of God. To this extent he bears pastoral responsibility for the whole Church and focuses in his person the whole mystery of the pastoral office. But he is Peter, not Mary. May we say, in this exalted context, that he is "only" Peter? Whereas, in her very womanhood, a woman participates in an aspect of the mystery of God and man that can never be known in quite such a way by a man, no matter what level of holiness he attains. For, of course, femininity is more than merely biological or psychological, says the (sacramentalist)

Church: the body and psyche of the woman suggest what she is. She is a woman—it is an ontological statement, prior to anatomy and psychology, but also declared and exhibited in anatomy and psychology. She does not have a neuter (or worse, androgynous) ghost renting her body temporarily. She is a woman; and for all eternity she will bear the aspect of the *imago Dei* disclosed by femininity, not masculinity.

But what of your ordinary laywoman? We began with the figure of the woman religious, the one whose virginity is consecrated to the Lord. Does what we say apply to every woman, lay or religious, virgin or mother?

Yes; of course, says the Church. To be woman at all is to be an icon of the divine image, under the particular aspect of femininity. May we venture that it is to have that profound Yes (*fiat mihi*) inscribed in the very secret of one's being? The man sets out from home, scouring and ransacking earth and heaven, inquiring, as it were, in his thousand enterprises—his sonnets written, his kingdoms conquered, his seas sailed—What is it? What is it? Who art thou? But to the woman, that which harries the man as a riddle to be cracked or a vista to be charted comes as a tap on the door, or as a still, small voice.

This is delicate language and, hence, perilous. It runs the risk, on the one hand, of tearing loose altogether from its moorings in plain reality and bobbing off into the ozone of fancy like a balloon dangling its string. And, on the other hand, it risks suggesting such a stark difference between man and woman that it would seem to be urging that all men must go forth and seize the god by force and all women must sit quietly and await the tap. To press things that far would, of course, to be falling into the fallacy of wringing the metaphor dry. No metaphor is completely successful. It will work only up to a point. The point hinted at in this manner of speaking about the man and the woman is only that it may be supposed, if things physical are indeed some sort of display of reality itself, that in the two sexes we may see two aspects of what it means to be Man, to be addressed by the Deity, that is.

Is there any sense, in other words, in which the man must learn from the woman how to say *Fiat mihi*? It is a point to be pondered.

But we were speaking of mothers and laywomen generally, whose response to the divine approach takes a form quite different from that at work in the cloister. Consecrated virginity is an especially vivid icon of wholehearted response to the divine, and one that not only does not exclude all notion of motherhood but rather transfigures the woman's potentiality as mother into forms of prayer and service not quite repeatable by the man. But what of laywomen, married and single?

The Catholic Church would call all women, as she calls all men, to consecrate their whole personhood to the Lord. If that consecration is not to take a specifically religious (cloistered, or other) shape, then it may, in the case of the single professional woman, take the form of a "secular" consecration. A woman—charwoman or chief executive officer—is invited by Grace to offer what she is, and *all* that she is (and she is a woman first), to God. Her station as a single person excludes, on the Christian view, the bearing of children, and also the physical intimacy with the man that is itself such a precious gift.

What shall she do, then, with her womanhood? An exact and "satisfactory" answer may never become apparent, for as long as she lives. All that is woman in her may appear to have been blighted by life's unfairness.

Here we approach holy ground not to be trodden upon by

busy and officious bystanders. Indeed, what *does* become of
the great treasure this woman has consecrated?

We can only, with the greatest diffidence, turn to the mystery shrouding the fate of all sacrifices. The holocaust goes
up in smoke. The offering is burned to ashes. Nothing is left.
The offerer is left empty-handed and abandoned.

Or so it would seem. But holocaust stands on the frontier
between the seen and the unseen. Faith clings to the notion
that what appears as ashes on the hither side of that frontier is
laid up as gold, silver, and precious stones on the farther side.

The trouble here is that no one wants to bustle in with
such meliorative remarks when someone is suffering. Who
am I to adjure this woman here to pluck up her spirits with
the thought that her offering is kept—"kept with fonder a
care, / Fonder a care kept than we could have kept it"—by
the Divine Spouse himself. It is too easy to whisk things
away from the plodding actuality of today's loneliness. We do
not regale the parents who must walk away from the tiny
coffin with news of the resurrection. We weep with them, in
silence, for the time being.

So it is here. Who is equal to speaking of such things? And
yet we do, somehow, want to hear the news from the far
country. And we also actually encounter, in some holy
woman, the immense tranquillity, generosity, and dignity that
follows upon her having in very truth consecrated her singleness to God.

In the case of a woman whose vocation is to the married
state, children may be vouchsafed. If this is so, then of course
she experiences under particularly vivid physical auspices
the meaning of the motherhood signaled by her womanhood. The bearing and suckling of children are privileges
reserved strictly to the woman, never to be experienced by
the man. Just as the mystery that attaches to our flesh and

blood is a mystery no angel can penetrate, so the mystery that attaches to physical motherhood is a mystery no man can grasp.

Why introduce the word *mystery* here, where all is perfectly clear? Anatomy, biology, and psychology tell us all there is to know about motherhood. It is a routine phenomenon that scarcely seems to call out for exalted vaporizings from eager bystanders.

On one level the objection is apt. But soon enough we all know that we ourselves, male or female, child or adult, married or single, are touched intimately, at the very wellspring of our being, by the phenomenon. We do not need to sentimentalize motherhood (the word itself seems to quiver with the threat of mawkishness, alas) in order to grasp this. For a start, we have no existence at all apart from motherhood. None of us sprang fully armed from the forehead of Zeus. Our mothers sheltered and nourished us from seedling to newborn infant. And, if they and we were fortunate, they nursed us with their own milk. They were, in other words, the custodians of our very existence.

Custodians. Does the word point to something that is true of woman and never quite true of man? Might there be a profound sense in which this custodianship is never altogether to be relinquished by the woman? On the one hand, of course, all mothers must relinquish their offspring if that offspring is ever to reach his own true freedom, stature, and identity. But is there a sense, almost enigmatic, in which womanhood remains the custodian of our very humanity itself?

Such a supposition would arise from what we can all see, all the time, including all the time back through history, namely, that the presence of woman is not only a palpable thing, but that from this presence there radiates something we can only call humanizing. It takes a thousand forms (many of which forms have come under attack in our own epoch, since, we hear, they belong to an image of woman we must repudiate). For example, when there were women present, men traditionally modified the profane and bawdy language that characteristically obtains in purely male haunts. What was this about? Surely it indicated the awareness, on the one hand, that such language was indeed harsh and perhaps, upon reflection, might have a sort of brutalizing effect on things, and, on the other, that women, by their very presence, call such harshness into question. (It is difficult even to speak of such a custom nowadays, since certainly this would be one of the customs most strenuously rejected by recent notions of womanhood. It is not uncommon to hear the legendary "four-letter words" issuing from the mouths of women now—and not, it may be remarked, only from the mouths of the harridans, viragos, and termagants who, as far back as Chaucer, have made themselves noteworthy by adopting such language.)

Or again, pornographic merchandise has traditionally been assumed to have men and boys for its market. Why? For whatever reasons (and it is this "whatever" that we are endeavoring to approach in this sequence) the presence of a woman seems somehow to introduce the note of shame into the otherwise gleeful atmosphere that presides over the men huddled over the glossy photographs or watching the film at the smoker. (Videotapes have greatly altered this scenario as of this writing.) A certain sheepishness colors the face of the man caught with the pictures. "Caught." Why "caught"? Again, for reasons that are now vigorously repudiated, this subject matter, especially when it is arranged specifically to stir up lust or leering looks, has seemed suddenly to take on a tawdry look the moment a woman arrives.

For to a woman, sex is far more than the random, not to say wholesale, means of gratification that a man, left to his own unbridled imagination, might enjoy supposing. There seem to be inscribed in the very stuff of womanhood the taboos that have from the beginning sheltered the sexual phenomenon against mere debauchery. Might it not be that we see at work here the "spouse" and "mother" for whom sex is knit seamlessly with the whole fabric of life itself, rather than appearing as spangles on that fabric, such as a man might fancy?

And yet again, what of the matter of masculine strife? Fisti-cuffs in a Dublin pub, duels on the outskirts of seventeenth-century Paris, the fracas at the street corner, shouts and threats splitting the domestic household: rightly or wrongly it has characteristically been the women who interpose themselves and plead for tranquillity. Or, perhaps we should qualify this, since not infrequently women have found themselves at the center of the fracas, themselves shouting imprecations and aiming blows, by saying that insofar as order has been restored, short of the arrival of the police, it will often have been the women who have led the attempt.

These examples are stereotypes, and, since such stereo-types have arisen from the very image of woman under as-sault in our time, namely, of woman as somehow gentler and even "softer" than man, we can only adduce the examples with a certain diffidence. Perhaps we need go no farther than to reiterate our "rightly or wrongly": we may all agree that such scenes do, in fact, belong to traditional notions of wom-anhood and manhood. If the traditional notions need to be recast, then of course we may gaze at the stereotypes with a patronizing gaze, as though to say, "Ha! That's how they used to think about things!"

To be Catholic, though, is to have the image of a certain

woman so deeply implanted in one's consciousness that one is not altogether free to jettison the stereotype. Indeed, one finds oneself wondering whether what we have in such scenes is not stereotype, which is a fairly superficial thing, but rather archetype. Does it belong to the woman immemorially (archetypally) to try to restore peace and order and to call the man back from his folly and fury? Does the woman have, in her very bones and marrow, so to speak, a commitment to peace and order, especially domestic peace and order, such that her whole instinct is to try to maintain, preserve, and restore this peace and order?

To be Catholic is to have a deeply rooted supposition that such indeed may be the case. For a Catholic always has the Mother of the Lord at the center of his vision as the one from among us mortals who was charged with the custodianship of the Child who, according to the Second Vatican Council, has "united himself in some sense with every man". In other words, the holy household at Nazareth forms a touchstone by which we may test our notions, not only of households, but of all circumstances that depend on peace and order for their well-being.

In this household, of course, the woman was not called upon to restrain the violence of the man: all we know of St. Joseph speaks of humility, dignity, fidelity, and true-heartedness. And this itself brings us closer to actuality and away from a picture of things that might unjustly be drawn from the examples we have ventured, namely, that the men are all violent and barbarian, and that it is only the women who have rescued things from havoc and collapse. Justly ordered, of course, masculinity exhibits the *imago Dei*, with all that this means of wisdom, grace, purity, and truth. And it would be to digress from our particular topic here to pursue just how the fall has affected that masculinity, as opposed to its effects on femininity. But perhaps we may say that disorder in the man commonly inclines him to spread that disorder into the exterior world (again, fisticuffs, shouts, tanks, and bombs), whereas the woman, whatever of the Fall tinctures her womanhood, nevertheless wants to protect life and to order surroundings in such a way that life is both safe and amenable.

A sacramentalist would see in the very anatomy of femininity the pattern of this. She is the bearer of a womb that is, in some sense, the archetypal "home". Safe; warm; intimate; nourishing; dependable; but above all safe. Her entire being attunes her to cherish this child with her very life. Indeed, her whole body is doing this in any case. She is also the bearer of breasts. These are soft, unlike the chest of a man, which is the locale of muscle primarily. They are vessels of nourishment, and of the blandest possible nourishment, namely, milk. It is from quiet pastures, fenced off from traffic and tumult, that milk comes. It is a drink whose very substance speaks of peace, unlike coffee, which issues from the roasting oven, and wine, which has undergone the winepress. And a woman's arms have been seen, immemorially, as the safest place, not only for her infant, but for her husband. They are not arms equipped first of all for the fight. We do not attach the notion of immense biceps and triceps to the arms of a woman, no matter what may be urged in the public realm in our own decade. It is not that a woman *can* not fight: anyone who threatens her infant will discover to his rue that there is no zeal like that of a woman whose child is in danger. But the woman of song, story, icon, and Scripture stands forth as mother.

But Deborah; Jael; Rahab; Priscilla: what of these? Is not at least part of the interest that collects around them that they were *women* who did what they did? That a woman should lead the troops against Sisera, and that a woman should put a peg through his temple, and that a woman should save the spies, and a woman be linked equally with a man like Aquila—one says, "See: who will insist that the woman cannot do such things?" But of course the very point we stress when commenting thus underscores what is so profoundly at work in the image of the Virgin Mary. No one says, "See! A woman can be a mother! A woman can tend the Son of God in her own household!" What she did *belongs* to womanhood, in some sense forever beyond the reach of the conflict of ideas and the struggle for power.

If all of this is so, then of course the redrawing of the image of womanhood in a way that obscures her identity as mother will rouse misgiving in the mind of a Catholic. Woman, on the one hand, is the only one who can be mother, he will think. No man, however well intentioned and even skilled in household work, can be mother. And, on the other hand, the language of the woman's whole body speaks of motherhood, at a level that cannot be altered by the altering of one century's ideas.

A Catholic will see no absolute anomaly in a woman's being chief executive officer or neurosurgeon or prime minister. What he will demur over would be the attempt to hold aloft the gaining of such offices as in some sense crucial to a woman's authenticating of herself and the corollary attempt to place the bearing and nurturing of children as in some sense a thralldom, or at least an activity ("parenting") that has little to do with what a woman is. This will appear to him as a disservice to the fundamental mystery of which woman is the icon.

Hence, also, a Catholic, at least a Catholic who is deeply committed to all that the Church has taught about the place of Mary in the entire drama of God and man and to all that

has been testified to in human identity from the beginning—
that we have no life at all without our mothers to start with,
and that we have a tragically blighted life if we are denied the
presence and care of our mothers, and that it is not good for
man to be alone, and that it has somehow been the women
who have protected human life from becoming altogether
brutish—such a Catholic will also demur when he hears
harsh and vulgar words issuing from the mouth of a woman
and sees the image of woman-as-policeman and woman-as-
tough and woman-as-soldier and woman-as-executive almost wholly supplanting the image of woman as spouse and
mother in public entertainment. Of course a woman can do
all of that, he will agree: but is there a more-than-neutral
agenda at work in this busy redrawing of the type, whether
that be stereo- or arche-!

In this sense, then, to be Catholic is to have one's notions
of womanhood and manhood rooted in a mystery that
reaches all the way to creation, when we both stepped onto
the stage in all the dignity that belonged to the two of us
severally.

13

Hiddenness

It may be fruitful to venture yet further reflection on the Marian mystery. We have spoken of the scant exposure given to her in the pages of the New Testament and have touched upon the matter of the silence in which she seems shrouded.

We may pursue this further by speaking of this silence under its aspect of hiddenness or obscurity.

In the *Magnificat*, our Lady pours out her gratitude to the Most High by saying, "For he hath regarded the lowliness of his handmaiden. . . . He that is mighty hath magnified me. . . . He hath scattered the proud. . . . He hath put down the mighty from their seat, and hath exalted the humble and meek. . . . The rich he hath sent empty away."

It is a song sung from the most profound depth of human obscurity. And we may recall in this connection that just such obscurity muffles almost every human being ever born into this world. Very few rise above the facelessness of the multitude. Few break through the hedge that hems in the conditions into which they were born. If we consider the aeons of human history and prehistory that elapsed before the internal combustion engine and the jet engine made universal travel available to almost everybody, and before global communications broke through the silence that heretofore had wrapped one's own province and neighborhood, we may grasp something of the obscurity that constitutes the lot of our humanity. Conquerors, explorers, poets, tsars, notables, and potentates of all sorts add up to a very slender list indeed when we compare that list with the immeasurable roster of us mortals. Who can even so much as conjure a picture of the hordes and hordes and hordes that struggle briefly across the dim rear of the stage only to disappear forever into vacuity? Ozymandias lies lost in the sand of the desert, his haughty bid for fame broken and fallen, like most such monuments. Tutankhamen is haled up from his repose under his pyramid, and his name restored to the lips of a century infinitely remote from his: But what of his ten thousand slaves? Where are their tombs? Who are they? Who will tell us their names? Who will announce the names of old Jewish women bundled out of Polish villages to be shot at the brink of mass graves? Who will find the names of the multitudes who went from their shops in Ukraine to the Gulag and thence to unmarked and frozen graves? Who will take the floor of the ocean for the men who dropped into that silence with the convoys sunk in the North Atlantic by the U-boats, or indeed of the U-boat crews who lie under the very next reef?

To call to mind the obscurity and anonymity that so effaces the very existence itself of nearly the whole race of men is to find oneself bemused. For in the wake of this obscurity and anonymity comes the specter of pointlessness. Vanity. What can possibly be the meaning of the whole pageant? What shall we put forward to pluck up the spirits of the child born into this world for the sole purpose, it seems, of rowing out the years of his maturity in the foetid hold of a Roman galley? Or of the infant born with twisted limbs, whose destiny is interminable years in a wheelchair? Or of the young virgin carried off at seventeen to the seraglio, there to idle away her womanhood among the twittering odalisques who await the rancid embraces of the caliph?

Vanity of vanities, says the Preacher. Thou turnest man to destruction. [He is] like grass. . . . In the morning it flourisheth, and groweth up; in the evening it is cut down, and withereth. We spend our years as a tale that is told, says the psalmist. Tomorrow and tomorrow and tomorrow. . . . It is a tale, told by an idiot, full of sound and fury, signifying nothing, says Macbeth. What is this quintessence of dust? . . . Weary, stale, flat, and unprofitable, says Hamlet. Solitary, poor, nasty, brutish, and short, says Thomas Hobbes. The sheer statistics of the thing—everyone falling into pointless graves—overthrow any efforts we might wish to mount in the interest of solace.

It is possible, to be sure, lacking such solace, for us mortals to devise tactics that, we hope, will enable us to surmount the dreary obscurity that seems appointed to most of us. Mercifully, of course, the prospect scarcely presents itself to the fortunate ones who are not much given to reflection. Many simply avert their eyes from the irony that grins at us all—we, that is, with brave notions about our uniqueness and destiny, doomed, it seems, to a drab and obscure sequence of days until the thread of our life has run itself out. One does not think of some superannuated Greek peasant sitting quietly on the bench under the vine leaves at the door of the taverna as hag-ridden with horror at the irony of human life, or of the valetudinarian Bantu woman, or of most people, for all of that, as paralyzed by the obscurity and apparent pointlessness of their lot. Mankind cannot bear much reality, said T. S. Eliot; the burden of inexplicability does not, thanks be to God, add its weight to the quotidian burdens that most men must carry. We simply get on with things as though there were some point to it all.

On the other hand, not a few of us resist obscurity and the anonymity from which it is so difficult to break out. I shall take measures, says the youth in a Herman Hesse novel, and so he sets out to find—to find what? Experience, perhaps: anything that will spice the otherwise bland pudding of life. But we do not need to go so far afield as Hesse's driven youths: what, we may ask ourselves, lies at the root of the immense industries in our own epoch of entertainment, fashion, cosmetics, travel, journalism, and almost everything else that hails us, shrilly and hourly? Do not all these enterprises supply us all with strategies by which we may divert ourselves, amuse ourselves, occupy ourselves, and keep from our ears the continuo that grumbles along beneath all that we do: "Your time is running out. You are almost no one. Nothing is happening. No one knows you are there."

Why should I hurry from shop to shop looking for the shoes, the pullover, the fabrics, cosmetics, or appurtenances that will flag everyone down with "Here is someone interesting. Here is someone beautiful. Here is someone *au courant*. This is not someone routine." Or why this *frisson* when I find myself swept into the entourage of someone rich and famous or when the opening that may turn out to be my big chance presents itself or when my name appears in a roster of notables, or near-notables, or at least of those who appear to promise notability. Why preen when I step forward to take up the dignity of some office to which I have been appointed or elected—school committee, say, or manager, or senior editor?

Because (I tell myself) here lies my route of escape from hiddenness. Inasmuch as I can garb myself à la mode, clink glasses with the great, or mantle myself in a little brief authority like Angelo in *Measure for Measure*, I can lay hold of the thing that alone will rescue my existence from the murk of obscurity, namely, an identity that is *known*, if not by the millions, at least by the few who form my world.

But to be Catholic is to have heard of a different ordering of things. It is to have glimpsed the state of affairs where our identity is not a thing to be sought in chic avenues or along the corridors of influence. It is to have been in attendance a thousand times at the obscure place where the young woman of no renown at all is hailed with the salutation that rings out, not from the avenues and corridors, but from the Sapphire Throne itself.

It is the salutation next to which the accolades and triumphs so sedulously sought by all the caesars, strivers, schemers, and ambitious men of history appear flat and vain, for it comes, not as the reward for my schemes, shot through as such schemes tend to be with venality, disingenuousness, and duplicity, but rather gratuitously, from the Most Highest, if we may borrow the Elizabethan superlative here. It is a salutation that crowns this woman with praise, honor, and glory never to be dimmed by the passing of aeons.

The Virgin of Nazareth, in all of her obscurity and anonymity, is, for Catholics, not only the chosen Mother of the Lord: she is also the icon in whom we mortals may glimpse the foretaste—the pledge, even—of what the Divine Mercy has in store for every man and woman who will say with her, *Fiat mihi*: Be it done unto me according to thy word. To be sure, the particular dignity with which that Mercy crowned the Virgin is unique: no other creature in heaven or earth has been so favored. On the other hand, the Divine Mercy calls Hail to every man and woman ever born. There is no poverty, no disfranchisement, no obscurity, nor any misfortune visited upon any man or woman by predators, circumstances, or suffering, that can interpose itself between any soul and that Hail. It is a salutation that comes, not in response to any influence that may be brought to bear upon it by riches, privilege, beauty, renown, power, or intelligence. It is the greeting that calls to every soul in the inmost secret of its being. We may say even that it is a greeting that comes to every soul only in its hiddenness.

To be Catholic is to affirm some such significance in the very obscurity that hides the figure of our Lady. We never see her in her youth and family. We see her only very rarely during the life of her Son. Actually there is only one glimpse of her, as there is of him, during the thirty or so years between the Presentation in the Temple, when he was a newborn infant, and the marriage at Cana of Galilee, when he had begun his ministry, namely, at the event invoked in the Rosary under the title the Finding in the Temple. A Catholic is not scandalized by the immense disparity that seems to stretch between the humility and obscurity of the Virgin, on the one hand, and her exaltation, on the other. The objection that too much is made of her in Catholic piety escapes him: What, exactly, do we suppose the Divine Mercy is all about to begin with, he wonders? Is it not precisely that it hails our mortal obscurity and bids it come into the precincts of great glory? He that is mighty hath magnified me. He hath regarded the lowliness of his handmaiden: so says every Christian soul. It is not for nothing that the Church has put the *Magnificat* in our mouths for every evening of our lives.

But what, exactly, might this great salutation mean to all of us who have not been appointed to the particularly glorious office to which the Virgin of Nazareth was appointed? Surely there is no such dignity in store for us, obscure as we all are?

No. Or rather, no *such* dignity. The dignity to be revealed as crowning each human soul is unique. There are no mere copies or repetitions in the retinue of the King of Kings.

There is no merely faceless horde attending on the Throne. Every man and woman, brought into being to begin with by the Word, which was in the beginning with God, is named with a name that so far is known only to God. It is a name inscribed on the white stone, to be given at the Last Day to those who, says St. John in his Apocalypse, overcome. We may guess that it is a name of such immense dignity that the one for whom it is reserved is not yet ready to bear it: hence our schooling in Charity here on earth and the completion of that schooling in Purgatory. My frame is not yet such that it can stand erect under the weight of that crown or that name. If it were given to me now, a grotesquery would become visible, since the figure thus named (me) is very far from corresponding yet to the dignity of the name. It would be like giving the name Plato to a parrot or Bach to a magpie: there is a hiatus between name and thing. In the City of God, the one named *is* the name: or, conversely, the name articulates accurately and wholly what (or who) the one named is.

When a Catholic places himself at the scene of the Annunciation in his prayers day by day, he hears the angelic salutation coming to this anonymous virgin, announcing her great destiny. And in her he sees, in a mystery, every soul who will say *Fiat mihi secundum verbum tuum*. To the slave in the galley and the child in the wheelchair and the girl in the harem and to all whose destiny leads, it would seem, to frozen and unmarked graves on the tundra, the Divine Mercy calls Hail! The voice of the angel pierces the fabric of anonymity, obscurity, and pointlessness that muffles our mortal existence and summons every soul with a bidding from the Throne itself.

Who knows what this summons will entail? For Noah it meant much carpentering, and thereby everlasting renown in the annals of salvation. For Gideon it meant leaving his little threshing floor, and also everlasting renown in these annals. For John the Baptist, a grisly end at the chopping block. But of course none of these tales opens onto the real destiny of the men who figure in them: we see only the earthly lot that was appointed to each one. How did Noah do as custodian of his eternal soul? Did Gideon persevere in the school of holiness? (In the case of John we may believe that his martyr's crown was, in some sense, the accolade given to him for having in very truth finished the course.) The Ark, and the Sword of the Lord and of Gideon allow us to glimpse brief events in the itinerary of a Noah or a Gideon. All else is hidden. We know nothing, really, of the longueurs that no doubt marked the life of these men, just as we know little or nothing of the longueurs attending the obscurity of nearly everyone's life. A brief breakthrough to renown, a few decades at the very most, and then silence. Dust to dust. J. S. Bach is given great gifts that bring him up from his obscurity and crown him with earthly renown (a just renown, as it happens): but then he goes on his way. Praise, honor, and glory come to a Duke of Marlborough, a Wellington, or a Nelson in the course of his earthly itinerary: But then what? Is "Hero of Trafalgar" all that is announced in the divine Hail that comes to the innermost being of a Nelson? We do not suppose so. Well, then: What *is* his destiny? "A far more exceeding and eternal weight of glory", laid up for him insofar as he will take his cue from the Virgin of Nazareth and, at some point, reply *Fiat mihi* to the salutation that comes to him as it comes to every soul.

Every soul? The child in the wheelchair? Indeed. Who knows what glory inhabits that enfeebled frame? What honor is incubating there, quite hidden from worldly eyes? Or what of the Down's syndrome child? What exquisite fruit is adumbrated in the sweetness and vulnerability that gild this child's limitations? The answer to such questions lies hidden among the secrets laid up by the Divine Mercy. We only know that words such as "glory" and "joy" and "freedom" are the best that language can do to strain forward and peer through the scrim.

But of one thing we may be sure: J. S. Bach himself, and Lord Nelson, will fall at the feet of such a child when the pall of its weakness has been lifted and its identity disclosed before the eyes of all heaven. What component necessary to the completion of heaven's glory now lies hidden in this child, waiting to be unveiled for the delectation of us all, we can only guess at. Bach was granted great gifts, and in his great fugues and concerti and chorales we glimpse the hem of the garment of heavenly bliss. In the courage and nobility granted to a Nelson we may dimly make out aspects of the stature to which a man may rise.

But what, then, of the anonymous hordes who seem so meagerly gifted and so little favored by fortune?

We come back to the hiddenness of the Virgin at Nazareth. "He hath regarded the lowliness of his handmaiden." We suspect that this lowliness was itself the very quality that fitted her for the dignity appointed her.

So: when Catholics are taxed with their Church's having made too much of the figure of Mary, they can only appeal to this realm of the Divine Mercy, which seems to function altogether apart from all worldly canons of celebrity, renown, and influence. The number of lines of text in the New Testament is very far from being an index of her dignity, they would urge. The very exiguity of the record is itself the clue. We do not add up the lines and reach a sum that qualifies her for great dignity. We see the unique office to which she was appointed, and we hear her response to the summons, and we meditate upon the mystery of it all, cloaked as that mystery is in silence, and we find ourselves eager to join the angel Gabriel with Hail! Highly favored!, and to echo Elizabeth's Who am I that the Mother of my Lord should visit me?, and to call out Amen! When we hear the Virgin herself say, He that is mighty has magnified me.

Magnified. It is the word that lies at the root of all the joyous piety that has fructified in the ancient Catholic Church in connection with the figure of the Mother of the Lord.

14

Tradition

To be Catholic is to be profoundly conscious of one's place in an immensely ancient tradition.

Tradition, of course, is the bond that holds together virtually every aspect of our mortal life. It is the matrix from which arises the varying shapes that we, in our varying tribes, give to our existence. The Bantus do it this way; the Finns do it this way; the Sumerians do it this way; the Jews, or the Irish, or the Latins do it this way.

What is this "it"? Well, human existence, we would all have to reply. Eating, drinking, marrying, dying, building, garbing: the mystery that lies at the root of our very identity as peoples steps into visibility in the shape that our tradition gives to all those activities. The efforts to shake off tradition discover that *some* shape must very quickly be given to all that the tradition has heretofore shaped: the revolutionaries in France at the end of the eighteenth century; the Bolsheviks; the hippies who collected in communal farms: they all found that we mortals cannot live together at all without some agreed-upon shape for things and that the attempt to hammer out fresh shapes has a melancholy tendency to present itself as a somewhat attenuated parody of what has been jettisoned, or worse, a travesty. Very little is gained by enthroning

Reason in Notre Dame Cathedral; and who will insist that the phalanx of commissars in heavy overcoats planted shoulder-to-shoulder on the loge of Lenin's tomb answers more auspiciously to our humanity than does the procession of archimandrites and archpriests with smoke and brocade and jeweled crowns? And is it to be urged that the draggled look that obtains in hippie sectors marks an advance on your traditional farm kitchen, with Grannie with her specs in the rocker by the hearth, the cat batting the ball of yarn, and Mother, all apple-cheeked and hearty, rolling out dough, befloured to the elbows?

Overstatement? Stereotype? Yes. The only point to be insisted upon in this connection would be that indeed we mortals do, in fact, over long periods of time, give a shape to things that somehow reveals aspects of our humanity itself and that it is very difficult to recreate such a shape in haste.

The same phenomenon may be seen in the religious aspect of life. Nay, we would all object: that is too flat a way of saying it. It is in the religious aspect of life that we may descry most sharply this property of tradition to disclose the most profound levels of our identity. What is it about the Northwest Indian tribes that takes shape in totem poles? Or about the Angles that takes shape in Anglican chant? Or the Spanish that will surge through the streets in the enormous processions of the Semana Santa?

This, of course, is a problematical line of thought. Pursued much further it would find itself obliged to insist that all religious traditions are somehow tied to ethnicity, but that is a line that will not hold through to the end. Does Lutheranism have the shape it has because it is German or because it is Lutheran? Is Hinduism Indian or Hindu? How necessarily Japanese is Shinto? What we may all observe without controversy, however, is that tradition gives a profoundly significant shape to human life and that religious tradition touches the depths of our identity as keenly as does any aspect of mortal existence.

To be Catholic is to be wholly at home in this awareness. This would seem to be laboring the obvious, except that there are forms of Christian profession that not only set virtually no store by tradition: they explicitly disallow any real authority to tradition. They speak of the ancient faith as though the Bible had swum into view just this morning and as though one's approach to it is simply to open it, read, and start running.

Once more, we find ourselves with a problematical line of thought before us. *May* not the Bible be thus used? Is it not perspicuous? Must we interpose prelates and pedants between the humble peasant and the Word of God?

And again, it is difficult to avoid overstatement and stereotype. Things do not always separate out into such tidy categories as humble peasants and pedants. Indeed the Bible is the Word of God, say all the churches, Roman and Orthodox as well as Calvinist and Anabaptist. And indeed it is to be sought out and ingested day by day. But when we have said that, we find ourselves with the next question, namely, who may teach this Bible? Marcion? Apollinarius? Joseph Smith? Socinius?

All of these profoundly serious readers of the Bible are looked upon by the principal churches in Christendom as in some sense heretical. You may not, if you wish to think of yourself as a Christian, as that word has been understood from the beginning, espouse their teachings.

Who says so? What court of appeal so rules?

The tradition of the Church, say the Catholics. And so say most Protestants, in one form or another. Socinius' reading of various texts was faulty and is not to be allowed: the correct understanding of the New Testament is that Jesus of Nazareth was the Second Person of the Blessed Trinity incarnate of the Virgin Mary. Socinius has it wrong. So says tradition.

But then what of the questions that bedevil "traditional" Christian groups? Did Jesus die for the elect or for the whole world? John Calvin will tell you one thing, John Wesley, another. Is the bread at the Lord's table only bread, or is it the Body of Christ? Zwingli will tell you one thing; Luther, another. Is the Church to be governed by elders and general assemblies or locally, by democratic vote of the congregation itself? The Presbyterians will tell you one thing, and the Congregationalists another. Will there be a "secret rapture" of believers exempting them from the great tribulation to come upon the world, or must the Church brace herself for just such tribulation? A hundred voices clamor here.

To be Catholic is to look to the teaching of the Church herself rather than to one's private efforts to piece Scripture together on such questions. This teaching, understood by Catholics, in the light of St. Paul's words in 1 Timothy 3:15, to be authoritative, is called the Magisterium of the Church. In this Magisterium a Catholic finds the authority granted by the Lord to the apostles guaranteed for as long as history lasts. Things did not suddenly fray out into a hermeneutical donnybrook when the last apostle died. The unction to teach continues, from the apostles to their successors the bishops. If it comes to a choice between Marcion and your bishop, then you as a Catholic must listen to your bishop. Both men will cite Scripture for you, just as both Zwingli and Luther will do in connection with the bread. Where does this leave you?

A Catholic finds himself in a tradition of teaching that stretches back to the beginning.

But tradition is such a human thing, it may be objected.

How can you tell when it has become destructive? Surely the Lord himself attacked with great vigor the traditions of the scribes and the Pharisees that had made a farce of God's revelation? And what about sinful bishops and popes, to be found right at the center of the tradition? How can you trust what they say?

A Catholic is aware of just such unhappy points. But he is also aware that just such anomalies have beleaguered God's purposes from the beginning: Noah, God's own servant and yet falling into debauchery; Jacob, very far from admirable quite often; David, the very psalmist himself, unfaithful; Israel herself, disobedient, idolatrous, perfidious, corrupt—and yet God's own Spouse.

It is often put to Catholics that it is mad for them to insist that this great juggernaut called the Roman Catholic Church, rumbling down through history heavy with paraphernalia, fat prelates, bric-a-brac, subtle diplomacy, and crusading armies—that this is to be understood as the Body of Christ. No one, surely, can adhere to a notion as manifestly absurd as that?

Well, yes, actually, says your Catholic. I do. Oh, the strictures are all too true, alas. It is a shabby record, full of sin, worldliness, ignorance, pride, avarice, venality, and cruelty. But let us recall God's people Israel: How can it be that the Most High is pleased to have His Name associated with that lot capering around the golden calf? But he does. *O populus meus*: my people. To be Catholic is to be keenly aware of just such an anomaly. The people of God is still the people of God, even when they are being licentious; and no one has the warrant to hive off and start Israel anew, ten miles away, in the interest of purity.

It is in such a light that a Catholic sees the history of the Church. The Christians have not done much better than the

Jews. If it is dreadful Borgia cardinals and popes you are thinking of, then what you have there (replies your Catholic, not proudly) is wolves in sheep's clothing, just as the New Testament anticipates. If it is ignorance, sin, worldliness, and terrible catechesis you are thinking of, then you have, alas, the Church as she emerged from the labor of the holy apostle St. Paul himself (see his letters to the Corinthian church). Multiply the shabby record those Christians achieved in a few years by 2,000, add a billion people, and you have the Roman Catholic Church.

And yet—and yet: outsiders, and her enemies, may well list such defects. But to be Catholic is to know that the spectacle of sheer holiness radiates in and from this ancient Church, in her Magisterium, in her liturgy, in her sacraments, and also in the lives of the faithful, that immense throng moving along through the history of this world, beginning with the apostles and followed by Polycarp, Felicity and Perpetua, Augustine, Benedict, Martin, Columban, Thomas, Dominic, Francis, Ignatius, Teresa, and the whole host of fathers, confessors, widows, virgins, doctors, and all the nameless faithful who remain in obedient, visible, and organic unity with the ancient see in Rome whither Peter and Paul brought the gospel.

A Catholic feels about the Church a sentiment not altogether dissimilar to the sentiment a Jew cherishes touching Jerusalem. There may be rats and offal in the streets, and jerry-built blocks of flats, and waste and corruption in the government: but if I forget thee, O Jerusalem, let my right hand forget her cunning. I shall wish thee prosperity. For a Jew there is no question of hiving off and building another Jerusalem somewhere, in order to get it right this time. For a Catholic there is no question of hiving off and building another Church somewhere, in order to get it right this time.

He is as much a part of this ancient tradition as the Jew is of Jerusalem's. There are not two Jerusalems, much less ten thousand. There is only one, for better or worse. But in that one, the Jew sees Zion, City of our God, dearly beloved of God on high. And in the one Church that there is, a Catholic sees the Body of Christ, or, in another figure, the Bride of Christ. No matter how deeply stained she may be now, she will step forth on the final Day, immaculate. (The sort of perception at work in this paradoxical, even absurd, Catholic attitude is called faith, which is the substance of things hoped for, the evidence of things not seen.)

Tradition implies a continuity developing slowly among a given people over a long period. You cannot create a tradition this morning. You may inaugurate something, but it will not be a tradition until many years have passed. A non-Catholic Christian may urge in this connection that he and his denomination have an august tradition five hundred years old. But to be Catholic is to find oneself with St. Augustine, who, as a Catholic bishop, had to defend the only Church there was against the inroads (or the exits, rather) of the Donatists, who wanted to split off and start the thing over in the interest of purity. No, says Augustine: you cannot do that. For, of course, the Church herself is infinitely more than a tradition, although she is full of tradition(s). She is a holy mystery, created by God himself and, like Israel, taking a specific, visible, single identity and shape in history. She is not an aggregate, or a network, or an association of associations. She is as visible and solid as Peter or Polycarp or Augustine.

The Church is full of traditions. Everyone, both Catholic and non-Catholic, knows that. Her structure, her teaching, her worship, her piety, her "constituency" are all profoundly traditional.

15

Catholics and Freedom

To be a Catholic (it is widely supposed) is to be shackled with heavy irons: rules, obligations, prohibitions, guilt. The great thing is to get out from under all this and to declare one's autonomy. "I don't want anyone telling me what I may or may not do." So might run the response if we were to ask someone why he had left the Catholic Church.

For many people, the issue is understood to be a matter of freedom. I must be free to shape my own destiny, and certainly free to make my own choices as I go along through life. After all, what is it to be human? Is it not to stand tall, take on the yoke of responsibility for one's own choices, and to be ready to bear the consequences? It is meddlesome, really, this way the Catholic Church has of laying down so many laws.

What might be the answer ventured by the Catholic Church to such a charge in this connection?

The whole question turns on the notion of freedom. Such would be the response put forward by the Catholic Church. And in so doing, ironically, she would not be appealing to anything we all do not already know and count upon. And she would cite a paradox here.

As we all know, any freedom is double-edged: the one edge

is the freedom *from* something, and the other is the freedom, thus gained, *to do* something. A man in jail wants to be free from his bars and free to go home. The exile wants to be free from his solitude and estrangement and free also to return to his own native land. The paraplegic would give almost anything to be granted freedom from his wheelchair and braces in order to have the freedom, which everyone else takes so blithely for granted, to walk and leap and praise God, like the man in the Gospel.

From the Christian point of view, this matter of freedom lies very close to the center of the whole drama of our redemption. *Christus Victor!* we cry. The Savior by his life, death, Resurrection, and Ascension has freed us all from the bondage of sin and death, which we brought on ourselves in Eden, and has set us free to enter into that race which, in St. Paul's metaphor, constitutes our progress toward the goal, when we will have won the capacity to bear the titanic ecstasy of the City of God, an ecstasy that would, in our present state, terrify us.

Our transition from bondage to freedom is marked initially at our baptism. But the freedom into which we now step is not *carte blanche* for a higgledy-piggledy manner of life, in which we celebrate our "freedom" by embarking like Nero or Caligula on the pursuit of every whim and appetite. All of us would no doubt agree that what we see in those emperors, not to mention hosts of others who have similarly pursued surfeit, is no human life at all. The man is making himself swinish, we might feel (not without reason), although charity ought to draw us beyond such a remark to the more authentic frame of mind that, in genuine solicitude for the man's well-being, wishes him well ("well", that is, in the sense of his abandoning destruction and seeking the true freedom with which our humanity is crowned).

Destruction. True freedom. Crowned. Where are we with this collection of terms?

We are at the point, mentioned a few paragraphs back, at which the Catholic Church would appeal to a paradox with which we are all long since familiar. It is the paradox in which obedience to rules, renunciation of various pleasures, and discipline turn out to be the very tactics by which freedom is gained. And further, it is the paradox in which this hard-won freedom turns out to be synonymous with joy and magnificence and perfection and beauty.

We may see these paradoxes at work at a thousand points. The ballet, for example: How has that ballerina achieved this supple and glorious mastery? Oh, would that my body looked like that and that I had the freedom to execute those breathtaking movements. How do they do it?

By obedience and renunciation and discipline. There is no other way. Thousands of hours, year after year, giving up this pleasure and that food, exercising in utter obscurity, placing oneself wholly under the rigorous direction of the master.

And the fruit of all that? Mastery. Control. Beauty. Perfection. And not only for the dancers themselves. The rest of us are the beneficiaries. Their prowess brings us joy. It hails us with truth in one of its modes, namely, the truth that attaches to man as body. In some sense, the form exhibited by Adam, new-made from clay, is a true form. We feel that the bodies of dancers are reminiscent of that form. The rest of us, full of potato chips and sour cream dips and nachos grande, must make shift to hobble about, wheezing and grunting, hauling our tremulous torsos and abdomens in and out of cars and up and down the stairs. Ah, would that I could move like that dancer, we mourn.

The same paradox is visible, of course, in gymnastics. Those godlike young men and these pixies from Hungary and China: How have they won through to this state of affairs in which discipline and mastery and control seem synonymous with beauty and freedom and perfection? It is a state of affairs altogether beyond the reach of all who do not feel it worth their while to abandon everything for the pursuit of this crown.

Or music. The tenor. The pianist. The oboist. They seem positively to exult in the challenge put to them by the score and to mount up with wings like eagles, transforming the impossible task into soaring and leaping joy. How did they win their way through to these precincts of freedom, while the rest of us croak and fumble with the keys in a melancholy way?

The paradox, of course, could be chased all through the fabric of human life. The freedom *to do* something is not easily won. The greater the perfection sought, the greater must be the remorselessness of our own self-abandon to the discipline that constitutes the steps up to the summit where freedom reigns in great bliss.

To be Catholic is to see the force of all this and to see all of it as testifying to that which is true of our humanity itself. Concupiscence has undone us. We can scarcely crawl, laden as we are with all sorts of venality and cravenness and pusillanimity and meagerness of spirit and sloth. But there, in the precincts where our humanity dances in all the glory with which it was invested when it was created and crowned with the *imago Dei*: Oh, that we were there! as the old carol puts it.

But how shall we get there? How be set free? How win through to the sheer muscularity and agility of spirit required by the choreography of that dance—or rather, that Dance. For it is, of course, *the* Dance, namely, Charity.

Charity? How did we get here?

To be Catholic is to see the goal toward which we struggle as that realm (it is called the Kingdom of Heaven) where that which was Law down here during our schooling on earth ("thou shalt not . . . thou shalt not") has been revealed for the blissful thing it is, namely, "Love does not . . . Love does not." Love does not kill, steal, lie, commit adultery. Love does unto its brother what it would wish for itself. Love lays down its life for its neighbor.

Oh. But I have many reservations about all of that. I have a difficult time, for example, in allowing this bodkin-tongued colleague of mine to get away with his remarks: I am rather deft at the withering reply. Or again, they didn't take me into consideration in their discussion: I enjoy registering my hurt by a slight frostiness. And again, that person who has roused my jealousy has run into bad luck: Am I not to enjoy, even in the teensiest way, a whiff of pleasure? And yet once more, I don't mind it being known that I know such-and-such a celebrity on fairly informal terms. This gives me a faint lead over the rest of you.

Alack. How am I, tumid with vanity and sloth, ever to gain that realm where sheer, joyous generosity of spirit seems to be the very choreography to which they all dance with never the smallest gasp or stumble? The name of the Dance is Charity: would that I had attended to my lessons with more assiduity over the years.

That state of affairs is, a Catholic would urge, exactly analogous to the agility and singleness of purpose and mastery we glimpse in a great dancer, gymnast, or artist. Somehow, in such precincts, discipline and practice and obedience to the rules have borne fruit, not in bondage and discouragement and meanness, but rather in suppleness and beauty and freedom. Whereas it is in the artists and athletes and others in whom we now may glimpse the paradox, it is in the saints that we may see the analogous thing in the region of final destiny. It is not the mastery of the oboe that is at work in our obedience down here (although heaven grant that there may indeed be great heavenly oboes): it is the mastery of our souls and the transformation of them into the image of Christ.

The image of Christ. That is a very taxing assignment.

Yes; but it is our assignment nevertheless. We will not have stepped up to the freedom for which we were made until we have reached "the measure of the stature of the fullness of Christ", as St. Paul puts it. Or we might say that the freedom in store for us may be glimpsed in the Beatitudes: When we have won the "blessed" crown that is given to those who have learned those difficult lessons, we will be free. Or in still another picture, when we can pass the litmus test of 1 Corinthians 13, that daunting hymn to Charity, we will be free.

It is in terms such as these that a Catholic understands the matter of freedom. We might say that freedom is a mere by-product of Charity's having wholly possessed one's being. No raw spots of irritability; no prickles of vanity; no pockets of self-pity. All is to be greatness of spirit, merriment, purity, serenity.

But of course it takes endless lessons in self-mastery if one hopes to achieve any such guerdon. The schooling in these lessons constitutes the whole ascetical life, on the Catholic view. Asceticism is not masochism. Rather, it is exactly analogous to the privations, disciplines, and exercises that a dancer, a gymnast, a violinist, or a tenor subjects himself to in order to master the thing he loves. Certainly one may have chocolate ice cream: What could be more innocent? But one may not have chocolate ice cream (or not much of it anyway) if one wants to dance. A flat stomach is called for. And certainly one may while away one's afternoons gossiping with one's friends: What could be more innocent? But one may not thus while away one's afternoons (or not many of them anyway) if one wants to play the violin like Itzhak Perlman. And so it goes.

Catholics fast, not because meat or eclairs are sinful or because the Church wishes to pinch off such small pleasures; rather, Catholics believe, as the ancient Church has always believed, that such small denials constitute excellent schooling. Fasting assists me to recall that the belly is not all. Actually, on its own level it reminds me of an immense principle, namely, that our appetites must be governed by Reason—by our power, that is, of judging and sorting out values and of making immediate choices in the light of the long view (which has freedom at its end). We all turn away in sadness from the spectacle of some old debauché who has been governed by appetite alone. Having gorged himself on food, drink, or sexual license, say, he must dribble away his last days weepy and full of regret, or worse, still leering and hiccoughing. On the other hand, we may come upon some old soul with merry eyes who is full of curiosity about how we are and what we have been doing and whose whole being radiates tranquillity and joy. How did she arrive there? The freedom that presides over her innermost being is a prize most sedulously to be desired. What has she denied herself? Probably more than chocolates. Who knows of the thousand times when she, stung by venomous remarks from some old person in her care, simply smiled and let the remark pass, with no doubt an inner aspiration, "Lord Jesus Christ, Son of God, have mercy on me, a sinner." Or who can tell what nights of vigil she has kept, offering up to the crucified Savior her own unfulfilled yearnings? Who will tally up her total of hours at the wheel, bogged down on the freeway, when what ascended from her was not a torrent of imprecations and fumings about how hopeless this all was but, rather, "*ora pro nobis peccatoribus, nunc et in hora mortis.*" Especially *nunc*.

There is no question about it. Strait is the gate. The aperture is as small as a needle's eye. We must through much tribulation enter into joy.

Tribulation? Surely this is to confuse things. Voluntary abstaining from some pleasure or other for the good of one's soul is one thing; but tribulation—say, being caught in bombed Warsaw, or in famine-ravaged Somalia, or in the path of Ghengis Khan's Mongols—that is something quite distinct.

Yes. But the thread that might connect my forgoing a piece of chocolate and our woman in the traffic jam and the Somali would be an attitude, surely? An attitude that is prepared to see all choices, and also all circumstances, even those that are beyond one's own choosing, as occasions put to one by the Divine Love, which may be transformed for one's own benefit. In such precincts, evil itself may be touched by the divine alchemy and turned to gold. You meant it (my kidnapping) for evil, says Joseph to his brothers, but God had good for all of us in mind. Or again, from his very ashheap, Job, victim of every conceivable undeserved ill, testifies to his stubborn conviction that God is good and not sadistic. Though he slay me, yet will I trust him. Polycarp goes with immense serenity to the stake. Thomas More goes to the Tower with vast dignity and solicitude for his wife.

Such attitudes are not won with the toss of a ball, like a gew-gaw at the traveling circus. (There are some reaches of Christendom where, to hear the teaching, one might conclude that indeed we may, just for the asking, achieve greatness of soul—"the measure of the stature of the fullness of Christ", that is. Just *ask!* it is urged. Or, "Pray through! The Lord will give you the victory!")

The Roman Catholic Church, which has been shepherding us mortals for two millennia now, does not have quite so breathless a notion of things. Nothing is won cheaply. Oh, to be sure, Jesus Christ won for us all what we could do nothing at all to win, namely, forgiveness and eternal life. But then begins our schooling in Charity.

For that is what it is, really. In the foregoing pages, the two words *freedom* and *charity* have been used almost interchangeably. On one level this is to use words carelessly. After all, the two words are not synonymous. On the other hand, as it turns out, the "law" in the City of God is indeed Charity, and that turns out to be a state of affairs so gloriously free that our wildest dreams of freedom here on earth are niggardly by comparison.

For that "law" (or "choreography", as we have called it, in a metaphor) may be said to indicate the clarity, precision, and enduring perfection of the City of God. That is, what we hear now as "Thou shalt not lie" hints at that City where sheer truth reigns and suffuses all. The lie is hell and was cast out of this City with Lucifer and his cohorts. The lie is sadness and wrath and strife, for it flings itself, forever impotently, against the everlasting solidity of the truth. It will not have the truth. It loathes the truth. And insofar as my being depends on the lie, even in the smallest degree, I am to that extent unfit and unready for the City of God. Its clarity, precision, and enduring perfection would crush me, enfeebled and deliquescent as I have made myself by living the lie or by depending on the lie.

What lie? The great lie, at bottom, that says with Lucifer, *Non serviam.* I will not serve. I will follow my own choreography. I will not obey the Choreographer. I will not submit to his law. I have my own morality.

To be Catholic is to hear in such words the voice of hell:

very plausible, very appealing, very bracing; but hell nonetheless.

One form in which such words often come to us all nowadays in the public realm touches on the matter of sexual behavior. This topic is, oddly, almost always suggestive of where a given civilization is at the moment. The public, colorful, and strident celebration of nakedness and of all the activities that suddenly boil up when people all take off their clothes may be trusted as an index of the state of the fabric of that civilization. There seem to be no exceptions in history. To be sure, the civilization does not always collapse outright: Victorian England, stuffy as it was, pulled itself together after the saturnalia of the Regency. We may tut-tut when Victoria's name comes up, but she at least wished to keep intact in her England the notion of the hiddenness that ought to guard the precincts where the man and the woman enact that "knowing" which seems to bring them both to the very center of the mystery by which, in their masculinity and femininity, they constitute that "one" which itself bears the image of God as no other creature in the universe does.

We have come quickly into deep waters here. The center of the mystery? Well, yes, a Catholic would urge (or, at least, a Catholic who has pondered the teaching of his Church on the matter). For it is in our sexuality that we may see that "language of the body", and that "spousal meaning of the body", taught by John Paul II. It is not difficult matter. The smallest children explore their bodies and find differences. And (time reveals) the one calls to the other. An invitation is implicit and insistent. The two forms do not exist side by side, inert and self-sufficient. There is an awakening and, soon enough, an almost irresistible bidding. I become more "alive", as it were, by following this awakening to its fruition in the other. The form of the body itself speaks its language to me: *this* is clearly made for *that*. He is made for her. She is made for him.

But because the union of the two forms is itself a case in point of the mystery of Man and Woman as Image of God, and because this union brings them both into that state of affairs where (literally, physically) the giving of oneself to the other who is not myself turns out to be joy—because such high and eternal stakes are at work here, stakes that first appeared at the creation, and that reach all the way to the Eschaton—because of all this, it is very meet and right, says the Church, that the ceremony be shrouded. There must be a veil protecting the holy place.

When that veil is ripped open, and the ogling public troop in, snickering and leering, then tragedy has come upon us.

But of course the Roman Catholic Church is not unique in her insistence on such a veil. All tribes, all cultures, and all civilizations have always known that the sexual phenomenon must be hidden. Tribes that go entirely naked about their daily tasks retire to some sequestered purlieu for the sexual act. Polygamous cultures (and even the sultan with his seraglio) acknowledge that *these* are *my* wives and not yours. There is no random traffic in this realm of the sexual.

But how did we get this far afield from our topic of freedom? We are not "afield" at all, of course. We are speaking of the rules, as it were, as paradoxically assisting us toward our freedom, the way the choreography does the dancer.

Thou shalt not commit adultery. Negative. Life-denying. Grim. So would run the verdict on such a prohibition in our own time. But a Catholic sees in this prohibition the same sort of warning as is constituted by "Danger: high tension", or "Keep back from the edge." No one complains that those warnings are negative. The negation is the smallest part of what they mean. They open out onto the awareness that your life is infinitely important to you and that you don't wish to be electrocuted just now. The negation celebrates that, and it joins you in your assessment of your own worth.

The negation in the rule against adultery is of this sort. Turn it around: to commit adultery is to destroy yourself, just as to jump onto the third rail is to do so.

Ha-ha! laugh many of our own time, winking and prodding each other with jocose knowledgeability. Hasn't Freud told us all about this sort of thing? And, having advanced many decades beyond old Sigmund, don't we now speak of "sexual preference" and of "life-styles", thereby drawing the sting from all of those otiose Victorian negations?

It may be worth remembering that Queen Victoria did not make up the prohibitions. Nor did the Puritans. Nor did the Roman Catholic Church. Nor did Christianity. Go to the bottom of the world, and you will find this profound awareness of the sacred character of the sexual phenomenon. What our epoch leaps insouciantly into is shrouded and hedged and hemmed in with the highest and thorniest hedges possible, in all tribes.

The man comes to the woman. They become one. Therefore shall a man leave his father and mother, and the two of them shall be one flesh. It is called marriage. It is called the holy sacrament of matrimony. It is not merchandise for the flea market or the frat house or the dormitory bedroom or the hugger-mugger assignation in the motel.

Why not?

Because (says the Church—says the rule—says, actually, Nature herself) insofar as you enter this shrine, and that one, and the other one (or the other dozens), you to that extent become a plunderer, for one thing, taking away the treasure of another personhood. And you incur the guilt of sacrilege: you have violated the shrine of the personhood (for that is what the body is). And you blind yourself to the glory of personhood, seeing in it solely soft and delectable surfaces and folds of flesh. And, lastly, you stultify your own personhood, snuffling and rooting into every shrine like a pig after truffles—like Odysseus' men under Circe's spell—and therefore wholly unfitted for the bliss of which this physical pleasure is the sketchiest and most diluted foretaste. That bliss will derive from the extent to which you have perceived in the body of the other the form of the personhood and have thereby honored that personhood. You will be as unfitted for that bliss as is a pig for the music of Johann Sebastian Bach.

So. Freedom and the rules. The negations are the very guardians of our true and ultimate freedom, and they act as our tutors now. Which of us knows all that is at stake, for example, in the mystery of the man's body and the woman's? Very few; very few. Well, then, we have the simple rule, embarrassing and almost insulting in its elementary flatness. Thou shalt not. The obedience brought to such a rule by the man or woman who looks, like Abraham, for a city whose builder and maker is God is like the obedience brought to the rule by a dancer or a musician. Here is how to do *that*. Do not stray from the rule.

It is thus with the whole moral law, says your Catholic. The rules point to joy, really—the joy that presides in that realm (it is the City of God) where we see finally what was guessed at in all of the aspects of our mortality (the ballet, gymnastics, art, and any sort of mastery), where obedience, discipline, renunciation, and effort yield the fruit of prowess, mastery, beauty, perfection, and freedom.

Such a picture of things calls into question the most shrilly insisted-upon maxims of our own epoch. Not so! is shouted from all sides. There is no such rule. Customs and taboos change from tribe to tribe and from century to century. And our own time has brought human freedom to the point where each man may pick the style that suits him most comfortably. A truly free society is the one that allows all such styles their full exercise.

Not altogether, replies our Catholic. We may consult once again the sexual realm in this connection. (It is not without interest that sexual taboos seem to be virtually the only taboos called into question by societies demanding "freedom": we seldom hear the freedom to lie, murder, steal, or cheat being touted.) From the Catholic point of view—and, it may be remarked, from the traditional Protestant and Jewish points of view—there is one context and one only for sexual activity, namely, that of heterosexual fidelity. The reason for this has been touched on above: in this act we find Man under his two aspects, male and female, enacting that knowledge of the other which opens him wholly to this other and which instructs him in the great mystery of self-donation. Since personhood is at stake here, the rite must be guarded. Marriage is the name of the bond that guards and hallows the man and the woman who have pledged themselves to this obedience. (To speak thus is to call down howls of incredulity and derision from the realm of "public discourse" in our own time. *No one* still talks that way! we hear. Well, again, yes, some do. The Roman Catholic Church does.)

But what, then, of all the alternative "styles" that appear to have stepped onto the public stage in the sexual realm now?

To be Catholic is to urge that each alternative must be tested by the tuning fork, so to speak, of heterosexual fidelity. Adultery, for example: the breakdown here is of the exclusive vow by which I bound myself to my spouse, knowing that it takes the whole of a man's life, in faithful attendance on the shrine of the spouse's personhood, to learn what it is all about. To steal away to a neighboring shrine is to pollute both with infidelity, one of the tawdriest of sins.

Well, fornication, then. Just two independent people, consenting ones at that. College students, shall we say.

Again, what is as costly as the crown jewels, namely, the personhood of the other, is treated like merchandise in the side show. A game. A *divertissement*. You can't do that, says the Catholic—or, you cannot do that and not stultify both you and your partner.

Sexual congress between two members of the same sex, then? The breakdown here is that there is the attempt at union with the other who is a mirror image of myself and not authentically "other". Catholicism celebrates the creation, when male and female created he them. The dance is not choreographed for two of the one kind. What you have there is futility and sterility. No fruit can issue from this congress. In reply to the shouts of protest arising at this point, a Catholic can only appeal to the sacramentalism of Catholic vision, which sees the physical as the icon of the spiritual. The body is not a random casing for my spirit, which is genderless. I *am* a man, or a woman, in some fundamental sense. It is the Manichaeans who will have it that the physical is merely an unfortunate ballast to our otherwise free-floating spirits. Sacramentalism takes seriously the iconography of the body. Hence the sexual act between two members of the same sex is futile, sterile, and disorderly.

There have not been put forward, as of this writing, the claims of bestiality as also a worthy alternative style, but if such a claim were advanced, a Catholic would see the matter as grotesque, of course, but, more than that, as the attempt at ghastly union with an other that is too utterly other than I. There is no possible union between a man and a sheep, say. The barrier is so high that ordinary human sensibility has always justly recoiled even from speaking of the attempt to surmount it.

What of autoeroticism? Here, of course, we all justly hesitate to speak too pompously. Who will inaugurate the vendetta here? But even here, the vision of our personhood as both cloaked and revealed in our body would discover a certain sadness. For has not that joy which is rightly perceived to gild the self-donation of myself to the other, my spouse—has not that joy been stolen off into a squalid corner here and detached from its true source? Again, few will wish to wax inquisitorial. But it is worth keeping alive the integrity of the sacramental and creational vision of personhood, of the language of the body, and of the spousal meaning of that body, even in such domestic and ubiquitous matters as this.

But this paradox of our freedom, and of the conditions that lead to it and guard it, is not exhausted by the rules, in the sense of the prohibitions and demands of the moral law. We find it also at work in the Church's adjurations to prayer, fasting, and alms.

None of these three activities would appear, on the surface, to tend toward freedom. Each one is a burden, in its own way. And each one asks something of me. Each one interrupts what otherwise might be a pleasantly self-serving *modus vivendi* that I had worked out for myself.

Prayer. We have already spoken of Catholics at prayer in another chapter. But we may at least recall in this context that prayer by its very nature draws me out of my self-absorption. In prayer I address the Most High, and I find myself addressed by him. In prayer I am introduced to the most profound mystery of being, namely that my "I" is addressed by, and is created to address, the "thou" who is God himself. Ego-centrism, which looks appealingly like freedom to most of us most of the time, is really another name for hell, since the center is not, in fact, ego (I).

The psalms furnish us with the most eloquent testimony to this state of the soul that has found its true freedom by discovering truth—the truth, principally, that it is God for whom I am made, and not for myself. "How amiable are thy tabernacles, O Lord of hosts." "One thing have I desired of the Lord . . . that I may dwell in the house of the Lord all the days of my life, to behold the beauty of the Lord, and to inquire in his temple." It is this, say the psalms, it is this, say the prophets, it is this, say the Law and the gospel and the Church and all the martyrs and saints, that our restless soul seeks. Any "freedom" sought elsewhere is worse than an illusion: it is a travesty and, finally, a ghastly cheat.

Prayer opens into this region where the human soul encounters the Most High for whom it was made. If my days do not have written over them as a superscript: Our Father . . . hallowed be thy name . . . thy will be done, then those days will turn out at last to have been Macbeth's dismal tomorrow and tomorrow and tomorrow.

The Church beckons us toward our true freedom by enjoining the discipline of prayer on us. And it beckons to us in its injunction to fast and abstinence.

Once again, on the surface of things it would appear that fasting and abstinence are just the sort of negations that gaunt religion is pleased to lay upon us mortals. Religion, and most especially the Roman Catholic Church, begrudges us all sorts of small diversions and indulgences that might otherwise spice up our lives, which are already difficult enough, heaven knows: so runs the plaint from our petulant souls in this connection. But it is a matter of our freedom—our true and whole freedom—that is at stake, the Church would remind us. Who is the free man? Or, to phrase it differently but to mean the same thing, what is the saint? Is he not the one who, like the ballet dancer and the gymnast and the violinist, has done his lessons, with all the discipline and self-denial that those lessons entail, *so that* he will attain to such and such an achievement, in this case the glorious freedom of the sons of God, as St. Paul phrases it. Since fasting and abstinence touch us at the very sensitive point of appetite, the exercise assists us toward that agility and prowess and grace which will enable us to execute magnificently and freely the steps demanded by the choreography of Love.

If we ask what, exactly, this might mean detached from this highly figurative language of the Dance, the Church would tell us that in order for us mortals to exhibit the great dignity with which we are crowned as Man, we must have brought our faculties into a just ordering, with Reason (or Will) presiding over affections and appetites. Affections and appetites open to us some of the richest delights of our existence: but in themselves they are somewhat random. Mere appetite (for food; for sexual pleasure; for any pleasure) cannot tell me whether the pleasure to which it inclines me at the moment is fitting. This may be the wrong time; or I may have had enough; or my station in life (married, say) excludes my satisfying this inclination to enjoy the body of some terribly appealing person who is not my spouse. The man who has been governed by appetite becomes swinish: even the pagan Greeks knew this. It did not take the Roman Catholic Church to tell us this. But in her holding out to us the discipline of fasting and abstinence, she is wise. We are reminded in these disciplines of what we are (man, not beast) and of our destiny (fitness for that City where Charity presides), and also, as it happens, of our need to reflect soberly on our myriad and habitual self-indulgences. This part of the matter is called penitence; and fasting and abstinence turn out to be excellent assistants in my efforts at penitence.

And alms. This intrudes on my right to my own money (most of the time it is money that is at stake, but time might also constitute a species of alms).

Yes. It does thus intrude. That is the whole point. For inasmuch as I am pleased to suppose that I have such and such a *right*, I am still, alas, an unhappy alien to the City of God. The word *rights* does not exist there. All is debt—exulted in with an exultation that can only be called worship. "Worthy is the Lamb that was slain and hath redeemed us to God by his blood", sings that City. "*Agnus Dei, qui tollis peccata mundi*", we all sing at Mass down here. We are debtors. God is our Savior. He has done all. Everything we have is owed to him. There is no one here who is not altogether a debtor—even the highest and best of us: My soul doth magnify the Lord . . . for he hath done great things for me . . . he hath exalted the humble and meek. *He* hath regarded. *He* hath done great things. *He* hath shown strength. *He* hath put down. *He* hath exalted. *He* hath filled.

Debt. Utter debt. But not, as it turns out in these precincts of joy, debt experienced as leaden and dolorous. No. Rather, this debt is transformed, by the divine alchemy, into the very substance of exultation. Read the psalms. Read the hymns of the redeemed in St. John's Apocalypse. Blessing, honor, glory, and power, be unto him . . . for he hath redeemed us.

It is a song to stick in the throat of the man who has spent his life squinting and tallying and calculating, making sure that his rights are never, ever called into question. What's mine's mine. It is hell's formula.

But, What's mine's thine: there is heaven's formula. All that I have is owed to thee, O my God; to thee, Paschal Lamb; to thee, Holy Ghost, Comforter. And hence, all this that is "mine" because of the divine largesse is thine, my brother, my sister. Especially my indigent brother and sister. Especially the beggar, the Lazarus at my gate (and is not my gate the whole world, now in this epoch of the global village?).

Alms. A discipline and a small renunciation enjoined upon me, not because Catholicism is niggardly, but rather because this ancient Church's whole ministry to me is to bring me to, and fit me for, joy. Freedom.

To be Catholic is to see the whole question of our freedom in terms such as these.

16

The Crucifix

No doubt the symbol that, above all others, even including that of the Madonna and Child, symbolizes the Christian religion to all the world is the Crucifix.

Crucifixes may, of course, be seen in museums. No museum curator would feel his collection of art to be anywhere near complete if it lacked the Crucifix—or a number of Crucifixes. One of the most profound and delicate indexes of our mortal sensibility is the shape we have given in our various cultures over the centuries to the Crucifix.

There is the young hero on the Cross, entering the fray to do battle with the Prince of Darkness and to overthrow him. The Old English poem "The Dream of the Rood" speaks in this way. The lines are spoken by the Cross itself:

> Then I saw the King of all mankind
> In brave mood hasting to mount upon me. . . .
> Then the young Warrior, God, the All-Wielder,
> Put off His raiment, steadfast and strong;
> With lordly mood in the sight of many
> He mounted the Cross to Redeem mankind.[1]

---

[1] Charles W. Kennedy, ed., *An Anthology of Old English Poetry* (New York, 1960), 145.

As the centuries pass, this heroic image finds itself gradually replaced by the Suffering Servant, more and more obviously the Victim, until we reach the late Middle Ages, with the twisted, emaciated, and blood-spattered figure on the Cross. (To pursue the changing image of the crucified Lord from century to century, and also from country to country, and to see what corollaries could be drawn between this and the greater or lesser emphasis on the Sacred Humanity of the Lord in Catholic devotion would furnish a rich task for some scholar.) Questions of sheer taste press in closely here, of course; and to sort out sentimental, or even saccharine, depictings from those that exhibit authenticity and fidelity to a devotion that is not simply lachrymose would be an infinitely delicate task, and one beleaguered with the danger of snobbery. For in the presence of the Crucifix we have moved beyond the frontier of the merely aesthetic to a region where canons of taste and artistic integrity falter.

There is a point of view, widespread among non-Catholic Christians, that dismisses the Crucifix with the remark, "Oh—we worship a Risen Christ." This stricture springs, no doubt, from a notion that is not in itself wholly false, namely, that Good Friday was not the end of the story. Easter followed forthwith. Indeed, indeed—the Christ we invoke in our prayers and supplications is not dead. He is alive in heaven, St. Paul teaches us; he makes intercession for us, he is at the right hand of the Father, and all authority in heaven and earth has been given to him. And he is alive in our hearts in the person of the Holy Ghost.

All of this is true. And, more than this, it has been the case that Catholic devotion, perhaps especially various forms of folk devotion, has from time to time seemed to focus with such ardor on the suffering Lord and his sorrowful Mother that the glorious mystery of the Resurrection has seemed to recede. Good Friday processions and obsequies have over-whelmed Easter.

But *abusus non tollit usus.* The abuse of a thing does not take away its proper use. If we find ourselves always trotting out our remark about worshipping a Risen Christ as a stricture against the propriety of the Crucifix and its centrality in Christian devotion, then we incur the guilt of impertinence. We have dismissed a great mystery with an airy slogan. It will not do.

For what the eye of faith perceives in the Crucifix is a mystery of such fathomless depth that the sun itself darkened and the rocks split apart. The Crucifix draws us to the point at which the Most High enters into the evil and suffering that despoils our humanity. And more than that: he enters into it *for us* ("This is my Body, broken for you") and, more even than that, is overwhelmed by it ("Eli, Eli . . . ?").

This is not an event to be set to one side in the interest of doctrinal punctilio. The fact that the Resurrection followed this dark event and brought it to fruition and filled it, para-doxically, with light and glory does not suggest to us that our devotion and our prayer ought not to unite themselves to this One in the very hour of his suffering when he most inti-mately bound himself to ours. It is a mistake to insist, with sprightly accuracy, that the One who thus suffered here is now risen, just as it is a mistake, with similar accuracy, to insist to the parents at the open grave of their child that we will all one day be raised. There is a time for everything un-der the sun, and in Catholic devotion we find this acknowl-edged. Such devotion is not fettered to chronology, which might say that because the Crucifixion followed the Nativity, we should therefore set that birth to one side, as an inappro-priate focus for our meditation and prayer, or that because the Resurrection followed the Crucifixion, we should similarly set the Cross, and the suffering figure on it, to one side since we must always exult in the victory of Easter. In other words, Catholic piety keeps alive every aspect of the Savior's work of redemption. Hence the Crucifix.

Suffering is the very condition of our humanity. Beatitude is our destiny, with all that is implied in that rich word: joy, fruition, bliss, freedom, glory. But there is no authentic living of mortal human life without suffering. (If there is that gay and unique person somewhere who would startle us all by claiming that life has never brought suffering to him, we need scarcely remind him that "all our yesterdays have lighted fools the way to dusty death" and that this happy exemption of his will come to an abrupt end one fine day with his dissolution.)

Suffering is the condition of our humanity. How far afield must we go in our canvass of this theme? Here is our neighbor, trying to carry on while his young wife dies slowly from cancer. Here is the infant orphan in the Romanian hospital (or the Iraqi, or the Rwandan, or the Vietnamese), dying of malnutrition without one single soul in this earth who knows so much as his name. Here is the woman, beaten daily by a churlish husband, doing what she can to make the word "home" have some rag of meaning for her children. Here is the child whose world has been wasted in the wake of his parents' acrimonious divorce, shuttling between households by order of the court. And there is the blind pauper with his tin cup sitting motionless by the curb in Tangier.

Not to mention the Pagliaccis, transvestites, chorus girls, sideshow freaks, and barroom pianists whose task it is to make us all laugh, or to divert us, while their disappointed hopes ache and all but cry out beneath the sequins and polka dots.

We may go so far as to urge, without mere sentimentalism, that even the suffering of the animals is "our" suffering, in a mystery, since it was our disobedience that brought on the Curse, for a start, and also since, as St. Paul teaches, the whole creation groans and travails in pain, awaiting the redemption, at which point (see Romans 8) we (humans) will be set free, thus signalling the liberation of the whole of nature from its suffering. The Alaskan brown bear gnawing off the foot caught in the steel trap; the wildebeeste galloping in clumsy terror from the cheetah, only to be brought down and torn in pieces; the lioness stalking the faint and emaciated gazelle as a meager dish for her famine-starved cubs; the dog, all trust and hope, looking to one passerby after the other, unaware that he has been abandoned; the mallard, circling and quacking as the turtles pull the last of her ducklings under.

Are we mawkish to think thus? We hope, most earnestly, that the suffering of animals is greatly dimmed by their limited capacity to think. We hope. But who can hear the scream of the rabbit seized by the cat, the frantic cheeping of the dispossessed wrens, or the howl of the dog tangled in his leash without groaning "*Kyrie, eleison!*"?

And where do we find ourselves when we thus groan?

At the Cross.

But it is not an empty cross with the work finished and done. Oh, to be sure, logic and chronology (and some rigorous theologies) will dictate that it is so. *Consummatum est.* Yes. We know that. We cling to that. But that which is thus "finished" remains present and actual in time—in the dimension, that is, under which we mortals must experience what it is to belong to the race of Adam. The victory of Easter, with its empty tomb and mighty risen Prince, cancels sin, suffering, and death: but we experience that canceling, not as a mathematical point that has no longevity, so to speak, but rather as the condition of our salvation, that is, the condition by which we are brought to glory. Brought: this bringing takes time. We live in time. We suffer in time. We see not yet all things put under Thee.

To be Catholic is to assume this paradox of "finished" and yet "still present". It is to draw upon the paradox as one prays. It is to place oneself at the feet of the Savior as he bears our sadness, sin, and suffering in his own body on the Tree.

It may be observed at this point that a similar paradox is at work in the Eucharist. Jesus Christ said to his disciples, as he broke the bread and blessed the cup, "Do this for a remembrance of me." A mere remembrance refers us to an incident fixed in the past, which we try to recall to mind. But the word the Lord used here, *anamnesis*, has the force of "a remembrance that is a making present". The Church has always understood the Eucharist to be just such a remembrance. The Mass is a true entering into the mystery of Calvary. The Sacrifice, offered once for all at the Cross, is "made present" in the Mass. The event, in time, is now past. But the Lamb slain there is the Lamb slain from the foundation of the world. The liturgy pierces the scrim that hangs between time and eternity, and past, present, and future are "made present" in the celebration. An idea not wholly unlike this is at work in the Crucifix. Yes, the body was taken down, buried, raised, ascended, and is now at God's right hand in heaven. But even in heaven, there appeared to the eyes of St. John "a Lamb, as it had been slain". This is what we see on the Cross as we gaze at the Crucifix.

The paradoxes ("mysteries" would be the word familiar to Catholic piety) multiply as we ponder it all. How can God suffer for us? What does this "substitution" mean—that St. Peter speaks of when he says, "He himself bore our sins in his body on the tree" (1 Pet 2:24)? The Church hears the same theme in the words of Isaiah: "By his stripes we are healed. . . . And the Lord hath laid on him the iniquity of us all. . . .

Surely he hath borne our griefs and carried our sorrows" (Is 53:5–6, 4). How can this be? In what sense is it true?

We ask such questions with particular earnestness when we find ourselves crushed with our own sorrow or confronted with some tragic scene, especially of the suffering innocence of children and animals. All the sorrow seems to be concentrated just here, or there, in the weeping women of Stalingrad, Warsaw, or Bosnia Herzegovina. Can there be any sorrow greater than this? In what sense has it been "borne" by the Savior?

Logic collapses in these precincts. Sympathy itself falters. Our bravest attempts to penetrate the mystery draw back. Faith itself staggers. Does it mean that we should no longer feel the weight of our sorrow, since Another has carried it? Some pert theologies speak as though this should be the case, but we know that this claim is a travesty. Sin, sorrow, and suffering, and death itself, were indeed taken away at the Cross, but we mortals must enter into the depths of this mystery in actual experience. The fact that the Savior bore all this for us does not mean that we bear nothing of it; rather, it means that we are invited in to that place (the Cross) where suffering is transfigured. We (the Church) are his Body, says St. Paul. As such, we "share" in his suffering for the life of the world.

This is what lies behind the old Catholic injunction to "offer it up." It is a phrase wholly unknown to Protestantism, with its rigorous and logical insistence on "the finished work of Christ": you can't offer anything to God except your sinful self, to be washed in the Blood of the Lamb.

This is accurate, technically. But Catholic piety wants to penetrate what St. Paul might mean when he speaks of "filling up that which is behind of the suffering of Christ" (Col 1:24) and of being crucified with Christ (Gal 2:20) and of "bearing about in my body the dying of the Lord Jesus" (2 Cor 4:10). All of this has been neatly reduced by Protestant theology. But the Ancient Church has never settled the matter so neatly.

"Offer it up." Catholics chuckle when they recall the nuns enjoining them thus to offer a hangnail or a lost glove or a skinned knee. Offer it up. To whom? Why?

Because Jesus Christ invites us to do so. He tells his followers that they will drink the cup of which he drank and be baptized with the baptism with which he was to be baptized (he was speaking specifically of his imminent suffering in Jerusalem). Where, suddenly, is the theology that teaches that because the Savior did it all, we thereby are reduced to the status of inert bystanders? Whether the sorrow of the moment is a lost glove or a lost spouse or a bombed city, I am invited by the Divine Mercy to unite this terrible loss (for the child, the loss of the glove may threaten the end of the world) with the suffering of the Savior at Calvary and thus to discover that my suffering is his suffering, and that—paradox of paradoxes—his is ours (again—we are his Body).

The pain is there. It has not suddenly evaporated. The Cross is the Cross, not a magician's wand. And on that Cross Catholic eyes see the One whose self-offering transfigured all suffering. Stalingrad is still rubble: the Cross did not avert the Panzer howitzers. But insofar as I will bring my burden of sorrow and suffering (*and* sin: sins are indeed washed away here; this *corpus* is the *Agnus Dei* who taketh away the sin of the world)—insofar as I will bring my burden here, fall on my knees, and cry out for help, to that extent I may know that the Savior is receiving what I offer up and making it one with his own offering here.

This is what the saints speak of when they speak of suffering. The Divine Mercy, like alchemy, transforms the leaden burden into precious substance. We cannot know just what the experience of the martyrs was as the red-hot iron entered their flesh, but we know that they were enabled to bear the pain and even, incredibly, to sing and rejoice. It is all opaque—nonsense, even—to the squint of logic, but we hear the testimony of a thousand saints who have suffered, either physically or in the inner man, and who tell us, not merely of consolations, but of joy.

There is no guarantee of joy, of course: the darkness that shrouds Calvary is thick, and it is scarcely believable that the Son of God himself had it all sunshine in his Passion. We go through that valley of the shadow of death with him.

But *with him*. With whom? Him—the Savior—the Agnus Dei—this figure on the Cross.

This is why the Roman Catholic Church keeps the Crucifix before our eyes and invites us not only to ponder the mystery but also to kneel and ask for succor. Do we importune a figure of wood or plaster when we do so? No—no more than a lover fools himself when he gazes at the portrait of his beloved.

The image assists us to gather our wayward thoughts and feelings. It focuses things. It may even come to our rescue if words fail: the corpus, bowed in agony but with arms stretched wide, says, not in sentences but in its very shape, "Come unto me, all ye that labor and are heavy laden, and I will give you rest. Take my yoke upon you. . . ."

My burden of the moment may be sorrow: Warsaw, or a son debauched by his own choice. It may be physical suffering: paralysis, painful hospital tests, or arthritis. Or it may be sin—my own, alas, or the evil that regales me wherever I look.

With respect to sin, to be Catholic to see both Judgment and Mercy crowning the figure on the Cross. Here is where sin is "taken away", as the sins of Israel were taken away by the slaughter of innocent lambs on their altars. (The truth there, of course, as the Book of Hebrews teaches us, is that the blood of lambs and goats could never take away sins but that the Sacrifice they anticipated, namely, this Sacrifice here on the altar of Calvary, does take our sins away.) We see the judgment of God in this Sacrifice: "Without the shedding of blood there is no remission of sins" (Heb 9:22). The blood of Jesus Christ is the "price" of my ransom (1 Tim 2:6). Hence, to be Catholic is to come and kneel, with penitence, and also with thanksgiving and the resolve to put away my sin. The Crucifix is a powerful emblem in the presence of which all of my truckling with sin is laid bare in all of its squalor.

But this Crucifix bids me also to the place where my exasperation or ire over others' sins must be forsworn in the name of the Mercy that God himself offers to the perpetrators of sin (I being the chief among them). What is it that rouses my ire in the passing scene? Someone cutting into the line at the ticket window? Bloody-mindedness on the part of some driver on the freeway? Cretinous inefficiency on the part of committees, boards, and panels of experts in local, state, or federal government? Monumental waste of taxpayers' money on all sides? Cruelty to children, animals, or the poor? Poisonous ingratitude and self-absorption on the part of some old person being cared for? The list goes on and on.

And my ire seethes. Swift vengeance is what we want here, I say. Oh, for the power to set things right forthwith and finally. If I were in control . . .

The words die on my tongue as the Crucifix looms. Ah, *Domine Deus.* Depart from me, Lord: I am only a sinful man. Lord, I am not worthy. "With what judgment ye judge, ye shall be judged" (Mt 7:2).

The judgment on my sins revealed itself at Calvary. Do I

wish a separate, and stricter, judgment to come upon everyone else? Can I maintain such a wish as the figure on the
Cross looks on me?

No. For in that look I am bidden to the region where all is
forgiveness and for which I have been invited to prepare myself every time I have said "and forgive us our trespasses, as
we forgive those who trespass against us." Not only have I
not been asked to participate in judging the sins of others: I
have been offered the noble opportunity to join my voice
with that of the Crucified as he cries out, "Father, forgive
them." That, and that alone, is to be my prayer as I think of
others' sins.

It is not an easy lesson. It may begin in me by my having,
by main force, by an act of sheer will, to *say* (loudly, it may
be—loud enough to drown out the vindictive voices clamor-
ing in my breast), "save us (all) from the fires of hell; lead all
souls to heaven, especially those in most need of Thy mercy"
(beginning with me, the vituperative one).

To be Catholic is to confront all of this in the presence of
the Crucifix. The image helps me. This is why the Roman
Catholic Church has kept the Crucifix before our eyes at all
times.

Envoi

Our theme has followed a track indicated by the phrase "To be Catholic is to. . . ." A number of milestones have presented themselves. Where does the track take us, finally? Do we leave things in midjourney, so to speak, or is there some sense in which we may stamp "Arrived" on the itinerary?

No religious man, surely, will ever make the claim to have arrived; or, if he does, the rest of us demur over what looks for all the world like presumption on his part. Perhaps he is a high-level initiate in some arcane Gnostic sect. So be it. But, for the general run of religious people, Jew and Muslim as well as Christian, the sense of being en route is very much to the fore.

It is certainly in the very forefront of the Catholic imagination. To be Catholic is to have, at the far end of one's picture of things, the Vision of God. The Beatific Vision. The supreme attempt on the part of human imagination to catch even the dimmest and most fugitive glimpse of this Vision will be found in Dante's *Paradiso*, where the imagery of light—of dazzle, even—suffuses all. Dante ends his immense saga of Hell, Purgatory, and Paradise by pointing us all to "The Love that moves the sun and other stars". It is that, really, toward which a Catholic sees himself moving.

Every aspect of the Catholic's religion bids him thence. His baptism: in this event he is taken "into Christ" and stamped with the indelible identity "Christian", that is, one of those who, by being found in Christ, will one day hear "Come, ye blessed of my Father, inherit the kingdom prepared for you from the foundation of the world."

All of the sacraments, baptism being the first that the new Christian encounters, stand on the cusp between the seen and the unseen, and mark him as one whose life—including his physical life (we look for the resurrection of the dead)—is destined for eternity and already participates in the eternal.

Prayer: here he finds himself among "the whole family in heaven and earth" (Eph 3:15)—angels, saints, all who have preceded him in death, all who accompany him on this earthly pilgrimage, the Mother of God herself, and our Great High Priest, Jesus Christ, into whose self-oblation we have all been drawn. Prayer locates him in this assembly.

The Church herself, for whom the Lord gave himself up and whom he loves as his Spouse: to be Catholic is to see her as in some sense "sacramental", in that she is both physical and visible in her membership and in her existence in time as a hierarchical structure, but also spiritual and unseen, insofar as only God knows just who from among her numbers is truly one of the redeemed.

The Church's Magisterium: to be Catholic is to rely on this exercise, apostolic in its character, of the Church's identity as "the pillar and ground of the truth" (1 Tim 3:15), and to be spared, as it were, the perpetual uncertainty that accompanies the notion of the Church as *only* invisible, to be found in the hectic clutter of conventicles, sects, denominations, and lately sprung associations, all claiming to be church. This awareness, far from permitting the smugness that says, "*We* are the One, True Church", with a sort of pharisaical hauteur, results, as it did for Augustine, who, as a Catholic bishop, strove mightily to recall the Donatists and other schismatics to this one Church, in the modesty that admits that she is very far from being "our" association, much less the creation of a sixteenth-century king or zealot: she is the Lord's. We have no warrant to take upon ourselves the authority to begin again, much as such a fresh start might recommend itself to us from time to time as we see widespread worldliness, ignorance, sin, and heresy in her ranks. But a Roman Catholic understands the teaching office of the Church to be guaranteed and protected by the Lord's promise that the gates of hell (in the form of heresy, falsehood, apostasy, or error) will not, for as long as time lasts, prevail against this Church. And he sees the Petrine See in Rome as bearing the authority that the Lord asked the apostles to exercise in his Church, and most especially that given to Peter. Peter, and the See that bears his name, is, for the Catholic, the "sacrament" of the Church's unity, again, for as long as time lasts.

And the Mass. The Mass draws the Catholic, day by day, up to the precincts at the summit of which, as it were, the seraphim cry "Holy!" around the Sapphire Throne. Down here on this earth, things may present themselves to his eye as a huddle of unlettered peasants in a plastered hovel of a church, all flaked and peeling, or as a knot of anxious soldiers tossing in a landing craft, or as the throng filling Chartres. But whatever the immediate look of the thing, to be Catholic is to find oneself gazing through the veil of contingency and temporality at the Lamb slain from the foundation of the world, so profoundly hinted at in van Eyck's great *Adoration of the Mystic Lamb* in Ghent. It is to find oneself bidden to "assist at" this great Sacrifice, which finds its origin in the counsels of the Holy Trinity before the world was, its pattern in the Upper Room, and its completion at Golgotha. *Consum-*

matum est. The Mass does not add to that one Oblation: it makes it uninterruptedly and actually present to the Church until the Lord returns.

To be Catholic is to see one's entire identity and calling to be nothing other than "configuration to" Christ and union with him, in his humiliation, his self-oblation, his Resurrection, his Ascension, and his intercessory office in behalf of the world. "For the life of the world": to be Catholic is to see oneself as *for*, not against, the world. "For God sent not his Son into the world to condemn the world, but that the world through him might be saved" (Jn 3:17). Patriarchs, prophets, kings, apostles, fathers, confessors, martyrs, virgins, widows, infants, and all the faithful from the beginning testify to this. To be Catholic is to share in this august identity.

This is the "glad tidings" of which we spoke in the first chapter of this book.